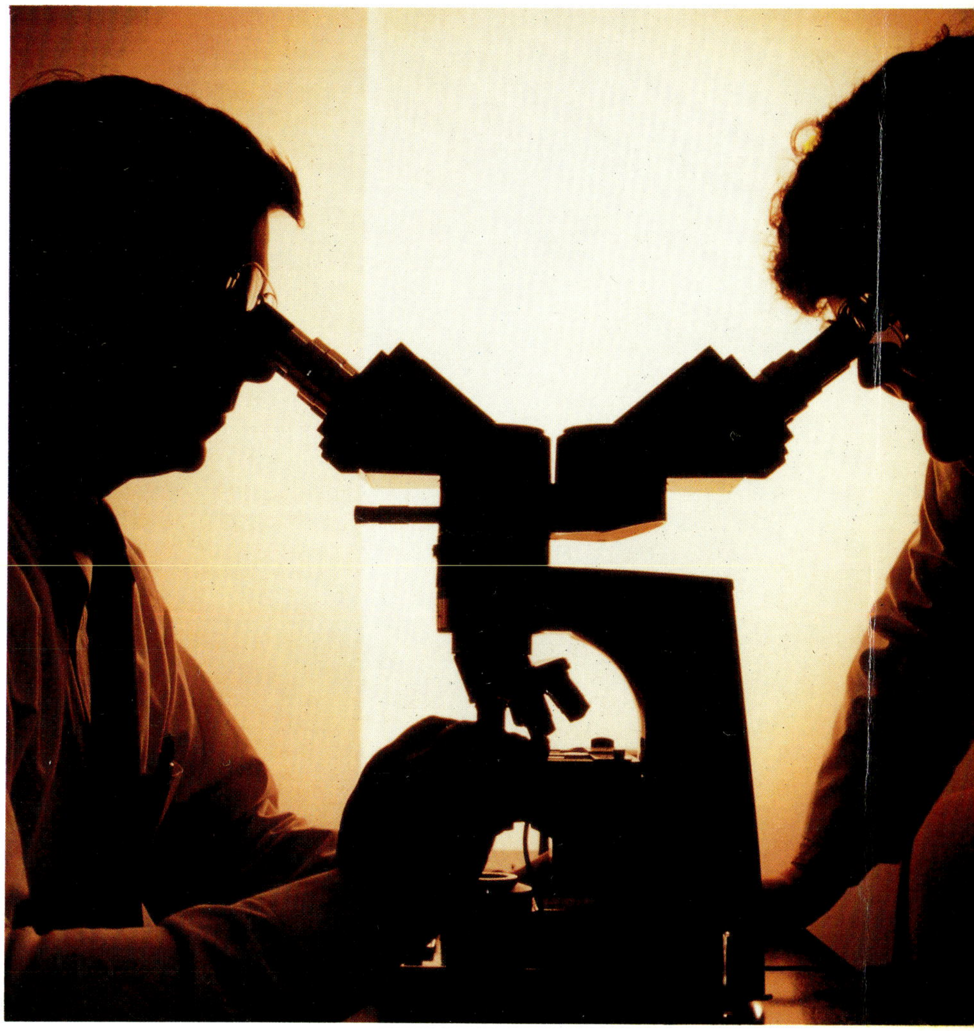

Mead

"Partners in Excellence" and "Commitment to Progress" chapters by John K. Waters and Teresa Zumwald

METROPOLITAN

DAYTON

FLYING HIGH

DIANA RANKIN

CONTENTS

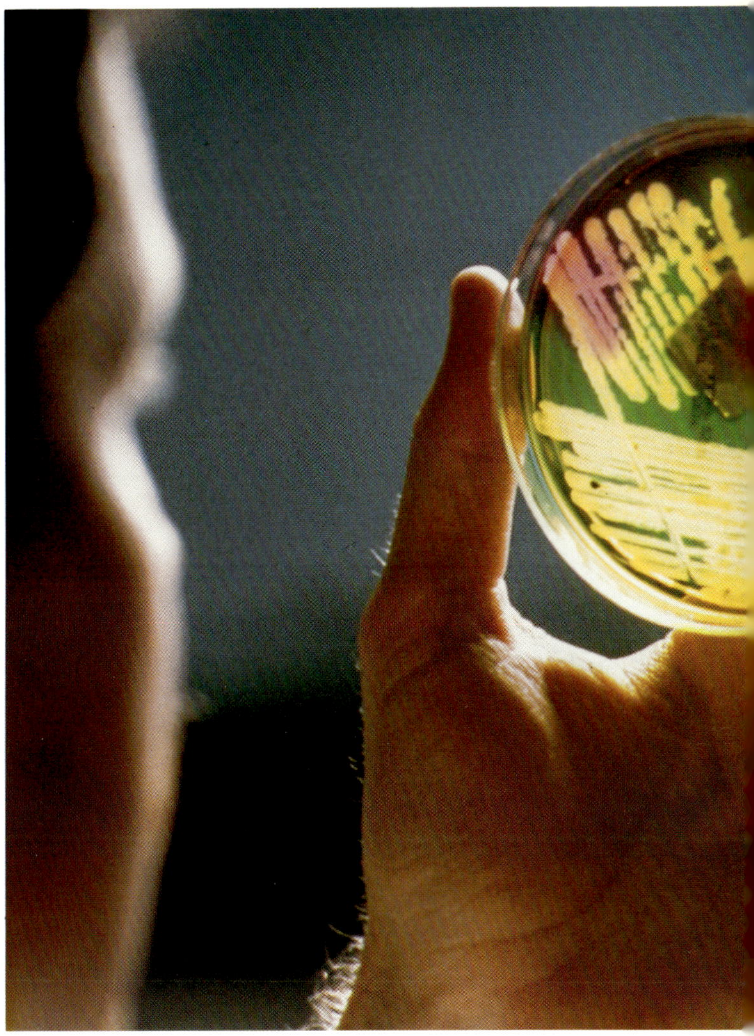

CHAPTER ONE

MIAMI VALLEY PERSPECTIVE

"What are you doing, Wil?"

"Watching that bird. I'd give anything to fly like that."

"You can fly in a balloon at the fair," said his brother Orville.

"No. Not in a balloon. Like that bird. I'm going to do it—no matter what."

This is the spirit of Dayton. On December 17, 1903, Orville and Wilbur Wright fulfilled that dream. With four successful flights, they proved flight was possible and forever changed the world. The Wright Brothers' airplane, James Ritty's cash register, Charles Kettering's automobile self-starter, Swinder Bahl's laminated charge plate, George Marinoff's ink-jet printer, John Janning's liquid crystals for digital watches and calculators—these are only a few of the Dayton area's multitude of world-renowned innovations. The auto headlight, flip-top can, parking meter, parachute, automated teller machine, cellophane tape, airplane ejection seat . . . the list goes on and on. In fact, since 1971 Dayton innovators have been issued over 8,000 patents, practically one patent per day.

Today, Dayton and the Miami Valley area offer one of the largest concentrations of technical experts in the world, particularly in aerospace and high technology—more than 23,000 scientists, computer specialists and technicians

Downtown's One Dayton Centre Tower stands in the heart of the eight-county Miami Valley. Andy Snow

work right here in the Dayton region. But Dayton is more than high-tech. The city of Dayton occupies the hub of an eight-county region with a population of over a million people. The different jurisdictions create a diverse, yet unified, metropolitan area that includes Fortune 500 firms, advanced technology companies, manufacturing, warehousing/distribution and service businesses, as well as agricultural enterprises.

The Miami Valley is diverse in the quality of life as well. An abundance of green space provides residents with more than 35,000 acres of reserves and nature centers. Each village, town and city offers a variety of recreational opportunities—parks, pools and country clubs—as well as celebrations unique to its own particular history and locale.

With so many different municipalities and so much to offer, the Dayton Area Chamber of Commerce and Wright State University decided it was time to tell the world about the Miami Valley. In 1989 leaders from the Chamber and Wright State developed a program called CHALLENGE 95, which sought to incorporate the multicounty region into a single, cohesive planning body.

Honoring the memory of those who served their country in battle is the Veterans Administration cemetery in Montgomery County. Bill Swartz/BBS Images

A steering committee of sixty leaders was formed and hundreds of people participated in open community forums. The result: an aggressive program designed to maintain the uniqueness of each community while stimulating the economy of the entire Miami Valley.

Communities such as Centerville in Montgomery County, dot the Miami Valley landscape, offering the avid shopper a blend of specialty boutiques and antique shops.
Andy Snow

MONTGOMERY COUNTY

Montgomery County, the largest county in the region, with a population of 574,000, includes the city of Dayton as well as fine suburban communities. Northern suburbs such as Englewood, Vandalia and Huber Heights are thriving housing developments. Oakwood, south of Dayton, offers manor homes and upscale shopping. Brookville, Trotwood, Union, New Lebanon, Miamisburg, Moraine and West Carrollton are located within a short drive—or a pleasurable bike ride—of downtown. Centerville and Kettering, to the south, are growing communities offering within their borders all the amenities of city life—shopping, the arts, prosperous businesses.

The diversity of Montgomery County's cities is also present in the industrial base. From automotive manufacturing to computer information services, Montgomery County is supported by an excellent infrastructure, including Dayton International Airport to the north. Yet, Montgomery County remains balanced, with working fields of wheat, beans and corn on the outskirts of the urban center.

Located in the heart of Montgomery County, Dayton, with a population of nearly 200,000, is the sixth largest city in Ohio. Dayton's wide, clean streets and extensive network of parks endow it with an air of old and new, upscale and down-home, fast-paced and unhurried.

Dayton is summer at Wegerzyn Horticultural Center. Dayton is sailing on Eastwood Lake or at

Standing today at the North Gateway of the Main Street Project in Dayton, the marble monument to Civil War soldier Private Fair was dedicated in 1884. Recast in bronze, the monument was rededicated on Memorial Day in 1991 and is situated one block south of its original location.
Bill Swartz/BBS Images

the Englewood Reserve. Dayton is Saturday night at the Victoria Theatre or the Dayton Ballet. Dayton is the opera, the Philharmonic, the Muse Machine and the Dayton Contemporary Dance Company. Dayton is jazz and the city's Neon District where the hot spots stay jumping all night and the greats of rhythm and blues perform at Gilly's. For folk music, it's the Canal Street Tavern. For comedy, it's Wiley's Comedy Club located in the historic Oregon District. Dayton is shopping downtown or at malls—one located north of town, one south and a new one east—and dozens of shopping centers.

Of course, Dayton is work. But not all work. Of the Daytonians who have jobs downtown, many gather around Courthouse Square for a leisurely outdoor lunch. On Friday after five the fun really gets cranking with the biweekly "Affair on the Square." Bands pump out music, vendors hawk sandwiches and soft drinks, farmers set up stands filled with fresh vegetables and hot-from-the-oven pastries. And every Fourth of July the city blocks off Main Street and throws a big bash, complete with a Dayton Philharmonic pops concert and a fireworks display that lights up the evening sky.

Since 1913 Dayton has been administered by a city-manager—the first large municipality in the nation to adopt this form of government. The city has five commissioners, one of whom serves as mayor. To ensure the betterment of the entire region, Dayton's commissioners work closely with officials of Montgomery County and the private sector.

GREENE COUNTY

With 267,000 acres and a population of 130,000, Greene County is Ohio's sixteenth largest county. It is home of Wright-Patterson Air Force Base, located in Fairborn, and the site of six colleges and universities, including world-famous Antioch College, Wright State University, Central State and Wilberforce.

From Xenia, the county seat, and in all directions, Greene County has enjoyed rapid growth. One of the fastest-growing areas is Beavercreek, along the Interstate 675 bypass east of Dayton. Bellbrook, in the southern part of the county, is home of unique shops and the annual Sugar Maple Festival. Nestled in the eastern part of the county is Jamestown.

When the workday is done, Greene County is just the place to exchange a business suit for a sweat suit and enjoy the outdoors, including twenty-four parks on 6,000 acres of recreational land. Walk the gorge that overlooks the Blue Hole in Clifton Gorge State Nature Preserve. Stop for lunch at the Clifton Mill, a working grist mill. Stroll trails filled with more than 340 species of wildflowers. Greene County is home to the U.S. Air Force Museum and the epic outdoor drama, Blue Jacket.

DARKE COUNTY

In Darke County, population 53,000, 92 percent of the land is devoted to agriculture. In 1990 total agricultural receipts equalled more than $200 million. Growing crops and raising livestock is a way of life—and a celebration of that life.

The Great Darke County Fair, a nine-day gala held in August at the county seat, Greenville, is the largest county fair in the state. Greenville is the birthplace of Annie Oakley, with a statue of the famous markswoman to prove it. Lowell Thomas, Sr., the famous broadcaster and world traveler, called Greenville home.

An approaching summer storm dramatically darkens the sky over a Darke County farm.

Richard Todd

Clifton Gorge State Nature Preserve in Greene County is just one of many reserves and parks in the Dayton region, which boasts more than 40,000 acres of green space for outdoor enthusiasts. C. Gatland Photography

Major industrial companies include Corning Inc., Cadillac Gage Co. (a unit of Textron), Whirlpool Corp. and many others.

Miami County

Life unfolds at a slower pace in the dozens of villages and small towns tucked just north of Dayton along Interstate 75. When the Milton-Union High School football team wins the big game, for example, the whole town gathers for a victory parade with the town fire truck leading the way, horns blaring and lights blazing.

Tipp City, Piqua and Troy—three of the county's largest municipalities—are historic canal towns from the days of the Miami-Erie Canal.

Seven thousand people make their home in Tipp City, which is closest to Dayton. Built along the Miami-Erie Canal in 1840, Tipp City boasts eighty-nine buildings on the National Register of Historic Places. Old Historic Tippecanoe, a downtown historic district, features hearty country cooking, rural country inns, art galleries and craft shops. There's even a clothing store that carries everything the well-dressed frontier pioneer might need. Autumn brings the Mum Festival and a parade down the center of town.

Piqua, located a few miles north of Troy, celebrates the annual Piqua Heritage Festival every Labor Day weekend.

Troy was settled in 1808 nearly thirty years before the Miami-Erie Canal cut right through the center of town. Located between Tipp City and Piqua, this city of 20,000

hosts the Strawberry Festival one weekend each June and settles back while more than 150,000 visitors sample all things strawberry. Troy, the county seat, is also home to industry giants such as PMI Food Equipment Group, Hobart Brothers Co. and American Matsushita Electronics Corp. (Panasonic).

Covered bridges and rural byways of Miami County recall an era of days past. Richard Todd

PREBLE COUNTY

Preble is picture-postcard country: silver silos jut into the sky; white farmhouses preside over planting and harvest; rows of corn bend in the wind.

A gracious community of nearly 40,000, Preble County was founded in the winter of 1808 by farmers and mill operators who used Seven-Mile Creek outside of Eaton to grind their grains into flour. The millers are long gone, but those who came to work the land left an enduring legacy.

Over 90 percent of Preble County is given to agriculture, with corn the primary crop. Farms are typically 165 acres and earn an average of approximately $50,000 per year, making them the ninth most prosperous farms in the state. Each of Preble's eight villages, from Camden, population 2,300, to West Manchester, population 490, have at least one park for the enjoyment of their citizens. In the county seat, the city of Eaton, population 7,500, people find time to stop and chat—about the weather, crops and the world situation. Life unfolds at a slower pace and residents like it that way.

WARREN COUNTY

Rural charm blooms in Warren County, located south on Interstate 75 along the Dayton-Cincinnati corridor. The Little Miami River meanders though the countryside here. The Little Miami Scenic State Park offers horseback riding, canoeing or picnicking.

Historic Clifton Mill in Greene County is the country's largest water-powered grist mill operating today. Tours are offered at this site along the Little Miami Scenic River. Dawson Jones

DAYTON
STREET
GULCH

But if you want razzle-dazzle . . .

There's Paramount King's Island Entertainment Center, the largest seasonal theme park in America, and The Beach, the Midwest's biggest water park. Try Waynesville, antique capital of the Midwest, featuring dozens of antique shops in refurbished turn-of-the-century homes. Or Pioneer Village, a reconstructed New England-style settlement dating back to the early 1800s. And Lebanon, home of the Golden Lamb, Ohio's oldest restaurant and inn, where ten presidents throughout America's history found a good meal and a comfortable bed. Warren County, one of the prime tourist destinations in America's heartland, is full of surprises, from award-winning vineyards and an ancient Indian burial ground to Caesar Creek State Park and more than 2,830 acres of lakes, beaches, picnicking and hiking.

Charming Lebanon in Warren County is home to Ohio's oldest restaurant and inn. Bill Swartz/BBS Images

CLARK COUNTY

Bordering Greene County, between Dayton and Columbus, Clark County includes 1,150 farms within 4,112 square miles of land. Ranked Ohio's number one cattle and calf producer and fourth in production of greenhouse and nursery plants, Clark County places ninth in the state for total cash receipts accruing from agricultural products. Farms average 201 acres. And more than 3,500 young people participate in area-sponsored Future Farmers of America and 4-H Clubs.

Nevertheless, Clark County possesses a vigorous industrial base. Twelve internationally owned corporations produce a range of products from marine gears and diesel engines to paper-pulp processing equipment. Still, the manufacture of farm machinery remains the

A thirsty bicyclist takes a break at a local Yellow Springs watering hole. Andy Snow

Truly part of America's heartland, Springboro in Warren County readies for Halloween. Bill Swartz/BBS Images

area's primary industrial product. Nearly 150 years ago the city of Springfield became the leader in production of reapers and harvesters. Today Navistar (formerly International Harvester Co.), still calls Springfield home, as it has since the turn of the century.

Springfield, the county seat, is located thirty minutes from Dayton—close enough for additional amenities, yet distant enough to maintain its own identity. Something unique is always available in Springfield. Like shopping at the Marketplace, a renovated turn-of-the-century mart filled with novel stores and restaurants. The Marketplace is one of seventeen county buildings listed on the National Historic Register.

Eaton is the county seat where the Preble County Courthouse echoes with pounding gavels from trials past and present. Lynn Funkhouser

Summertime is filled with activities. The Springfield Symphony Orchestra performs lawn concerts during lunchtime. The Springfield Arts Council holds the Annual Summer Arts Festival, where outdoor programs are staged in the amphitheater of Veterans Park. For water sports, Buck Creek State Park's provides nearly 4,000 acres of forest and lake.

CLINTON COUNTY

Located in the heart of Southern Ohio, Clinton County is comprised of several communities: Wilmington, Blanchester, Sabrina, New Vienna, Clarksville and Port William. Clinton is close enough to Cincinnati, Columbus and Dayton to enjoy the urban culture, while still retaining the pace of small-time life.

Over fifty industrial firms are involved in a variety of businesses from mobile homes and machine tools to ceramics and auto parts. Industry in the area revolves around the Wilmington Industrial Air Park and Airborne Commerce Park, where more than thirty businesses are located. Agriculture

The thriving industrial base of Clark County is evident in the growing city of Springfield. Bill Swartz/BBS Images

has also always been important to the economic life of the county. In 1990 the county had 920 farms spread over 236,000 acres, which generated nearly $64 million in cash receipts.

In close proximity to the urban centers of Dayton, Cincinnati and Columbus, the community of Wilmington in Clinton County still enjoys the pace of small-town life. Bill Swartz/BBS Images

MIAMI VALLEY HISTORY

Around 14,000 years ago, as the Wisconsin Glacier retreated from Southwestern Ohio, it gouged deep river valleys and high cliffs from the 425-million-year-old sedimentary rock blocking its path.

The retreating glacier provided the ancient Paleo-Indians with a lush home of plants and animals. Hunters and nomads, the Paleo-Indians left behind little evidence of their existence, save for a few flint tools, spear points, knives and scrapers used to hunt the now-extinct mastodon. Around 8,000 B.C., as the climate continued to warm, the Archaic Indians settled in the valley. They hunted, fished and lived on the grains, fruits and nuts that prospered due to the climatic change. Their culture, which lasted until about 1,000 B.C., yielded to the Adena, the first generation of Woodland Indians.

The Adena built elaborate mounds to bury their dead. And the evidence remains today. The Miamisburg Mound, the largest Indian mound in Ohio, located just south of Dayton, measures sixty-eight feet high and 850 feet around. In West Carrollton, between Miamisburg and Dayton, the Hopewell Indians built an earthwork that covered thirty-one acres with circles and squares.

The enactment in 1787 of the Northwest Ordinance opened up the country to a hardy stock of pioneers. In 1796 Dayton's founders—Benjamin Van Cleve, Daniel Cooper, Colonel George Newcomb and Jonathan Dayton—traveled across the Ohio Valley and up the Great Miami River to a site

Clark County is home to the scenic campus of Wittenberg University. Bill Swartz/BBS Images

located at the juncture of three rivers—a perfect place for settlement. They quickly built a shelter, Newcomb's Tavern, which still stands today in Dayton's Carillon Historical Park. Dayton township was soon formed, comprising much of what is today the Miami Valley.

The confluence of three bodies of water—the Great Miami, Stillwater and Mad Rivers—all but ensured a prosperous future for the new township. A series of canals that followed the Great Miami and connected Lake Erie with the Ohio River made shipping on flat-bottomed boats possible,

Modest, strong lines of St. Mary's Episcopal Church in Warren County reflect the dedicated spirit of the Miami Valley people. Bill Swartz/BBS Images

creating a thriving economy for the villages and towns situated along the river. Today the rivers are used mostly for recreation. At the Piqua Historic Area in Miami County, for example, mules still pull the General Harrison canal boat and its passengers along a restored mile-long segment of the Miami-Erie Canal.

When Daniel Cooper built a grist mill in 1799, Dayton was destined to become an industrial leader. And indeed it did. To keep his bartenders honest, James Ritty, owner of the Empire Restaurant, tinkered around and invented the cash register. John H. Patterson took the idea and marketed it to other bar owners. It was a tough sell. After all, why replace a one-cent pencil and an inexpensive strong box with a $125 machine? Today Ritty's idea and Patterson's company—NCR Corporation—has evolved into one of the world's leading electronics and computer companies.

The 1815 Johnston Farm, located in the Piqua Historical Area, is the only remaining Indian agent house in Ohio. Richard Todd

Across the street from NCR, Carillon Historical Park features sixty-five acres and fifty-one historical exhibits. There's a replica of Colonel Edward Deeds's barn, where Charles Kettering and "The Barn Gang," as they came to be known, invented the first automobile self-starter, which led to the creation of DELCO, Dayton Electric Laboratory Co.

And, of course, there's that modest bicycle shop on Hawthorne Street where Orville and Wilbur Wright gave Dayton its greatest legacy: the airplane.

From renovated Victorians to luxury townhomes, the Dayton region has something for everyone. Dawson Jones

CHAPTER TWO

THE WRIGHT PLACE

December 17, 1903, Orville Wright flew 120 feet. Although he spent only 12 seconds in the air, Orville and his brother Wilbur had succeeded in giving us wings.

Dayton's proud history of aviation technology, research and advancement is well recorded. From the birth of flight to the testing of advanced aircraft at Wright-Patterson Air Force Base, Dayton remains an important center of the aviation-aerospace industry.

Back in 1909 Dayton Wright Airplane Company, owned by the famous brothers, was already manufacturing airplanes. By the following year, the company had added a second building and was producing four planes a month, more than any other aircraft factory in the world. From the tinkerings in a modest Dayton bicycle shop, the genius and ingenuity of the Wright Brothers bestowed on the Miami Valley a legacy of innovation. Today the region has one of the greatest concentrations of aerospace/high-technology companies in the United States.

Wright-Patterson Air Force Base is the largest, most diverse and organizationally complex military base in the world. It was commissioned in 1948

Research and development for the F-117A stealth fighter was done at Wright-Patterson Air Force Base, the largest and most important military complex in the U.S. Air Force. U.S. Air Force

The 65-acre Carillon Historical Park honors the inventors and inventions that contributed to the growth of the Miami Valley, including Wilbur and Orville Wright, whose genius and ingenuity advanced the field of aviation. Jim Baron/Image Finders

from three World War I-era army installations: Wilbur Wright Field, Fairfield Air Depot and McCook Field—an engineering division that continued to test aircraft after the end of the war. During the twenties, numerous speed and maneuverability records were set at McCook, including many by James Doolittle, the famed aviator who led World War II's first bombing raids over Tokyo.

The aviation visionaries of the Miami Valley are well remembered through a variety of museums and historical sites. The Aviation Trail, a self-guided tour, tells the story of the area's contribution to flight. The Wright Cycle Shop is where Wilbur and Orville built their flying machine. Hawthorne Hill mansion in Oakwood is the last home of the Wright family, where they entertained such fellow visionaries as Alexander Graham Bell, Thomas A. Edison, Henry and Edsel Ford, Charles A. Lindbergh and Paul Laurence Dunbar—Dayton's famous black poet and childhood friend of Orville, Wilbur and their sister, Katharine. The International Women's Air & Space Museum, located in Centerville, is planning a new facility near downtown Dayton. And the 1806 home of Asahel Wright, Wilbur and Orville's great-uncle, is filled with memorabilia commemorating the contributions of women in flight.

Near downtown Dayton at Carillon Historical Park, which features sixty-five acres of historic exhibits, visitors snap photos of the Wright Flyer III.

The last home of the Wright Brothers, stately Hawthorne Hill, still stands today in the suburban community of Oakwood. Gregory C. Sundra

Because of the complexity of the controls, Orville considered the Wright III the most important plane the two brothers ever built. The park also features a replica of the Wright Bicycle Shop.

Huffman Prairie, where the brothers held their flying school and perfected the techniques of flight, later became part of the U.S. Army's Wilbur Wright Field. Today Huffman Prairie is part of Wright-Patterson Air Force Base.

More than 200 aircraft and missiles are on display at the United States Air Force Museum. William A. Holmes/Image Finders

From a helicopter model based on a design by Leonardo DaVinci to the Apollo 15 space capsule, which circled the moon in 1971, the United States Air Force Museum—the oldest and largest aviation museum in the world—is a testament to the men and women who created flight.

Located on the grounds of Wright-Patterson, the museum attracts over 1.5 millon visitors annually. Visitors can walk through presidential airplanes, get a look at rare foreign aircraft, see what life was like in a World War II prisoner-of-war camp and snap photos of more than 200 aircraft and missiles. "It felt really neat seeing the DC-3, the plane I flew in as a stewardess for American Airlines in the 1940s," says Betty Shea, who now lives in California. "My son and his wife may be the reason we get to Dayton, but once there, we wouldn't miss the Air Force Museum."

"Our economy is tied to aviation, aerospace and the related technologies," says Brad Tillson. "Our future is driven by it." Mr. Tillson is a board member of the National Aviation Hall of Fame and vice-chairman of the 2003 Fund, a group of more

than seventy Miami Valley citizens who are preparing for the year 2003—the 100-year anniversary of powered flight. The group has worked with the National Park Service to have three locations certified as historical landmarks: Huffman Prairie, site of many early Wright Brother test flights; the Wright Flyer III; and the Wright Bicycle Shop. Also on the list: the Hoover Building, site of the Wright Brothers' printing business and Hawthorne Hill, the Wright family home. The Dayton Aviation Heritage National Park is being planned with passage of Congressional legislation.

UNITED STATES AIR AND TRADE SHOW

The United States Air and Trade Show is the event that provides the U.S. aerospace industry with a "home court" advantage and is recognized as the only international trade exposition of its kind for North America. Starting with a rally and a parade of fifty hot-air balloons, everything from historic airplanes to space-age technology is on display. The week-long event, held in July in even-numbered years, hosts 300 domestic and international aerospace and related high-tech businesses and organizations in more than 100,000 square feet of display and conference space. Exhibitors read like a who's who of aerospace—General Dynamics, McDonnell Douglas, United Technologies, Boeing, Rockwell, Northrop. Major product announcements are made that attract international media and trade press. The show also features a forum for the discussion of global aerospace issues.

The highlight of the event is the colorful, exciting and renowned air show, described by most knowledgeable observers as the "best in the world." This high-flying exhibition is held every summer at Dayton International Airport as part of the U.S. Air and Trade Show or, in odd-numbered years as the Dayton Air Show.

People from all over the U.S.—and the world—come to spread their blankets across the grass and watch the spectacular Air Force Thunderbirds and the Navy Blue Angels execute thrilling precision maneuvers high in the sky. Crowds are held breathless by wing-walkers balancing on historic biplanes or the blasts of machine-gun fire blazing from the cannons of combat jets simulating tactical assaults.

On the ground, dozens of exhibits from the old to the new delight visitors of all ages. Volunteers dressed in World War II leather bomber jackets, Mae West life vests and flight helmets with goggles direct sightseers through a B-24 bomber. Inside the main pavilion, NASA's display features the Hubble telescope and the space station.

Enthusiastic parade-goers celebrate during the week-long U.S. Air and Trade Show.
C. Gatland Photography

For the 1990 United States Air and Trade Show—and the sixteenth annual Air Show exhibition—Russian jets swept into Dayton. An American flag flew from the cockpit window of a Russian Ilyushen IL-76 cargo jet. Two Russian MiG-29 fighter planes zoomed overhead. "The most important air show in America is in Dayton. I'm glad to be here," said Roman Taskaev, a Russian MiG-29 pilot. "We come from Moscow on a goodwill air show tour. This is beautiful," agreed Y. G. Yermakov, also a MiG pilot. "We heard much about the air show in Dayton," added Anatoly Belosvet, deputy chief designer of MiG aircraft, "and we are aware that this is the most prestigious air show in the U.S.A."

Not to be outdone by the Russians, the United States Air Force zoomed in flying F-117A Stealth fighters and the forward-swept-wing X-29 research plane. In a sense, the Stealth was coming home. All the research and development for the secret plane had been done at Wright-Patterson. "This is a fabulous show. It's our first civilian appearance," said Lt. Col. John Zink, a Stealth pilot. "I'm glad to be here. The air show people are treating us well. It's the Midwestern friendliness."

Sanctioned by the United States Department of Commerce, the U.S. Air and Trade Show is also supported by the Department of Defense, National Aeronautics and

Crowds are thrilled by precision maneuvers of U.S. Air Force Thunderbirds at the U.S. Air and Trade Show, the fastest-growing aerospace event in the country. William A. Holmes/Image Finders

Space Administration (NASA) and the Federal Aviation Administration (FAA). *World Airshow News* said Dayton has "an outstanding air show organization and production." The show has earned the Governor's Award for "excellence of achievement benefiting mankind and improving the quality of life for all Ohioans."

Of course, air shows have been held in Dayton since the beginning of flight. The Wright Brothers flew aerial exhibitions, many of them over the Huffman Prairie. In 1924 the International Air Races drew about 100,000 spectators to Fairfield Air Immediate Depot and the Wilbur Wright Field, now part of Wright-Patterson Air Force Base. Lt. James Doolittle, one of those early daredevils, delighted spectators with his aerial feats.

Shows continued throughout the years, the largest occurring in 1945, when more than one million visitors from the U.S. and abroad came to the Army Air Forces Fair for the first postwar show. Today's international show originated in the 1970s, when General Aviation Day was held at Dayton General Airport, a small Montgomery County-owned airport south of Dayton. The idea took hold and the Dayton Air Fair was born. The 1975 Dayton Air Fair, held at Dayton Municipal Airport, now Dayton International Airport, was sponsored by the Dayton Area Chamber of Commerce, the city of Dayton and its Department of Aviation. Opening the gates to 65,000 people, it was the first air show in the nation to offer a combination of entertainment to the general public and sales information to the aviation industry. Today, the United States Air and Trade Show regularly attracts crowds of 300,000 visitors.

THE NATIONAL AVIATION HALL OF FAME

The National Aviation Hall of Fame immortalizes the men and women whose vision opened the skies. Launched October 5, 1962, by the Dayton Area Chamber of Commerce, James W. Jacobs, Gregory C. Karas, John A. Lombard, Larry E. O'Neil and Gerald E. Weller, the first National Aviation Hall of Fame Enshrinement Ceremony was held in December of that year. The National Aviation Hall of Fame is the only exclusively aviation-related organization chartered by the Congress of the United States. In recognition of its importance to the nation, Congress created the organization through passage of Public Law 88-372. The bill was signed into law by President Lyndon B. Johnson in 1964.

Once a year, in conjunction with the United States Air and Trade Show/Dayton Air Show, the National Aviation Hall of Fame sponsors a black-tie affair at the Dayton Convention Center and formally inducts men and women who have advanced the science of flight. Among the dreamers and doers who have been enshrined for their contributions to flight: Orville and Wilbur Wright (inducted in 1962), Amelia Earhart Putnam (1968), Charles Yeager (1973),

A parade of some 50 hot-air balloons kicks off the festivities at Dayton's U.S. Air and Trade Show.
C. Gatland Photography

Howard Hughes (1973), John Glenn (1976), Clyde Cessna (1978), Neil Armstrong (1979), Henry Ford (1984) and Dr. Hans P. von Ohain (1990). The list goes on and on. Portraits of the inductees were drawn by former Daytonian Milton Caniff, creator of comic strips "Steve Canyon" and "Terry and the Pirates."

The National Aviation Hall of Fame learning center, to be located in downtown Dayton, will feature 52,000 square feet of hands-on exhibits, displays, scientific demonstrations and live performances. Aviation thinkers, tinkerers and heroes will come to life and visitors will see how the earth looked to pilots like Lindbergh and Earhart. The $12 million fund-raising campaign to build the center began with a $1 million contribution from the state of Ohio at the 1990 Enshrinement Ceremony.

Everything from historic aircraft to state-of-the-art technology is on display at the renowned U.S. Air and Trade Show. Here, a flight crew is dressed in World War II flying attire.
Dan Tyrpak

James M. Cox Dayton International Airport

Surrounded by 4,000 acres of farmland and low-density housing, the James M. Cox Dayton International Airport is located eleven miles north of downtown Dayton near the suburb of Vandalia, at the intersection of Interstates 70 and 75. Evolving from a private airfield founded in 1924, Dayton International is owned by the city of Dayton and operated by the Department of Aviation. A three-year renovation project completed in 1989 has allowed Dayton International to keep pace with the region's growing economy and expanding need for air services. Financed by a city-

sponsored, $31.2 million revenue-bond offering—with federal airport improvement funds making up the difference—the expansion progressed at no cost to taxpayers.

Dayton International, one of the few airports in the nation with a dual-runway system, offers three all-weather lighted runways: a 10,900-foot primary runway, an 8,500-foot parallel runway and a 7,000-foot cross-wind runway.

Perhaps it's only fitting for the city that gave the world flight to have one of the nation's busiest airports. More than 200 flights depart Dayton International daily. Twelve commercial airlines provide nonstop service to sixty-five cities and carry 4.8 million passengers annually. Eight air-freight carriers serve the region. Each night, Emery Worldwide Air Freight processes more than 2.3 million pounds of letters and cargo at the $90 million Emery Worldwide Starbase Superhub, making Dayton one of the largest air-freight facilities in the world. Smaller regional airports—Class I and

The U.S. Air and Trade Show regularly attracts some 300,000 visitors, and remains a tribute to Dayton and the Wright Brothers. Bill Swartz/BBS Images

James M. Cox International Airport is situated on 4,000 acres, just a few minutes north of downtown Dayton. Andy Snow

Class II—are also available in Clark, Montgomery, Greene, Darke, Miami and Warren counties.

WRIGHT-PATTERSON AIR FORCE BASE

Located on 8,145 acres, Wright-Patterson Air Force Base is the largest, most important and organizationally complex military installation in the U.S. Air Force. Wright-Patterson is headquarters for the research-and-development center and a vast worldwide logistics system.

Wright-Patt is home of the new Air Force Materiel Command (AFMC) which brings research, development, procurement and maintenance under one command. AFMC is responsible for managing more than 50 percent of the U.S. Air Force budget annually.

Wright-Patterson also houses over 100 organizations representing a broad spectrum of Department of Defense activities, including the the Air Force Institute of Technology, Wright Laboratory and the newly created Joint Logistics Systems Center, which manages the development, requisition and installation of new computer systems for all military services and the Defense Logistics Agency. The JLSC will manage about $260 million in contracts for computer systems and software.

With 28,500 employees, Wright-Patterson Air Force Base is the area's largest employer. The presence of the base has created 26,800 secondary jobs within a fifty-mile commuting radius.

In fiscal year 1991, the economic impact of the base was $3.6 billion on the surrounding eighteen coun-

With more than 200 flights departing each day, Dayton International is one of the nation's busiest airports. C. Gatland Photography

ties. Some of these dollars are funneled into the local economy via contract awards for research and development. In one year, for example, the Aeronautical Systems Division awarded $119 million to fund R & D operations at large and small businesses and educational institutions in the Dayton area.

Contract awards through Wright-Patterson Contracting Center totaled close to $680 million in fiscal 1991 within the Dayton region. The Joint Logistics Systems Center has recently begun awarding contracts, although its impact on the local area economy is not yet known.

With an annual budget of $1 billion and a staff of more than 2,000 scientists and engineers, Wright Laboratory is the world's premier center for basic and applied research of aeronautical systems. Many of the scientists and engineers are recognized world leaders in their diverse fields. The wealth of expertise at work at Wright Laboratory includes a variety of fields such as aeronautical, chemical, electronic and mechanical engineering, physics, chemistry, mathematics, computer science, psychology and physiology.

While research and development of aerospace technology is the mission of Wright Laboratory, the U.S. Air Force and other government entities are not the exclusive benefactors of these resources. Most of the technology is available for immediate commercial application and industrial problem-solving. Examples of commercial

Dayton International features one of the few dual-runway systems in operation in the country, which allows simultaneous use of both the main and crosswind runways. This system helps to ensure on-time arrivals and departures. Bill Swartz/BBS Images

spin-offs of Wright Laboratory technology are: graphite composite fishing rods, tennis/racquetball rackets, golf clubs, artificial hip joints, brake discs, exhaust gas analysis, fire-resistant fabrics, electronic blood/breath analyzers and much more.

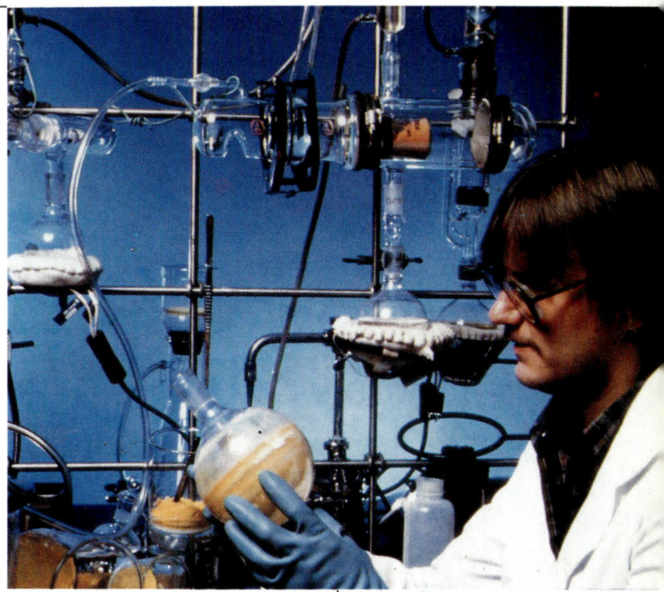

Research and development of nonmetallic, electromagnetic, metallic and ceramic materials is conducted through the Materials Directorate, one of seven major technology directorates in operation at Wright-Patterson. U.S. Air Force

AEROSPACE INDUSTRY

Since the pioneering days of flying, Dayton's pursuit of the business of flight has never abated. Back in 1910, Phillip O. Parmalee, an exhibition pilot for the Wright Brothers flew two packages of Salome silk, each weighing 200 pounds, from Dayton to Columbus. Commercial cargo flight was born.

In 1917 Edward A. Deeds and Charles F. Kettering formed the Dayton Wright Company to manufacture warplanes for World War I. NCR pitched in, too, building airspeed indicators and tachometers. Today more than 800 advanced technology companies are located throughout the Miami Valley. Many of these companies are aerospace-related.

Since 1946 B. F. Goodrich Aerospace has conducted business from the city of Troy, in Miami County. Today the company occupies a 312,000-square-foot facility and employs 800 skilled workers who produce wheels and brakes for sophisticated aircraft such as the Boeing 747-400 jetliner, the massive C-5A/B military transport and NASA's fleet of space shuttles.

Hobart Brothers Company, incorporated in Troy in 1917, has made important contributions to the space program through development of new metal alloys and advanced arc-welding technology that has been used to weld the space shuttle's massive fuel tanks.

Back in 1917, when R. N. Hartzell manufactured a walnut propeller for his neighbors Orville and Wilbur Wright, he never dreamed that his products would one day go into space. But when the Voyager program needed a specialized type of propeller, they came to the city of

Recognized as the world's largest and oldest military aviation museum, the U.S. Air Force Museum is located on the grounds of Wright-Patterson Air Force Base. William A. Holmes/Image Finders

Wright-Patterson is home to the 906th Tactical Fighter Group, which is authorized for F-16A Fighting Falcon aircraft. U.S. Air Force

B. F. Goodrich Aerospace in Troy manufactures wheels and brakes for today's sophisticated aircraft. Andy Snow

Piqua and Hartzell Propeller Inc. Today the company manufactures aluminum and graphite props for Cessna and Beech aircraft.

Elano Corp., established in Xenia in 1950 by Ervin J. Nutter, fabricates metal for the aerospace, defense and aviation industries. A wholly owned subsidiary of General Electric, the Greene County company has earned FAA approval as a certified repair station for tubular and sheet metal jet engine ducting.

Consultants such as Dayton Aerospace Associates, Inc. and Digital Concepts Inc., advise private industry and the Department of Defense on a variety of projects.

The goal of any company, of course, is to see one's products perform flawlessly. Ulysses, a joint U.S.-European space program that sent an information-gathering satellite into orbit around the sun, drew its electrical power from a system built by General Electric and tested at the Department of Energy's Mound Plant in the Dayton suburb of Miamisburg. The Galileo Program, which put a satellite in orbit around Jupiter, carried a similar electrical power system.

AVIATION/AEROSPACE EDUCATION

Situated at the center of an educational corridor of twenty-six colleges and universities, Dayton offers a consortium of aerospace educational resources unlike anywhere else.

According to the Ohio Aerospace Institute, the University of Dayton—among the nation's top 100 engineering schools—leads the state in all university aerospace research. Since 1949 UD has conducted more than a quarter of a billion dollars worth of research for the Air Force, making it Wright-Patterson's top university contractor. UD has also conducted projects for the

The Air Force Institute of Technology directly supports national defense through specialized education programs. U.S. Air Force

Army, NASA and private industry.

The University of Dayton offers a strong aerospace program, with professors who are considered leaders in their fields. Hans von Ohain, designer of the jet engine, is a senior research engineer in the University of Dayton Research Institute (UDRI). Jim Roley, one of the 100 semifinalists for the Teacher in Space program, is an assistant professor of teacher education.

Dubbed the MIT of the Midwest, the Air Force Institute of Technology (AFIT), located on Wright-Patterson Air Force Base, is responsible for graduate-level education that meets the strict requirements of the Air Force and the Department of Defense.

Lightning strikes are tested on the F-16 fighter jet by Krug International—another fascinating element of Miami Valley's aerospace industry.
Dawson Jones

The Air Force's only degree-granting technical institute, AFIT offers master's degree programs through three resident schools: the School of Systems and Logistics; the School of Engineering; and the School of Civil Engineering and Services. Each year AFIT educates some 25,000 students; nearly one-third of all general officers on active duty hold AFIT-sponsored degrees. But entrance requirements are stiff. To earn a degree students must complete seventy-two credit hours in eighteen months and conduct original research. More than thirty U.S. astronauts have graduated from AFIT programs.

Since 1978 a select number of young physicians from all over the world have come to Wright State University School of Medicine for their residency in aerospace medicine—the only civilian aerospace medicine program offered anywhere in the United States. Affiliated with Good Samaritan Hospital in Dayton and the Armstrong Labs at Wright-Patterson, young physicians learn from the unique slant of the space environment. Residents study weightlessness, acceleration, fire and radiation, nutrition, aging and oxygen deficiencies as they affect the human body during flight and space travel. Doctors undergo the same rigorous survival course required of pilots.

CHAPTER THREE

TECHNOLOGY AND INDUSTRIAL WEALTH

Fortune magazine cites Dayton as one of the nation's best cities for business. "Based on Fortune's statistics," says Richard Clay Dixon, mayor of Dayton, "our city generally outshone most Midwest and Northeast cities and more than held its own against the strong Sunbelt communities."

That wasn't always the case. In the 1970s, Dayton was hard hit by the economic woes of the nation. Dayton lost 35,000 manufacturing jobs. During that period the state of Ohio had one of the highest unemployment rates in the nation. Convinced that only economic diversity would sustain Dayton through recessionary periods, city leaders planned a future that would include a mix of service, manufacturing and high-technology jobs.

Indeed, an ever-expanding service industry supports Dayton's manufacturers with nationally recognized printing services, banks, convention centers, hotels and a host of other service-related businesses. Over the last two decades, services has been the fastest-growing sector in the region. Services employ the most people—26 percent, or 118,000 persons.

With one of the highest concentrations of scientists, engineers, computer specialists and technicians of any city in the United States, Dayton is a mecca of advanced technology resources and ambitious scientists from all over the world.

Robotic welders let the sparks fly at the GM Truck and Bus Group Moraine Assembly facility. Dawson Jones

Approximately 26 percent of the region's manufacturing firms are considered high-tech, with more than 800 companies engaged in leading-edge products. Biotechnology, computer software development and aerospace, for example, represent about ten percent of the region's total labor force.

Manufacturing still provides many of the jobs in the area. In 1991, 98,000 people were employed in manufacturing, or 22 percent of the total work force of 443,000 persons. Nine of the nation's largest firms, along with some 15,000 smaller companies, comprise the Miami Valley's extensive manufacturing base. Services employ the most people—26 percent, or 118,000 persons.

From Springboro to Tipp City, the Dayton area has garnered a growing reputation as the automotive component capital of the world. Automotive sales generate more than $7 billion each year. Customers are located throughout the United States, Canada, Europe and Asia. Moreover, the concentration of the region's highly skilled work force has enticed more auto-related firms to relocate into the area. Scores of highly skilled tool-and-die makers service the six General Motors manufacturing plants and wide-scope high-technology industry of the region. General Motors has the second largest concentration of its employees located in the Dayton area. Chrysler, Honda, Ford and Navistar also operate assembly and component plants in the Miami Valley. "No better union craft

A skilled worker at the pharmaceutical firm of AH Robins in Vandalia operates equipment that manufactures time-release pills.
Dawson Jones

people exist in the tool-and-die industry than in the Miami Valley," says Tom Heine, president of the Dayton Area Chamber of Commerce.

Dayton's economy has a world perspective that accounts for more than $1.5 billion in exports per year. Estimates of the gross product associated with international business are 12 to 15 percent. Approximately 550 manufacturing firms employ nearly 70,000 workers in export-related industries.

With more than 56,000 people worldwide, NCR is one of the top five employers in the Miami Valley. The scenic NCR World Headquarters is located on the south side of downtown Dayton. Jim Baron/Image Finders

For more than 100 years, NCR Corporation has operated internationally; the Bob Hipple Laboratory for Cancer Research in Dayton was designated as an International Cancer Research Institute by the government of Japan. Mel Enting, founder and owner of Enting Water Conditioning, Inc.—manufacturers and distributors of water purification systems—spoke at the former Soviet Union's 117th conference and addressed environmental problems regarding the Aral Sea. One of the first foreigners invited to the conference by the Geography of the Academy of Sciences, he donated an Enting Reverse Osmosis Water Purification system to a children's hospital in the area, where one child in ten does not survive the first year, partly due to the region's contaminated water. The Russians were so impressed with the system that when an "ABC News" team arrived to film a documentary on the Aral Sea, the Academy had them purchase two of the Enting systems for the people of Nukus in Uzbekistan.

Located along the Interstate 75 corridor from Springboro to Troy, Japanese companies such as Panasonic, Fujitech Industries, Inc. and Pioneer Electronics have also discovered the advantages of the Dayton area. By 1989 approximately 120 Japanese-affiliated companies employed

Shortening cans roll off the line at Sonoco Products in Piqua. Dawson Jones

close to 19,000 Ohioans, representing more than a $4 billion boost to the state's economy. Almost one-third of all Japanese-owned or joint-venture companies in Ohio are located within fifty miles of Dayton.

Dayton's expertise in the sciences has earned the city an international reputation as the technological capital of the Midwest—and a major player to be reckoned with in the global economic development of the nineties. With all the resources of a major metropolitan area and the openness of America's heartland, the Dayton region remains a great place to conduct business.

YESTERDAY'S VISION, TODAY'S MEGA-CORPORATION

While Daytonians never tire of telling the story of Wilbur and Orville, the Wright brothers aren't the sole industrial geniuses to come out of the Miami Valley.

By the late 1870s, tavern owner James Ritty was looking for a way to prevent dishonest bartenders from shortchanging the till. In 1879 he invented the cash register. However, it was a hard sell because few tavern owners wanted to spend over a hundred dollars on a machine that replaced an inexpensive cash box. In 1884 John Henry Patterson bought the floundering cash register company. Starting with thirteen employees and 3,200 square feet, Patterson called it the National Cash Register Company. Patterson, who had a genius for marketing and advertising, set up a distributorship in Liverpool, England, in 1885 to become one of America's first multinational corporations. By 1906, NCR operated 271 overseas offices.

Today, NCR World Headquarters, located in a parklike setting on the south side of downtown Dayton, employs 56,000 people worldwide and the familiar red-and-white NCR logo

GM's Inland Fisher Guide Division designs and manufactures automotive body hardware components and systems. Andy Snow

can be seen on computer workstations in the retail, financial and business sectors across the nation and around the world. On May 6, 1991, after a five-month takeover battle, NCR Corporation became AT&T's computer division in a $7.4 billion buyout.

NCR also had an indirect hand in creating another Miami Valley industrial giant. A few years after the turn of the century Colonel Edward A. Deeds and Charles F. Kettering, both employees of National Cash Register, met in a barn behind Deeds's Central Avenue house in Dayton, with William A. Chryst. The three men designed an electric ignition system that rendered the hand-cranked automobile engine obsolete. Henry Leland of Cadillac ordered 8,000 of the new ignition systems for the 1910 model and the Dayton Engineering Laboratories Company (Delco) was founded.

In 1912 Cadillac ordered 12,000 self-starters—another Kettering invention—and Delco opened its first factory on Fourth and Sinclair streets in Dayton. Six years later, Colonel Deeds sold

Twilight settles over the Dayton skyline and the Woolpert headquarters building (left). Woolpert is a leader in the field of geographic computer graphics and is one of the largest mapping firms in the nation. Woolpert Consultants

the company to United Motors Corporation—owned by General Motors founder W. C. Durant—for $8 million. General Motors had come to Dayton. Colonel Deeds and Boss Kettering, who later became GM vice-president of research, hired gifted engineers and inventors and began building GM and the United States into the greatest automobile manufacturer in the world.

Boss Kettering, as he came to be known, was a prodigious inventor, outranked only by Thomas Edison in the total number of patents granted over his lifetime. Another Boss Kettering invention of the early 1900s—a self-oiling porous metal bearing that required no additional lubrication during the lifetime of the part—became the basis of GM's Moraine Division, recognized globally for advanced brake technology. Today, Delco Chassis Division, based in Dayton, includes Delco Moraine NDH and Delco Products. Delco Chassis has plants and offices in more than fifteen countries and employs nearly 30,000 people. A part of GM since 1918, Delco Products manufactures suspension systems around the world.

In 1923 Inland took over a facility originally designed by the Wright Brothers for the world's first airplane factory, the Dayton Wright Airplane Company and 225 Inland employees began making laminated steering wheels for automobiles. Inland Fisher Guide Division now is a world leader in the design and manufacture of automotive body hardware components and systems, molding and trim. Comprised of twenty manufacturing facilities around the world, Inland Fisher Guide consistently ranks highest among all GM divisions in the number of patents it generates.

Alfred Mellowes, a native Daytonian who was living in Indiana, built the first self-contained electric refrigerator for household use. The Guardian Frigidaire Co., forerunner of Frigidaire, produced less than forty of the Mellowes units

Newly assembled GM S-10 pickups await shipment to dealers around the world.
Dawson Jones

before Durant purchased it for General Motors. By 1921 the first Dayton-produced Frigidaire refrigerators came off the production line and another GM division was born. In the late 1920s, Kettering and his engineers produced freon, which boosted sales of the refrigerator and made possible the room air conditioner.

During World War II, General Doolittle's famous raid over Tokyo was in part made possible by thirty-five different Frigidaire-produced hydraulic controls on his B-25 aircraft, and Frigidaire played a vital part in the nation's war efforts. In the late 1970s, GM sold the division to White Consolidated Industries. Today that plant has evolved into two Dayton GM divisions: the Harrison Division and the GM Truck and Bus Group.

Dayton's newest GM Division, the GM Power Train Division, opened in early 1991. Producers of the 6.2 and 6.5 V-8 diesel engines, the division is also responsible for the vehicle that was used so successfully during the Gulf War.

The Mead Corporation, headquartered in downtown Dayton, is a $5 billion forest products company that employs 22,000 people nationwide. Today Mead is at the forefront of electronic publishing and color imaging. LEXPAT, a Mead service, provides electronic access to a full text of all United States patents since 1975. In the seventies, Mead Data Central introduced LEXIS and NEXIS electronic information bases. Since then more than one million users have signed on.

Optical scanners read a billion characters of written text annually, converting printed words

Mead's electronic information networks: LEXIS provides up-to-the-minute legal research services, and NEXIS relays breaking news reports to businesses and news correspondents around the world. More than one million users have signed on since their introduction in the 1970s. Dawson Jones

to electronic updates of LEXIS, the computer-assisted legal research service. Daily, the laser beam optical scanners read three-quarters of a million words of legal documents, which makes new judicial opinions available nationwide weeks or months ahead of their printed publications. United States Supreme Court decisions are now available in full text through LEXIS service within three hours after they are announced in Washington, D.C. Within minutes, NEXIS provides Atlanta-based CNN's research team with comprehensive background information that can then be relayed to the organization's correspondents around the world. In business, corporations such as Ford Motor Company use NEXIS for access to news reports on major competitors.

The same Mead vision and innovation also produced Mead Imaging Cycolor products, which provide high-quality, low-cost, full-color images.

Dayton-based Standard Register Company is the second-largest business forms company in the world today.
Dawson Jones

Mead's vision and technology carry into its paper products as well. One of the world's largest manufacturers of paper, Mead produces more than 1.2 million tons annually, with a billion-dollar-plus distribution. Mead began the 1990s with a $560 million expansion in coated board. In a ninety-second dash through pumps, presses, coaters and dryers, billions of fibers form a precisely engineered sheet that is made into cartons for packaging. Few offices and fewer schools are without Mead-produced notebooks, typing paper and copy paper. And many homes have been decorated with Mead laminating papers.

Sensitive to the environment, Mead invested $193 million in the past twenty years to protect environmental quality. Nearly all Mead products are recyclable, even the water that is used in the thousand-a-ton-a-day coated-board mill. In 1989 more than 28 million trees

were planted by the company. Research teams continue to explore ways to use more recycled fiber in paper and paperboard without sacrificing strength and printability.

One of the 75 largest contractors in the country, Danis Industries is a prominent Dayton business whose construction trailers are familiar sights across the Miami Valley. Andy Snow

Dayton-based Woolpert, a world leader in interactive computer graphics for geographic information services, was founded in 1911 by Charles D. Putnam as a civil engineering, land surveying and landscaping company. Today, Woolpert has grown into one of the largest and most respected mapping firms in the country, with twelve offices in nine states and corporate headquarters located along the Miami River. Woolpert's Geographic Information Services Division uses aerial photography, surveying, photogrammetry and geographic information services to build data bases and produce computer mapping for the infrastructure management of many American cities.

The Reynolds and Reynolds Co., a $600 million corporation, is also headquartered in downtown Dayton. Founded in 1866 by Lucius D. Reynolds, the company supplies information management systems and related professional services to markets worldwide. Originally selling business forms and paper-based accounting systems, Reynolds and Reynolds grew into the major supplier of electronic forms and systems to the automotive dealer market. The company is the fifth largest supplier of stock continuous forms in North America.

Dayton-based Standard Register Company was founded in 1912 with two products—pinfeed autographic registers and marginally-punched continuous forms, both innovations at the time. Standard Register today is a $700 million international company—the second largest company in the $8 billion business-forms market.

The Berry Company—one of the largest subsidiaries of BellSouth—is a world leader in telephone directory services. It began in 1910 when Indiana-born Loren M. Berry, newly married and ambitious, moved to

Approximately 22 percent of the area's work force is employed in manufacturing. Dawson Jones

Dayton to sell advertising for the local phone company's directory.

Danis Industries Corporation, located north of the Miami River in downtown Dayton, is a construction, real estate and environmental services firm with annual sales approaching $400 million. Founded in 1916 by B. G. Danis, Jr., the corporation has grown into five operating construction and real estate groups. Among the seventy-five largest contractors in the United States, Danis Industries employs more than 2,500 people and manages $500,000 to $50 million projects. The red-white-and-blue Danis construction trailers are familiar sites throughout the Miami Valley as well as the Midwest, Mid-Atlantic and Southeast.

The Miller-Valentine Group, another leading real estate developer headquartered in the Dayton region, was founded in 1963 by Gerald M. Miller. The company applied its knowledge of concrete construction to buildings, then nationally franchised the Con/Steel Building System. The innovative tilt-up building system uses site-cast, independent, reinforced-concrete panels fabricated to the specifications of each project. Over the past twenty-five years, the Miller-Valentine group, a partnership of interrelated companies, has built

Heavy industry still provides much of the region's employment. These Dayton workers pour liquid iron in the manufacture of machine tools. Dawson Jones

Isotec in Miamisburg is a leading chemical manufacturer.
Bill Swartz/BBS Images

more than 20 million square feet of office space.

The Huffy Corporation, Miamisburg, is a leader in advanced bicycle styling and technology. Building bikes in Dayton since 1934, Huffy uses computer-aided design, aerospace metallurgy, wind-tunnel testing and biomechanical data to manufacture the world's foremost high-tech bikes—built from 100 percent American-produced components. Riding Huffy bicycles in the 1984 Olympics, the United States team took home the gold for the first time since 1912. Huffy's divisions produce everything from infant carriers and diaper bags to lawn and garden tools.

Commitment to technology has made Dayton and the Miami Valley a formidable industrial location. The Miami Valley Research Foundation, a private, nonprofit corporation, seeks to continue that tradition by relocating high-tech companies from around the world to the Miami Valley Research Park, a 1,500-acre site at the convergence of Montgomery and Greene counties.

The Research Park is home to such companies as Mission Research Corporation, an aerospace research company; Kodak's nonimpact ink-jet printing technology center; Edison Materials Technology Center; the Center for Artificial Intelligence; the Wright State University's Center for Rehabilitative Engineering; Dayton Power and Light Company's Research and Service Center; BDM Corporation; and the Ohio Advanced Technology Center. Also at the research park is the Ohio Computer Technology Center (OCTC). This is a consortium of computer and information technology companies and institutions that transfer technology developed by members to commercial customers as marketable products and services and military and governmental technology to members

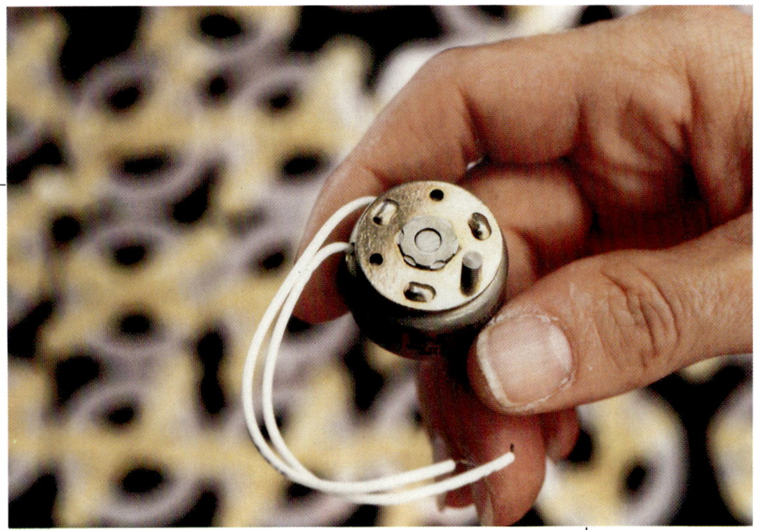

for utilization in the development of commercial products.

Small and mid-size businesses are also vital to the Dayton-area economy. Herbert Saiger Designs of Troy, for example, a one-man operation, designs casual furniture for hotels such as the plush Hotel Del Coronado in San Diego.

Warehouse Beer Systems Company, a drive-through beer warehouse, boasts nineteen facilities and annual sales of $10 million. Color Q, a nationally recognized specialist in four-color reproductions and original art works, attracts business from all over the country.

Agriculture is also an important part of the area's economy. In Ohio, farm assets equaled $28.3 billion in 1990, with farm debt of $3.3 billion, which leaves Ohio farmers with $25 billion in equity. In 1990 the Ohio cash receipts from marketing livestock agriculture were $4.1 billion. The Valley's Darke County led the state in cash receipts for agriculture, with nearly $200 million. Clark County, with nearly $80 million, was ninth in the state.

In the eight-county area of the Miami Valley, there are 8,730 farms, with an average size of 175 acres. Crops include soybeans, corn, wheat, oats, hay and tomatoes. Livestock includes beef and dairy cattle, calves, hogs, sheep, poultry and bees.

It seems that almost everything from trucks and bicycles to computers and high technology is produced in the Greater Dayton area. Dawson Jones

Miami Paper operates on the banks of the Great Miami River in West Carrollton. Andy Snow

THE BUSINESS OF DAYTON IS BUSINESS

Dayton has ample room to grow. The Miami Valley offers nearly six million square feet of industrial warehouse space, five million square feet of office space in more than 130 office centers, ranging from downtown high-rise towers to suburban office complexes. Downtown Dayton alone contains approximately 1.2

Some 9,000 farms operate in the eight counties of the Miami Valley, adding a significant contribution to Ohio's nearly $30-billion agricultural industry. Bill Swartz/BBS Images

million square feet of office space, including two new Class A twenty-story office towers. The region also provides forty-eight industrial parks reserved for light manufacturing and nine for heavy manufacturing.

Dayton's financial community, one of the most vigorous in the nation, strongly supports local business, from start-up to major corporate expansions. Bank One, Dayton, began operations 175 years ago as the Dayton Manufacturing Company, with total assets of $123,505.21. The vagaries of the nation's economy led it through several ownerships and name changes. At one time the Winters family—relations of actor Jonathan Winters—owned the bank. Known as Winters National Bank of Dayton, the bank had more than seventy branches located throughout Ohio and assets of $1.5 billion. During the 1980s, Winters merged with Banc One Corporation, a bank holding company that owns fifty affiliate banks operating 823 offices in seven states.

Today Bank One, Dayton, NA, is a nationally chartered, full-service bank offering financial services and products primarily in a seven-county area of Southern Ohio. With headquarters in the Kettering Tower, 40 North Main Street, Dayton, the bank operates fifty banking offices in its seven-county area and employs more than 1,500 people. It has over $2.8 billion in assets and $2.3 billion in deposits, making it the largest bank in its market area.

Society Bank's strong ties with Dayton's booming commercial and manufacturing community were established during the 19th century when it was known as Second National Bank. In 1925, Second National became Third National Bank and continued operation under that name until 1984, when Society Corporation acquired Third National's holding company. Society Bank is an affiliate of Society Corporation, one of the largest bank holding companies in the nation.

Based on successful banking traditions, Society Bank has enjoyed regional prosperity and experienced continual growth while fulfilling its commitment as a conscientious corporate citizen. Society's operating philosophy is echoed throughout the organization. With Dayton roots dating back to the mid-1800s, customers feel secure in knowing that Society Bank will continue its obligation to the Dayton area. Employees take pride in the ability to recognize ways to enhance the quality of life. The bank operates 70 offices in its southern region, which includes the Dayton, Springfield, Cincinnati and Celina areas.

National City Bank also is a formidable force in the Dayton community, with nearly forty area offices and seventy Money Station locations. The roots of National City Bank run back to the post-Civil War era in 1871, when Merchants National Bank received its charter. After a series of mergers and acquisitions, the bank was renamed First National Bank in 1966. In 1977 First National joined National City Corporation, the strong, highly respected, Ohio-based

Downtown Dayton boasts more than 1.2 million square feet of office space with room for continued growth.
Bill Swartz/BBS Images

Old and new stand side-by-side in downtown Dayton with the Victoria Theatre built in 1866 and the Citizens Federal Centre built in 1989.
Gregory C. Sundra

regional bank holding company. The bank continued to grow and nearly doubled in size prior to its acquisition of the 100-year-old Dayton-based Gem Savings in 1991. The marriage of these two well-respected financial institutions created a major banking force with $2 billion dollars in assets. In the spring of 1993, First National was renamed National City Bank, Dayton.

"Many of our customers have a long tradition with our bank—their parents and grandparents still bank here," says Fred Schantz, president of National City Bank, Dayton. "The strength of National City Corporation, coupled with our local decision making, adds great depth to the ability of our local bank to serve its communities."

Dayton's Star Bank, founded in 1866 by H. Groby & Company, was ranked in the largest top one hundred performing banks by an Olsen Research study. With $70 million in assets, Star is significant in the greater Dayton area and the dominant bank in many of the surrounding communities.

Citizens Federal Bank is the largest financial institution headquartered in Dayton and offers twenty-one branches in the Greater Miami Valley. Widely recognized by its Rainbow logo, Citizens Federal has been serving customers in Southwestern Ohio since 1934.

The bank's wholly owned subsidiary, CitFed Mortgage Corporation, specializes in one-to-four-family residential mortgage loans and has seven origination offices located in Dayton, Cincinnati and Columbus. Citizens Federal became a publicly held corporation in January 1992 through its holding company, CitFed Bancorp, Inc.

Fifth Third Bank is one of ten affiliate banks of Fifth Third Bancorp. The Bancorp, which is headquartered in Cincinnati, has more than $9.9 billion in assets and 249 Banking Centers located primarily in Ohio, Kentucky and Indiana, including fifty-three locations in select grocery stores, which are open seven days a week. The Bancorp has been consistently praised by analysts for its performance. *Financial World* magazine named the bank as one of the strongest in the nation.

NBD Bank, Dayton's newest bank, opened operations in late 1990. A principal subsidiary of NBD Bancorp., NBD is one of the twenty largest banks in the country, with operations across the Midwest and the Southeast as well as abroad.

Dayton's business community understands that it carries the mantle of social responsibility. When a flood devastated Dayton in 1913, John H. Patterson marshaled his forces at NCR. The "Cash" temporarily stopped operations and went to work to save their city. Motorcycle messengers drove south to buy food; NCR's woodworking shop turned out lifesaving boats in hours; a tent city sprang up on the company's lawn to house employees who lost their homes in the flood. The Cash became hotel, restaurant and hospital.

That same spirit of concern for the community still exists today. In 1991 the United Way of the Greater Dayton Area collected donations of more than $20 million. Vigorous in support of local charities, the arts, public schools and local universities, the business community takes an active role in contributing to the quality of life in Dayton.

Established in 1866, Star Bank is a leading Miami Valley bank, with some $70 million in assets.
Richard Todd

Mead

CHAPTER FOUR

SUPPORT SYSTEMS FOR SUCCESS

Dayton's diversity provides the region a leading role in the nation's economic growth. A region in renaissance, Dayton passes the economic litmus test with scores high in natural resources and development of economic programs.

The city's reputation as both a transportation center and a tourist center for aviation enthusiasts has grown steadily while the technology, manufacturing and service arenas continue to build a secure future. Cooperation among the academic community, government and the private sector creates an unusual atmosphere of advanced technology research that will carry Dayton—and much of the world—into the twenty-first century.

Strategically located near the intersection of the nation's most traveled highways—Interstate I-70 (east/west) and I-75 (north/south)—Dayton is the nation's largest ninety-minute market by air and one of the largest by land. Ninety minutes represents the time it takes to offer cost-efficient service. Traveling the interstates, it's possible to reach 5.6 million of the nation's population within ninety minutes. By air, 55 percent of the U.S. population and more than 56 percent of the nation's income can be reached within ninety minutes.

Reflective of the Miami Valley's growing economy is Dayton's shining skyline. Andy Snow

The region's highway transportation network connects to more than 300 cities and towns within a 90-minute radius. Here, the busy thoroughfares of Interstate 75 and U.S. 35 intersect.
Dawson Jones

At the apex of a triangle between Cincinnati and Columbus, Dayton is only an hour away from both cities and only a few hours away from most of the Midwest's major cities, including Indianapolis (117 miles), Louisville (150 miles), Lexington (132 miles), Cleveland (202 miles), Toledo (150 miles), Detroit (215 miles) and Chicago (312 miles).

I-675 connects the southern and eastern suburbs with I-70, which runs past the Dayton International Airport and through the northern suburbs. U.S. 35 connects the eastern suburbs with I-75 and with downtown. America's oldest highway, the National Road (U.S. 40) runs through the northern part of the Miami Valley and the city of Vandalia.

More than thirty trucking companies have terminals within the region, providing transportation of manufactured goods throughout Ohio and across the United States. Dayton's second-morning-market encompasses a 600-mile radius, serving more than 130 million people. Three major rail systems are in the Dayton area: CSX, with a 2,500-car switching yard; Conrail, with a 1,000-car switching yard; and Grand Truck Western, offering liquid or dry bulk service.

Throughout the metropolitan area, the Miami Valley Regional Transit Authority (RTA) provides bus service and operates electric trolleys that run on overhead wire tracks—as they have for more than 100 years. Dayton is one of only five U.S. cities with running electric trolleys. Long-distance bus service is provided by the merged Greyhound-Trailways system.

Dayton is viewed as one of the best product test market areas in the United States because of the large consumer market and diversified distribution facilities. The median age in Dayton is 33.5 years, with about 25 percent of the population under eighteen, 21 percent between 35 and 49, and nearly 25 percent over 50. Effective buying income for the region is greater than the average income in Ohio and the rest of the U.S. Twenty-seven percent of the population has an effective buying income of $20,000 to $34,999; almost 19 percent is rated $35,000 to $49,000; and more than 18 percent has an effective buying income of $50,000 or more.

Economic Development Plans for a Strong Future

Dayton's leaders recognize the importance of economic development throughout the entire Miami Valley. Several programs ensure the continuing revitalization of downtown and the city's neighborhoods. Nationally recognized as a leader in financial planning, Dayton uses a multilevel approach that enables the city to accumulate cash reserves in growth periods, then use the reserves during recessionary periods. After budget review, the city commissioners adopt a six-year plan of policy goals and objectives on which they base policy decisions. Economic vitality within the city is enhanced by an extensive infrastructure; a strong downtown area; development and support for both the business community and Dayton's neighborhoods; and corporate leadership.

Located in the geographic center of the Miami Valley, downtown Dayton serves as the region's preeminent center of commerce and community life. Downtown Dayton has half of the region's commercial office space, in excess of 5 million square feet. Well over 1,000 businesses employ more than 25,000 people in the region's center.

- The Downtown Retail Opportunities Program, a push to draw shoppers downtown and

Dayton's vast rail system features Conrail, which operates a 1,000-car switching yard. Dawson Jones

to assist downtown businesses, jointly markets downtown stores, restaurants and service businesses.

• DaytonTomorrow is the city's strategic plan. By combining the ideas of 1,000 Daytonians in fifty-five focus groups, 8,500 ideas were generated, then distilled to twenty issues of concern in five key areas: marketing, leadership, the people, the economy and Dayton as the region's hub. The mission statement for Dayton Tomorrow: "To enhance the total quality of life in Dayton neighborhoods through targeted service delivery and negotiated partnerships in the Dayton area."

• City Summit Report is an outgrowth of the Miami Valley Arts Council and Arts Summit and Cityscape that identifies key issues. The council believes that creative solutions are generated through the arts.

• Downtown Dayton Partnership is a permanent downtown management corporation formed to coordinate all the strategies for downtown as the hub and strength of the entire Miami Valley.

• In 1983 Dayton adopted the Enterprise Zone Program, which allows agreement to be made between the city and business and industry. It provides local and state incentives in the form of real personal and franchise tax abatement and tax credits for training and child care. Intended to promote business investment and increase overall employment, Dayton's Enterprise Zone has created or retained more than 2,300 jobs. Ninety-nine agreements have been approved, resulting in an investment of more than $125 million into the community, with pledges of an additional $544.5 million in land, buildings and other inventory.

• CityWide Development Corporation offers business and real estate development consulting, financial assistance and direct loans within the Dayton city limits. CityWide also administers the State of Ohio's Regional 166 loan program and the SBA 504 fixed-asset loan program. Nearly $300 million in private funds has been invested in Dayton with the assistance of CityWide.

Founded in 1972 in response to the major loss in manufacturing jobs, CityWide was created by business and neighborhood leaders and government as an investment in the city's future through venture capital programs, packaging financial programs and financial feasibility studies. CityWide

may invest venture capital in merging or start-up businesses, act as a gap lender or help a company put together a package that is attractive to local banks and lenders. CityWide is also involved in housing packages for an upscale market, creating more affordable housing and providing home improvement and home ownership programs that have revitalized Dayton neighborhoods.

CityWide contributed venture capital to Dayton filmmaker Julia Reichert's first feature film and her production company, the Last Resort Production Company. Filmed locally in 1990 in the city, the film *The Last Resort* received critical acclaim when it opened nationwide and from Daytonians when it played at the Neon Movies, another CityWide project. Reichert and her former partner, Jim Klein, are well known for their documentaries, which have earned Emmy nominations.

Employment in Dayton's service sector has increased dramatically since the mid-1980s. Jim Baron/Image Finders

CityWide Development Corporation was established in 1972 to invest in housing and business within the city of Dayton. One of its many successful projects is the popular Diner on St. Clair. Dawson Jones

• COUNTY CORP is the economic development arm of Montgomery County. The organization offers fixed-asset financing programs to growing businesses throughout a six-county region, including Greene, Clark, Darke, Miami, Preble and Montgomery counties. COUNTY CORP is a private, nonprofit corporation that was started in 1979. Certified by the U.S. Small Business Administration and the Ohio Department of Development, it offers below-market rate financing for fixed-asset expansions.

• The Dayton Business Committee (DBC), consisting of top officers from eighteen major corporations in the area, promotes more aggressive and streamlined economic development in the Miami Valley. DBC concentrates corporate clout on four primary areas within the region: leadership, downtown development, Wright-Patterson Air Force Base and education.

• North I-70 Development Association is a consortium of ten suburbs and cities in the northern area of the Miami Valley that banded together to promote their area nationally and internationally. The communities include: Covington, Englewood, Huber Heights, Piqua, Tipp City, Trotwood, Troy, Union, Vandalia and West Milton.

• Private citizens are often the region's best ambassadors to attract new business and assist in economic development. William Hobart, president of Hobart Brothers, a $300 million company in Troy, was instrumental in the decision of several foreign firms to locate in this region. Manufacturers of welding equipment and passenger loading systems for airports, Hobart Brothers had a long-standing relationship with Panasonic. "When they came they were impressed with our quality of life and work ethic," Mr. Hobart says. Panasonic also needed water, a million-plus gallons a day, and the region offers that luxury.

• Montgomery County's tax-sharing and economic development program, ED/GE, calls for $50 million to be spent among cooperating jurisdictions. Growing communities share a limited amount of money from new development; static or declining communities share in the expanding tax base of growing areas. Participating communities can spend the money in a number of different ways, such as for roads, sewer lines or other big-ticket items that businesses coming into an area may require.

• The Dayton Area Chamber of Commerce sponsors numerous programs that promote economic development within the region. Strategic planning was undertaken with Challenge 95, which pulled together nearly 500 people from all walks of life throughout the Miami Valley. To promote regional cooperation, the chamber established two regional partnerships designed to enhance economic and community development in the Valley.

Through the chamber's Small Business Development Center nearly 300 businesses were helped in 1992 alone. Business retention and expansion is the focus of the chamber's Dayton Development Council and Dayton/Montgomery County Convention and Visitors Bureau. Working with the private and public

Economic growth in the Miami Valley is evident in the construction of new commercial and residential development.
Bill Swartz/BBS Images

sectors in both Washington, D.C., and in Columbus at the state capital, the chamber obtains approval for numerous projects for the Dayton region.

To help Dayton-area businesses, the chamber annually offers more than 100 seminars designed to increase knowledge on timely business topics. Seminars explain the components of a business plan or help companies improve their bottom line. The chamber's Leadership Dayton is a program designed to identify, educate and develop a select group of citizens for positions of community leadership. Nearly 500 graduates have taken positions of leadership within the community since the program's inception in 1975.

Programs to infuse vitality into the local business climate have met with great success. Jim Baron/Image Finders

PROVIDING VITAL SERVICES

The Dayton Power and Light Company, Inc. (DP&L), the principal supplier of electricity and natural gas to the region, adds greatly to the area's economic development. DP&L's eight generating plants consistently rate in the top ten of all plants in the country for productivity and efficiency as the company manages the balance between economic growth and the environment. DP&L's tradition of effective management of resources in electric power resulted in a heat rate that ranks fourth in the nation. Heat rate is a measure of efficiency that shows how much fuel is converted into electricity in relation to being lost to the environment. DP&L's heat rate represents a $4 million five-year savings for its customers.

Headquartered in downtown Dayton, DP&L serves twenty-four counties covering 6,000 square miles in West Central Ohio and employs more than 3,100 people.

Water has always been important to the economic development and quality of life of the Dayton region. An abundant supply of high-purity water in underground storage assures the region of clean, safe water. Most of the Dayton water supply comes from a vast aquifer system, pumped from more than ninety wells, averaging fifty to 210 feet in depth. The city actually sits over the Teays Stage Hamilton River, a massive underground river at the bottom of a 400-foot-deep valley.

The confluence of three rivers—the Great Miami, Stillwater and Mad rivers—long ago set the destiny of Dayton's prosperity. A series of canals built in the 1820s that paralleled the Great Miami and connected Lake Erie with the Ohio River made shipping on flat-bottomed barges possible, assuring a bright future.

Water also nearly destroyed Dayton when a devastating flood wrecked the city in 1913. The flood, which came when three days of constant rain dropped eight to eleven inches on the region, caused more than $100 million in property damage and cost more than 300 lives. In the aftermath, more than $2 million was donated by 23,000 citizens to solve the flooding problem. Through efforts by community leaders from the Miami Valley, the Ohio Legislature passed the Ohio Conservancy Act, in 1914, which allowed for the creation of conservancy districts.

The official plan of the Miami Conservancy District included five earthen retention basins that were formed by large dams. Quantity of the flow of water is controlled by the fixed size of the outlet conduits, with no gates or other means to manually control the flow. In addition, fifty-five miles of levees and thirty-five miles of improved channels protect nine cities—including Dayton—along the Great Miami River.

Completion of the $31 million project came in 1922, yet these same five dams—Englewood, Germantown, Huffman, Lockington and Taylorsville—still protect the citizens and property in the Dayton region from floodwaters today. Surrounded by wooded reserves and operated by

Dayton/Montgomery County Park District, the dams are popular recreation areas for picnicking, fishing, canoeing, hiking and camping.

The Great Miami Buried Valley Aquifer system, designated in 1988 as a sole-source aquifer, supplies drinking water to approximately 1.5 million people throughout Southwestern Ohio. A vast natural aquifer, the deep underground buried valleys were formed around 14,000 years ago when the Wisconsin Glacier retreated. Replenished through the rivers and underground streams, the aquifer assures the region of a plentiful, clean water supply.

"An underground system is less subject to contamination and the quality is more stable," says George Crosby, superintendent, Division of Water Supply and Treatment for the Department of Water, city of Dayton. "We have a chance to react and convert any containment," Crosby explains. The underground aquifer also means the quality is more stable. Drinking water has a better taste; the temperature doesn't fluctuate radically and there is no odor, qualities important to everyone.

The city of Dayton, which supplies water to about 400,000 people within the city and suburbs, has undertaken a variety of measures to enhance the potable water quality. These include operation of an early warning well-monitoring network, installation of interim

Regional cooperation has proved invaluable in Dayton's commercial expansion. C. Gatland Photography

HILTON
DAYTON DAILY NEWS

Completed in the early 1920s, Taylorsville is just one of five major Miami Valley dams that still protect residents and property from floodwaters today.
C. Gatland Photography

remedial measures to mitigate ground-water contamination and construction of activated-carbon facilities for emergency treatment of potable water. Additionally, the Dayton City Commission established a comprehensive multijurisdictional Well Field Protection Program (WFPP) in recognition of the sensitivity and vulnerability of ground water and the need to be proactive in the protection of public health.

Well field protection is a priority. Dayton's WFPP program includes prevention of increased risk to the public water supply and the reduction of existing risk to the water. Prevention is accomplished through land-use control zoning; reduction of existing risk is accomplished through ground-water remediation efforts, emergency preparedness and improved management of hazardous materials.

Water protection is also important in Dayton's waste-water treatment program. Since 1983 more than $100 million has been spent expanding and advancing the waste-water treatment plant to comply with all federal and state regulations. A leader in environmental protection, the waste-water protection plant generates enough electricity to provide all the heat and one-third of the electricity used in the plant, through conversion of the methane gas produced by treatment of sludge.

Convention Arenas Impact Dayton's Economy

More than 2.8 million people visited the Dayton area in 1992 as recreational travelers and conference delegates—an estimated economic impact of $278 million.

In 1983 the Dayton/Montgomery County Convention and Visitors Bureau opened a satellite office in the state capital, Columbus. Since Columbus is the headquarters city for over 95 percent of the State Association market, the Bureau's daily presence has maximized its market share of state business.

A magnet for many trade shows and conventions, the Convention Center was renovated into a spacious, state-of-the-art facility where multiple events can be held simultaneously without inconvenience or crowding. Housed behind the atrium-style lobby, the center's main floor features 77,000 square feet of exhibit space, room for more than 400 booths. There are also twenty-two meeting rooms. Pop concerts by the Dayton Philharmonic orchestra, the black-tie dinner for the National Aviation Hall of Fame, aerospace trade shows, aviation reunions, political rallies, medical conventions and local festivals are all held at the Convention Center. Every November the full-service kitchen is put to the test when the Dayton tradition of serving Thanksgiving dinner to 6,000 takes place. Started by retailer Arthur Beerman twenty-two years ago, the dinner exemplifies the spirit of those who make up the Dayton community.

Attached to the center via skywalk is a 1,500-space lighted parking garage and the 300-room luxury Stouffer Center Plaza Hotel. Another 7,000 rooms are available within a fifteen-minute walk or a short taxi ride.

Hara Arena Conference and Exhibition Center consists of six buildings under one roof, making it one of the largest exhibition complexes in Ohio and in the top 100 nationally. A 5,500-permanent-seat facility that expands to seat 7,000, Hara hosts everything from family entertainment shows to business conventions to concerts to elegant formal banquets and wedding receptions. The kitchen facilities are ready to cater dinners for up to 1,500 peo-

A major player in the economy of the Miami Valley region is the Dayton Power and Light Company, Inc.

Andy Snow

ple. Hara mounts a variety of gatherings, including Hamvention, a gathering of 30,000 amateur radio operators from around the world, Walt Disney's Magic Kingdom on Ice and the Miami Valley Boat Show. Annually, 1.5 million people visit the attractions held at Hara. More than twenty acres of parking for 4,000 cars surround the sprawling complex. Located 15 minutes north of downtown and within close proximity to I-70 and I-75 and the Dayton International Airport, Hara Arena is delightfully situated in a wooded setting, once the site of the Wampler family fruit farm. Still actively involved, the family combines the personal care and concern of a family business with the professionalism of a major exhibition and conference center in a metropolitan area. Hara is one of the few privately owned businesses of its kind in the country.

In 1990 Wright State University opened its $34.5 million multipurpose entertainment and sports complex, the Ervin J. Nutter Center. With a seating capacity of up to 13,000, the economic impact on the region is $20 million in ticket sales alone. Billed as the largest sports and entertainment complex in the Miami Valley, the Nutter Center includes four basketball courts, a recreation running track, a multipurpose room and 30,000 square feet of exhibition space for trade and con-

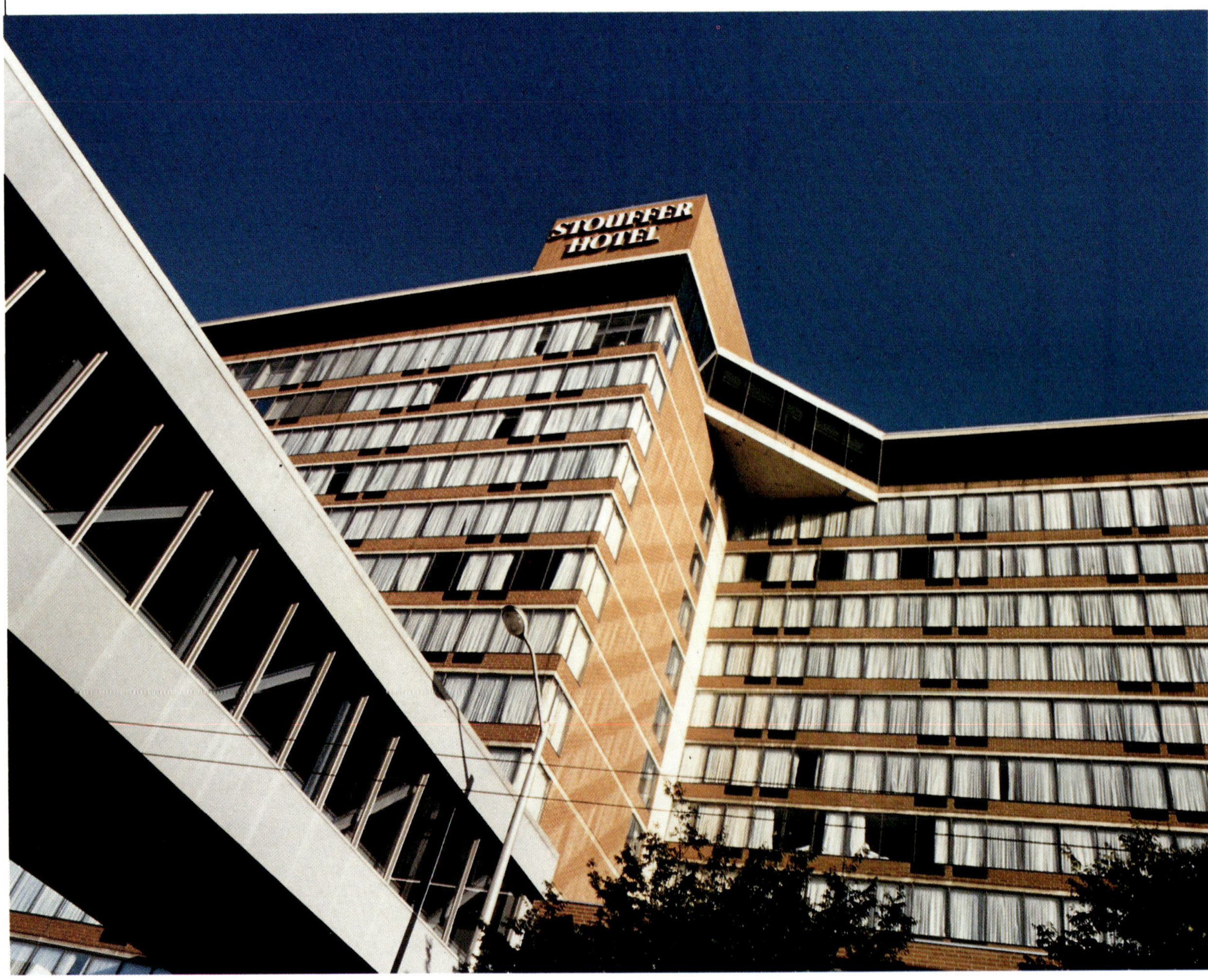

The luxurious Stouffer Center Plaza Hotel features 300 rooms for Dayton area travelers and is conveniently connected to the Dayton Convention Center. Andy Snow

sumer shows. Teleconferences and televised games are transmitted nationwide. Located throughout the complex are state-of-the-art color animated scoreboards and message centers. Overlooking the main arena is the John Berry Room, where 300 can be seated for dinner. Located adjacent to I-675, the center is on the Wright State University campus, near Wright-Patterson Air Force Base. The center also hosts concerts and family entertainment, such as Frank Sinatra's Golden Jubilee Tour and the Ice Capades.

Other well-equipped, user-friendly facilities include the University of Dayton Arena, suitable for sporting events, concerts, seminars and meetings, with seating for up to 14,200. In Troy, Hobart Arena seats 4,500 for concerts, sporting events and trade and consumer shows. And many of the region's hotels provide convention facilities for business meetings and seminars.

Diverse in its offerings of convention and exhibition space, the Dayton region rolls out the red carpet to visitors to the Miami Valley. Working together, the hospitality industry and the Dayton/Montgomery County Convention & Visitors Bureau have increasingly added to the economic diversity and the economic development of the area.

Some 77,000 square feet of exhibit space and 22 meeting rooms make the Dayton Convention Center an ideal place for local, regional and national events.

Dawson Jones

CHAPTER FIVE

ENSURING QUALITY OF LIFE

The Miami Valley has always made fine living its highest priority. And no wonder, with the finest medical care available anywhere and with the highest concentration of colleges and universities in the nation—twenty-six within a fifty-mile radius of Dayton.

Service industries in the Dayton area are projected to add 43,000 new jobs, with health care leading the field. Quality medical care is within minutes of nearly every corner of the Miami Valley. On the leading edge of medical technology, the work of many Dayton scientists and health care professionals has reached international distinction, with far-reaching medical significance.

The region's third largest employer, second only to Wright-Patterson Air Force Base and General Motors, the Greater Dayton hospitals employ some 23,000 people who earn an annual payroll of $400 million. An additional 19,000 jobs are generated in indirect employment such as laboratories, film processing, printing, food, linens, supply houses, packaging deliveries and advertising, including agencies and the media. An estimated $100 million is spent locally in goods and services by the hospitals.

Active in wellness programs, many hospitals have mobile units that

Wittenberg University is one of 26 institutions of higher learning in the Greater Dayton area. Andy Snow/Wittenberg University

provide free or minimum-charge screenings at local fairs, festivals and shopping malls. The hospitals initiate neighborhood revitalization programs and sponsorship of the arts. They spend approximately $30 million to provide education for medical residents and fellows, nurses and allied personnel.

Within the Miami Valley, nineteen hospitals provide about 5,500 hospital beds and nearly another 300 nursery beds. Competition among the Dayton hospitals is keen, since most of the hospitals offer similar services and technologies. Yet each is in the enviable position of good financial health. "The Dayton area has one of the best hospital systems in the country," says Gregory Sample, director of Public Affairs of the Greater Dayton Area Hospital Association. "Efficient delivery of health care services allows the hospitals to provide the best in medical care while meeting their mission to treat everyone regardless of the ability to pay."

Kettering Medical Center (KMC) is a regional acute-care center comprised of the 461-bed Charles F. Kettering Memorial Hospital, the 191-bed Sycamore Hospital, the Kettering College of Medical Arts and Sycamore Glen Retirement Community, as well as affiliated services. In addition to highly respected programs in neurology, pulmonary care, oncology and ophthalmology, Kettering is recognized as a major cardiac care center and is known for pioneering high-technology medicine in Southwestern Ohio. KMC is an integral part of the Seventh-day Adventist health care mission.

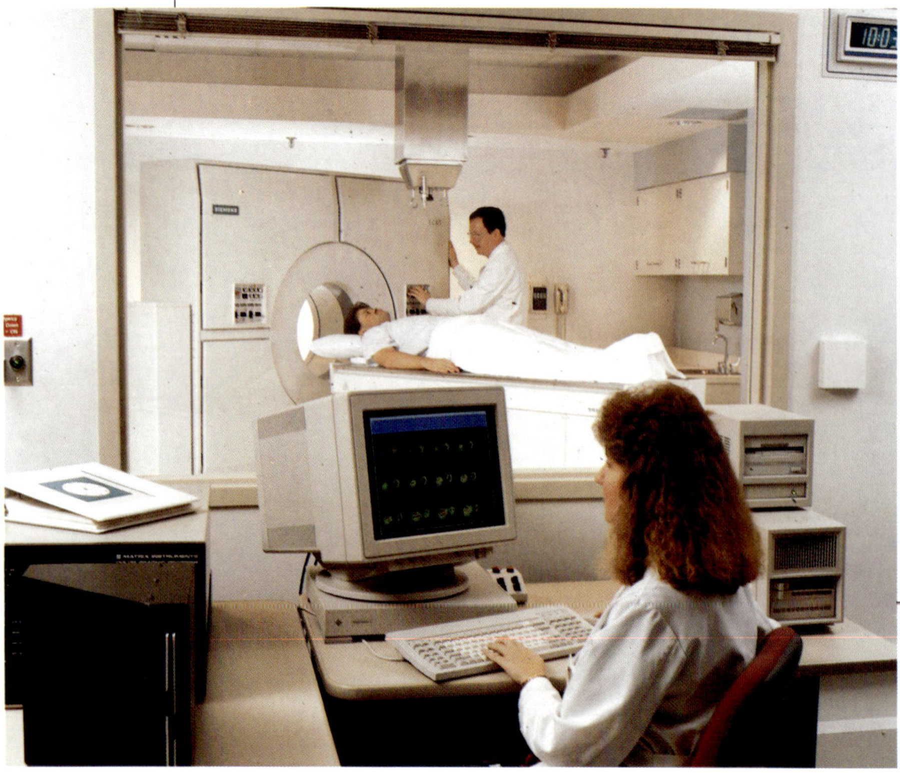

Kettering Memorial Hospital features advanced diagnostics, including Positron Emission Tomography (PET), which allows physicians to examine internal organs without the need of traditional surgery. Kettering Medical Center

Kettering was the first area hospital to install a positron emission tomography scanning machine (PET), a highly sophisticated imaging device that allows physicians to examine the function of organs in the body without surgery. KMC was also a pioneer in magnetic resonance imaging (MRI) and jointly operates an MRI research unit with the Wright State University School of

Medicine. The first freestanding pulmonary intensive care unit in the nation was established at KMC. Recognized as the leader in outpatient eye surgeries, KMC performs ophthalmology services such as corneal transplants, intraocular lens implantation and retinal laser therapy. Kettering College of Medical Arts, adjacent to Kettering Memorial Hospital, offers associate degrees in allied health and general education programs.

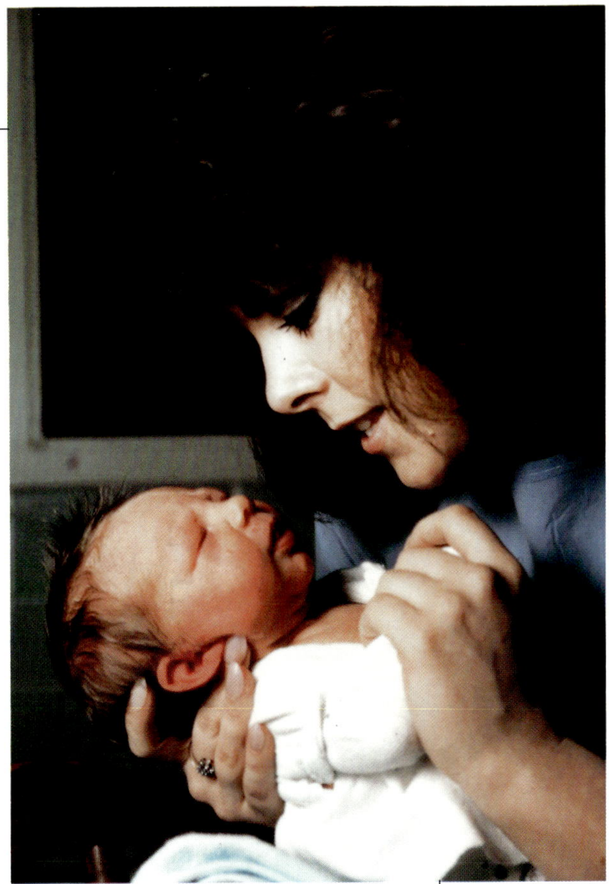

Established in 1878, St. Elizabeth Medical Center is well-respected for its rehabilitation, oncology and sports medicine programs, as well as other major health services like maternity and newborn care.
Dawson Jones

Dayton's first hospital was founded in 1878 by two Franciscan Sisters of the Poor who followed a mission of serving the community. This twelve-bed hospital has today grown into St. Elizabeth Medical Center, a 631-bed facility. A member of the Franciscan Health System of Dayton, St. Elizabeth Medical Center is well known for rehabilitation, oncology and sports medicine programs. The St. Elizabeth HeartCare Center offers the area's first bi-plane cardiac catheterization unit, as well as a full range of advanced diagnostic and treatment options for heart disease. The St. Elizabeth Digestive Disorders Center is the first designated center in Dayton to focus on the diagnosis of gastrointestinal disorders. Other major health services offered at the medical center include maternity, home care, senior services and psychiatry services.

With 772 beds and a staff of nearly 1,000 physicians representing thirty-four medical and surgical specialties, Dayton's Miami Valley Hospital (MVH) ranks in size among the nation's top 100 hospitals. Operating Dayton's only Level I Emergency and Trauma Center, the hospital also offers Dayton's only twenty-four-hour air ambulance service, which provides advanced life-support and skilled nursing care within a 150-mile radius. MVH's Regional Chronic Kidney Dialysis and Transplant Center performs 31,000 hemodialysis and peritoneal dialyses each year. The hospital's Regional Adult Burn Unit is the recognized facility for the treatment of patients in West Central Ohio. At the hospital's Fertility Center, the only center of its kind in the region, couples with little

CareFlight, Miami Valley Hospital's 24-hour air ambulance service, celebrates its 10th year of operation in 1993. Miami Valley Hospital

hope of having children realize their dreams with the help of medical technology. Through in vitro fertilization, gamete intrafallopian transfer, zygote intrafallopian transfer, or cryopreservation of the egg, pregnancies are resulting and babies being added to Dayton's population. Also a family maternity center, MVH has the highest number of maternity births in Montgomery County, with more than 5,000 births in 1992. Miami Valley Hospital began service to the community in 1891. The Rehabilitation Institute of Ohio and David L. Rike Cancer Center are also part of MVH.

Grandview Hospital and Medical Center and Southview Hospital and Family Health Center, together, comprise one of the nation's largest and most prestigious osteopathic health care systems. Featuring 496 beds, Grandview and Southview are acute-care hospitals with over 300 physicians on the medical staff. Grandview and Southview maintain leadership positions in specialties such as orthopedics and vascular surgery. In fact, surgeons at Grandview were the first in southwestern Ohio to perform the miraculous laserprobe surgery to unblock clogged leg arteries.

The newly opened Southview Medical Arts Center houses physicians' offices for outpatient renal dialysis, neurosurgery, and allergy and asthma treatment. Dayton's only three-dimensional CT scanner with exceptional imaging capability for improved diagnosis is located at Southview, and a new, stereotactic breast biopsy system is available for the most accurate breast cancer detection in Dayton. As a regional center for osteopathic medical eduction, Grandview and Southview Hospitals are affiliated with the Ohio University College of Osteopathic Medicine.

Well-established as community resources, both hospitals are known for offering a wide variety of special programs and support groups, including the Crohn's and Colitis Support Group—the only one of its kind in Dayton—plus diabetes education classes, a chronic-fatigue syndrome support group, free health check screenings and many other community programs.

Good Samaritan Hospital and Health Center is a 560-bed, tertiary care facility known for its extensive regional Heart Center and comprehensive videoscope and laser surgery program. The Good Samaritan Counseling and Treatment Centers offer a rare blend of inpatient and outpatient programs tailored to the needs of each individual. And the Family Birthing Center, which is a model birthing facility in Ohio, features family-centered care in spacious private rooms. Good Samaritan Hospital was founded in 1932 and is a member of the Sisters of Charity Health Care Systems.

Located in Sidney, Wilson Memorial Hospital is a patient-oriented, 112-bed acute-care hospital that also provides outpatient services, support groups, home health care, hospice services and an occupational medicine facility. Wilson's mission is to serve the community's health care needs and to provide leadership to continually assess and enhance the chalth of all those served. Expanded facilities, advanced medical equipment and procedures, a growing family of highly skilled health professionals and dedicated physicians assure that Wilson provides an environment of excellence for health care delivery to the community.

Wayne Hospital is a modern ninety-two-bed nonprofit acute-care hospital located in Greenville. Wayne offers a full range of inpatient and outpatient services within the structure of a small community hospital that focuses on providing personalized patient care with a holistic family-centered approach.

Serving the residents of the communities in the eastern region of the Miami Valley, Greene Memorial Hospital (GMH), in Xenia, provides all the sophisticated technology and services necessary in today's world of medicine to deliver quality health care. Individuals can receive intensive rehabilitation following a debilitating illness or injury within GMH's Physical Medicine

Known for its extensive regional Heart Center, Good Samaritan Hospital and Health Center uses state-of-the-art angioplasty in the treatment of heart disease.
Dawson Jones

Two young respiratory patients receive tender care at The Children's Medical Center, which specializes in a wide variety of care for infants, children and adolescents. Andy Snow

and Rehabilitation program. GMH's Mental Health Unit is a pioneer in the use of nurses as case managers and stresses the importance of family involvement. As the first hospital-based treatment center in the Miami Valley, Greene Hall is the area leader in the treatment of alcoholism and chemical dependency, with both inpatient and outpatient programs.

The Children's Medical Center (CMC) provides innovative pediatric services. The region's only full-service, 155-bed pediatric hospital, CMC employs medical science's latest technology to save young lives and improve the quality of others. In 1990 the "Children's Miracle Network Telethon" chose Dayton's Ahad Israfil, a CMC patient, as the national miracle child. Ahad has recovered from an accidental gunshot wound that destroyed twenty-five percent of his skull and brain. An advanced Critical Care Complex houses a pediatric intensive care unit, progressive care unit, burn unit and sleeping rooms for parents. Children's operates more than forty specialty and general pediatric clinics, providing a broad range of services to sick and healthy children. Nearly seventy-five percent of all surgeries at CMC are done on an outpatient basis through the day surgery program and an innovative unit called Almost Home, which provides medical observation without admittance to the hospital. The Ronald McDonald house is also nearby for families of hospitalized children.

The Dartmouth Hospital is the Miami Valley's only private psychiatric hospital. Dartmouth offers a complete, comprehensive continuum of mental health and addiction treatment to children, adolescents, adults and senior adults. The care continuum is provided at three locations—a sixty-bed acute care hospital that also provides partial hospitalization and intensive outpatient services, a thirty-eight-bed long-term residential facility for children and adolescents and an outpatient center that specializes in diagnostic services, family, group and individual therapy.

In the northern area of the Miami Valley is Upper Valley Medical Centers (UVMC), a 920-bed not-for-profit health care system encompassing two acute care hospitals, a speciality hospital, four long-term care centers and multiple satellite facilities. The umbrella organization was founded in 1986 from the merger of Miami County's three hospitals: Stouder Memorial Hospital and Dettmer Hospital in Troy and Piqua Memorial Medical Center in Piqua. This combination made it possible to reduce duplication of services and bring more advanced medical care to the region.

At Piqua Memorial and Stouder hospitals, UVMC provides comprehensive acute care. In addition, Rebound at Piqua serves traumatic brain-injury patients during the coma stages of recovery. Piqua also houses an enhanced pediatric department enlisting the management expertise of The Children's Medical Center (CMC). Also with the support of CMC is an inpatient children's rehabilitation unit at Stouder designated to care for children with ongoing therapeutic and medical needs. The Midwest Center for Head Pain Management at Stouder provides inpatient and outpatient treatment for chronic migraine and other severe head pain.

One of the largest, most comprehensive providers of behavioral medicine services in Ohio, Dettmer Hospital offers treatment programs for adult and adolescent chemical dependency and adult, adolescent and child psychiatry. Adjacent to Dettmer is the Jacob Dettmer Residence and the Adolescent Residential Center. Jacob Dettmer provides a cost-effective transitional step between traditional inpatient and outpatient chemical dependency services. The Adolescent Residential Center solves the growing need for specialized services for emotionally disordered, chemically dependent or dual-diagnosed adolescents. A Rebound second-stage rehabilitation unit for traumatic brain injury/coma patients is also located at Dettmer.

Two major federal medical centers are also located in Dayton. The USAF Medical Center, Wright-Patterson is a 300-

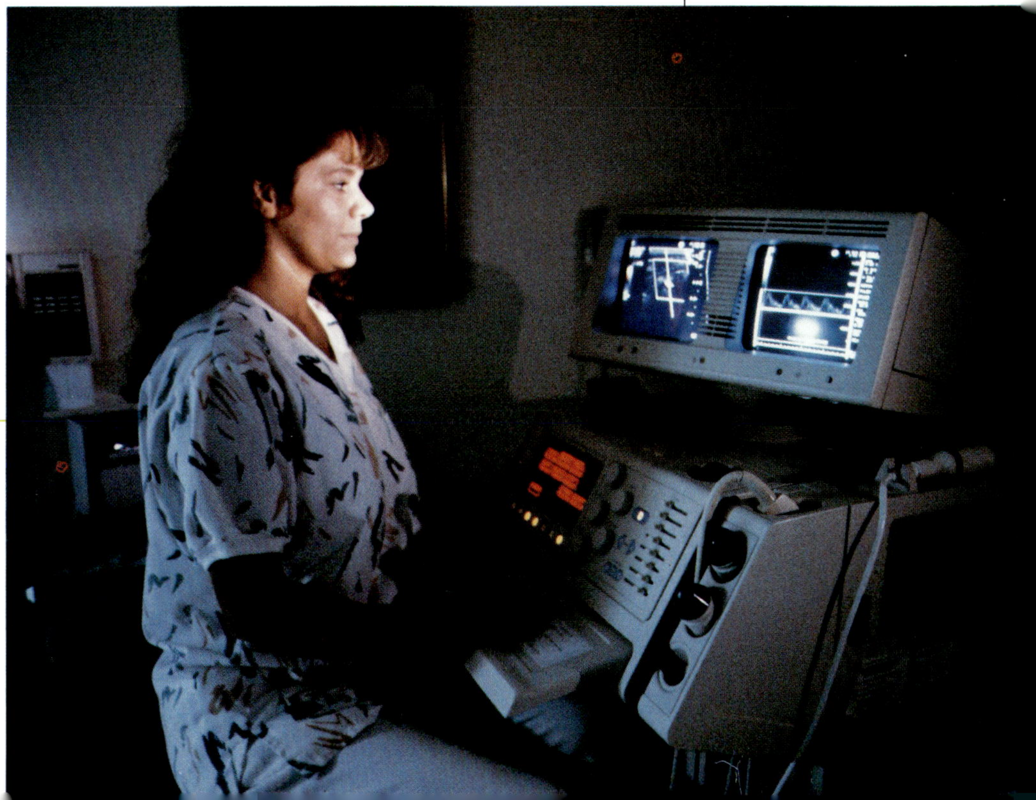

Upper Valley Medical Centers offers the most advanced diagnostic imaging capabilities available today. Here, a technologist operates the ATL Ultra Mark IX Ultrasound.

Richard Todd

bed multispeciality facility that offers and arranges for comprehensive community health and dental care in more than forty specialties. The medical center receives referral patients from the upper Midwest region and around the world three times weekly via the Department of Defense (DOD) aeromedical evacuation system. It serves 50,000 beneficiaries at WPAFB and the Miami Valley as well as more than 900,000 beneficiaries who live in the ten upper Midwest states that comprise the Department of Defense Region VI.

Education and training are emphasized at the medical center, which is integrated with Wright State University. Physicians are offered fully accredited medical training in a variety of programs. The medical center also offers clinical experience to Sinclair Community College nursing students. An active clinical investigations program, including more than 100 research protocols, supports the training mission and makes possible state-of-the-art treatment for cancer and rare eye disorders. Other hospital services include the Hyperbaric Medicine Clinic, the largest clinical chamber in the world, which acts as a worldwide referral center for DOD and provides emergency care for the local community. The organizational motto "Dedicated to Mission, Committed to Excellence" reflects a complete commitment to continuous improvement through Total Quality Management (TQM).

The medical center can expand by 132 beds during wartime or peacetime national emergency and is a key member of the National Disaster Medical System (NDMS). As such, it is responsible for eleven federal and fifty-three civilian medical institutions totaling 8,000 beds, or nearly 10 percent of all beds committed to NDMS.

Dayton's other federal hospital is the Department of Veterans Affairs Medical Center (VAMC), serving more than 382,000 veterans. The third oldest VA facility in the nation, Dayton's VA Medical Center has been an important health care provider to veterans since 1867. The medical center serves twenty-eight Ohio counties and one Indiana county. Comprehensive programs of primary, secondary and most levels of tertiary care are provided at the medical center. A complete continuum of ambulatory, acute and extended care is provided. Ambulatory care is provided through thirty-five clinics. Within the medical center is a 456-bed general medical, surgical and psychiatric

A statue of Hippocrates stands at the Wright State School of Medicine. William A. Holmes/Image Finders

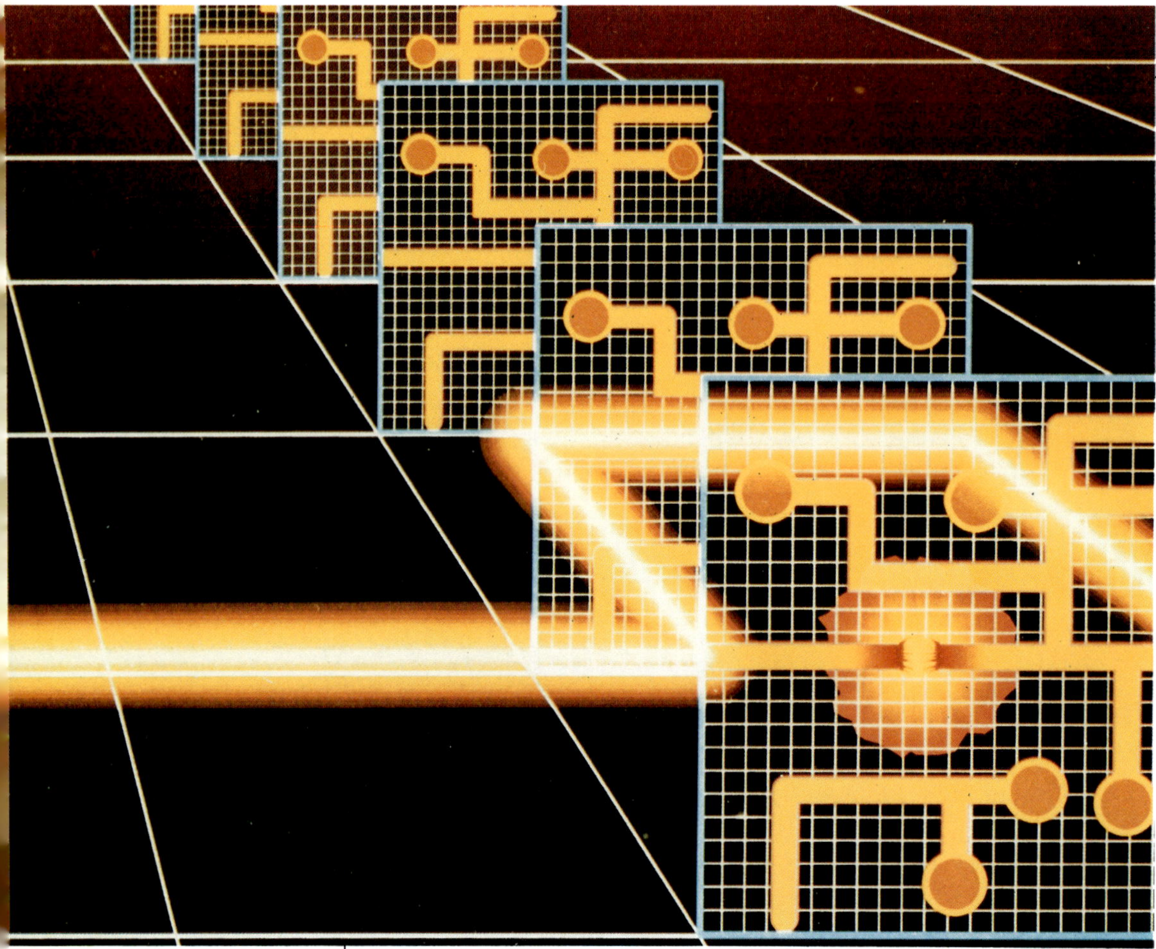

hospital; a 284-bed nursing home; and a 545-bed domiciliary. A Hospitality House, for families of critically or terminally ill patients, is the first in the nation to be operated on the grounds of a VA medical center by a veterans service organization. The VA's newest facility, an $82.5 million patient tower, is a ten-level, 426-bed hospital that houses state-of-the-art technology for modern, sophisticated medical care.

A primary teaching facility for Wright State University School of Medicine, the affiliation facilitates enhanced physician staffing and a high percentage of board-certified physicians. An agreement with the Air Force Medical Center provides interagency access to additional VA high-tech equipment, specialized laboratory studies and specialty consultants.

Located on 382 acres at the western edge of Dayton, the VA medical center's property also houses a ninety-acre National Cemetery, the only one in Ohio. A number of historic structures still stand at what was once known as the Old Soldiers' Home, constructed in the aftermath of the Civil War. One of them, the Protestant chapel erected in 1868, is still used. It is believed to be the oldest permanent place of worship constructed by the United States government.

Dozens of quality nursing homes for all levels of care, including skilled care, provide interim or permanent medical care for the region's residents. Several retirement centers, offering both inde-

The Center for Artificial Intelligence Applications develops solutions to operational challenges of the U.S. Air Force and industry in the Miami Valley. Center for Artifical Intelligence Applications

pendent and assisted living, are scattered throughout the region, many of them connected with major Dayton hospitals.

Through research, education and community service, the Hipple Cancer Research Center examines the molecular and genetic nature of cancer, contributing to the early detection, successful treatment and, ultimately, prevention of the disease. One of only sixteen autonomous cancer centers in the United States, the Hipple Center reached national prominence through its pioneering research in cell cloning, developing this valuable technique as a tool to examine and test colonies of malignant cells outside the human body.

National recognition has also come to Hipple scientists because of a technique developed at the cancer center for preserving bone marrow in a special solution that allows physicians to remove and store a patient's healthy marrow. Now used around the world, the technology helped in the treatment of radiation victims of the Chernobyl nuclear reactor accident. Hipple scientists also identified and purified a natural sustance that triggers the growth of white blood cells, boosting the immune system of patients at risk of infection after surgery or chemotherapy.

Hipple cancer scientists work to forge a better understanding of the molecular and genetic nature of cancer. With support from the National Cancer Institute, Hipple Cancer Center scientists developed a revolutionary new computer-driven microscope, the Cap-Scan. Using a laser beam for illumination, the Cap-Scan counts colonies of cloned cancer cells grown in small, glass microcapillary tubes. This first automated microscope in existence worldwide has numerous distinct advantages

These Wright State University students are enrolled in an introductory robotics class, where they study the mathematics, programming and control of robots.

Wright State University

over petri dishes.

The region's hospitals and medical centers add a great deal to the economy, but this is secondary to their primary purpose—providing every Daytonian with the highest quality medical care available anywhere.

EDUCATION FOR A GLOBAL FUTURE

Economic development within the Dayton region depends heavily on the area's high-tech community. Working together in Dayton, the federal, state and local governments, along with the academic community and the private sector, contribute significantly to the advancement of aerospace research and development. Ohio's academic engineering community currently participates in more than $100 million of cooperative aerospace research and development contracts from Wright-Patterson Air Force Base.

Advanced technology research and development flourishes in the Miami Valley, much of it in connection with the area's twenty-six colleges and universities. Federal and state funds invested in Dayton's academic community sponsor programs that ensure the region's success in a global economic future. These programs include:

- The Center for Artificial Intelligence Applications—The center, created with a $10 million, five-year contract from the Air Force, works toward applying artificial intelligence-based solutions to Air Force problems through research in collaboration with Miami Valley colleges and universities.
- The Dayton Area Technology Network—A group of Miami Valley science and engineering entrepreneurs who work to encourage technology transfer between government and industry to establish lines between universities and technology-based firms and to

Founded in 1887, Cedarville College enrolls nearly 2,000 students in 75 different areas of study. Bill Swartz/BBS Images

attract new technology-based companies to locate in the area.

• Edison Materials Technology Center—One of the nine Ohio Edison Centers created by the state as a nonprofit organization that brings together industry, university and federal resources to solve technical problems relating to materials and industrial processing. Members include nine local universities and fifty companies.

• Miami Valley Research Institute—A consortium of local colleges and universities that work together to attract university contacts and grants and to bring technology-based companies to the Miami Valley Research Park.

• The Ohio Advanced Technology Center—A nonprofit organization formed to facilitate transfer of Wright-Patterson Air Force Base technology to Ohio's private sector, particularly in the Dayton-Cincinnati-Columbus area.

The University of Dayton is part of the nongovernment, nonprofit Miami Valley Research Institute, a five-member consortium. Jeff B. Miller/University of Dayton

• The Ohio Computer Technology Center—A nonprofit organization of more than forty computer-related companies that support the Air Force Logistics Command at Wright-Patterson Air Force Base. The organization's purpose is to commercialize and market computer software products provided by the Air Force Logistics Command.

• The University Center for Electro-Optics—One of the three largest research centers of its kind in the country, where electrical-engineering and physics students analyze and harness the power of light.

• The University of Dayton Research Institute—This university-based facility conducts more than $31 million in research annually, most of it contracted by Wright-Patterson Air Force Base. UDRI also directs troubleshooting research in response to specific requests by local

industries.

• Wright State University's Biomedical and Human Factors Engineering Department—A department within Wright State's College of Engineering and Computer Science where electrical, mechanical and computer engineering is used to help rehabilitate people with paralyzing disease or injury.

Cooperation within the higher education institutions is at its strongest with the Miami Valley Research Institute (MVRI). A nongovernment, nonprofit corporation, MVRI is a consortium of the University of Dayton, Wright State University, Central State University and Sinclair Community College. The Air Force Institute of Technology, located at Wright-Patterson Air Force Base, is an associate member. Located in the 1,250-acre Miami Valley Research Park, MVRI conducts research in eight scientific-technology specialties.

At Wright State University, research has led to improved materials and products capable of high performance, often in harsh environments, such as thermally stable polymer adhesives and a titanium-alloy engine disk with controlled microstructure. Research has led to fire-retardant coatings and improved aerospace-alloy brazes and brazing methods, for example.

Environmental stresses are studied at MVRI member institutions to gain greater understanding of how pollutants and toxicants work in the ecosystem. One of the country's most sophisticated mass spectrometric facilities designed for research in the environmental sciences is housed at the Brehm Environmental Laboratory at Wright State University. A basic goal of the environmental research being conducted at MVRI member institutions is to ensure the Miami Valley—and the

The 1,250-acre Miami Valley Research Park is home to many of the region's high technology companies and organizations, including the renowned Miami Valley Research Institute. Andy Snow

country—of an abundant and continuing supply of clear water.

This nation's energy needs require more effectiveuse of existing energy supplies and new techniques for energy production. At Wright State University, the focus is on improving the yield from existing energy sources; at the University of Dayton, the emphasis is on the development of energy sources.

In 1961 the University of Dayton began offering one of the first bachelor's degree programs in computer science in the country. Computer and information science maintains its cutting edge at MVRI. Equipped with an array of computer models and architectures and staffed by highly skilled scientists and technicians, MVRI can accommodate nearly any research purpose and proposal.

Biomedical and human factors engineering at MVRI seeks to design equipment that meets with human capabilities and allows for the most effective coordination of humans and machines. At the Air Force Institute of Technology, computer-applied research is conducted in the relationship and interchange of computer language and human speech. MVRI contributes to the health care communities by its capacity to conduct virtually any type of basic, applied or clinical research to medicine. Centered in the School of Medicine at Wright State University and the Biology Department of the University of Dayton, the research extends to such fields as pharmacology, immunology, toxicology and aerospace medicine. At Wright State University, scientists are developing a microprocessor stimulator device that may restore the ability of paraplegics to stand and

Cooperation among Dayton's educational facilities and the Miami Valley Research Institute has led to incredible advances in the research and development of high technology.
Jeff B. Miller/ University of Dayton

walk.

Through either teaching or working arrangements, MVRI members are linked to all major area health facilities, which provide for clinical testing and evaluation of laboratory hypotheses. Biomedical science work at Wright State benefits from the School of Medicine's association with three local research institutions: the Cox Heart Institute, the Fels Research Institute and the Bob Hipple Laboratory for Cancer Research.

Greene Street Daycare and Pre-school in Piqua nurtures the Miami Valley's future scholars.
Richard Todd

Applied mathematics within MVRI members is a mathematical and a computer strength. At the University of Dayton, for example, mathematical models of the impact force of bird strikes on differently designed aircraft canopies are computerized to determine a design that combines maximum pilot visibility with maximum safety. Mathematical models and computer technology are used in research on frost accumulation on aircraft and the resulting drag and life penalties that require modifying takeoff procedures. Research at the university is also conducted to determine the effects of heavy rain on aircraft during takeoff and landing.

Substantial contributions are also made by MVRI member institutions in aeronautical, astronautical and applied sciences. At Wright State University, spectral techniques were developed for the Air Force to address problems of contamination in gyroscopes and linear accelerometers contained in the advanced guidance and control packages of intercontinental ballistic missiles. Research in laser spectroscopy at the University of Dayton has developed a remote optical diagnostic tool that evaluates combustion streams from gas turbine engines and other combustion devices that may be used where direct instrumentation is not practical. The University of Dayton and the

Conveniently located in downtown Dayton, Sinclair Community College offers associate degrees in fields such as allied health care, engineering and performing arts. Dawson Jones

Air Force Institute of Technology are among the nation's leaders in the application of laser optics.

Located within the same complex—the Miami Valley Research Park—is Edison Materials Technology Center (EMTEC), part of Ohio's Thomas Edison Program. EMTEC is one of several centers established to improve the competitiveness of Ohio industry. Specifically, EMTEC encourages the development and deployment of new industrial materials and technologies by Ohio companies. EMTEC deals in industrial base materials and the processes that convert these materials into products. Regardless of size, both member and nonmember companies have access to the EMTEC network of resources, including university research and development, direct application of existing technology from federal and other sources, short-term problem solving, technical consulting, training and technology transfer programs and excellent forums for communicating technical ideas, concepts and know-how. Perhaps the most important outcome of EMTEC's work is the formation of effective, integrated teams of industry, academia and government to assure the future competitiveness of Ohio's materials and processing industry.

Dayton and the entire Miami Valley share the same pursuit of excellence for education at all levels. From day care centers through highly specialized postgraduate degrees, area students receive quality education through innovative programs. Fifty public school districts provide education to the children of the Miami Valley. These are augmented by nearly thirty religious schools that represent several faiths.

The city of Dayton School District's strategic plan calls for graduation or successful completion of an individual achievement program of 100 percent of the district's students. Additionally, the objec-

Wittenberg University is considered to be the Midwest's leading regional liberal arts college. Andy Snow

tives include that within six months of graduation or completion of the education program, every student will be pursuing further education, serving in the military, gainfully employed or pursuing a career. The five-year plan, "The Choice is Transformation," is a model for many districts throughout the nation.

Dayton Public Schools implemented programs that include magnet schools, Partners in Education, National Merit scholars, foreign exchange opportunities and the Kiser Space Symposium, which has received support from the aerospace community locally and nationally. Partnerships among the schools and the business community assist students in preparation for their future through work programs and educational programs specially designed to respond to the needs of the community.

Established in 1856, Wilberforce is the oldest, private, African-American liberal arts college in the nation. Bill Swartz/BBS Images

The magnet program covers fourteen distinctive disciplines, such as the arts, international studies, math and science, and vocational training. Specially developed curricula that relate to these themes provide students with in-depth study and training in their chosen field. Students also receive exposure to community resources and enriched educational experiences.

At the Challenger Center, students take computer-simulated voyages to Halley's Comet and the moon. A living memorial to the Challenger astronauts who died on January 28, 1986, the center was designed by their families for children to apply math, science and problem-solving skills in a high-tech space lab located at Kiser Middle School for Environmental Science/Space Studies to learn the wonders of space development. The center received national attention when a CBS News crew filmed a segment for Charles Kuralt's "School's In."

Whether learning to be future astronauts, engineers or artists, the region's children are exposed to the vanguard of education. School districts of the Miami

Graduates of Wright State University celebrate the end of their studies. Wright State University

Valley offer the finest education available anywhere in the country. In several of the area's districts more than 80 percent of the students enter college. Average SAT scores are 962 in the city and 1007 in the suburbs.

Many of the area's graduating seniors continue their education locally at Sinclair Community College in downtown Dayton, which covers fifty-three acres and is growing. National recognition has come to Sinclair through the caliber of its nearly 120,000 students as well as its academic achievements. Sinclair is one of four community colleges in the Miami Valley. Edison State College in Piqua serves the junior college students in Miami County, Clark Technical College in Springfield serves those in Clark County and Southern State Community College in Wilmington serves Clinton County.

Scenic Wilmington College in Clinton County offers a liberal arts curriculum with 22 majors and specialized programs. Bill Swartz/BBS Images

The nation's oldest black college, Wilberforce University, founded in 1856, is a privately owned church university. It is Central State University, Ohio's only predominantly black institution of higher education. Established in 1887, Central State's program in Water Resources Management is linked with international water resources in Israel and throughout the world. Central State's colleges offer degrees in approximately sixty majors.

The University of Dayton, the largest independent university in Ohio, offers seventy undergraduate and sixty graduate programs of study. Located on eighty acres near downtown, the university was established in 1850. It is one of the ten largest Catholic universities in the nation, with an enrollment of 6,500 undergraduates and 3,500 graduate and law students.

The University of Dayton Research Institute (UDRI) focuses on the advanced research-and-development needs of government and private-sector sponsors. During the past thirty-five years, research totaled more than $250 million, with more than thirty ongoing contracts valued at

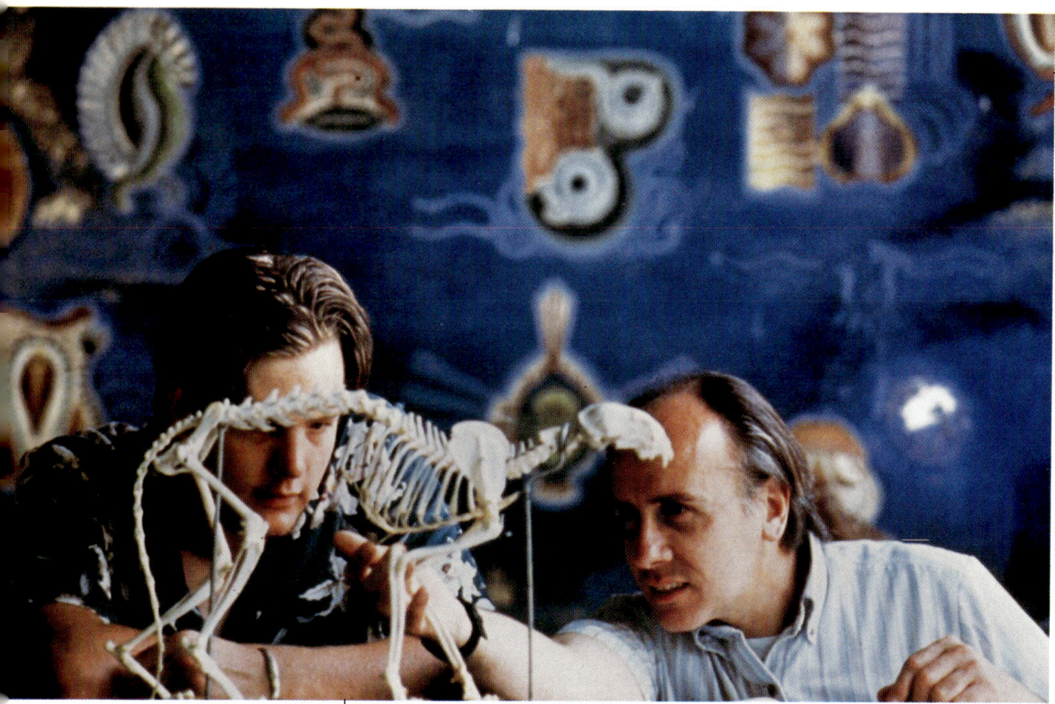

approximately $30 million.

Founded in 1964, Wright State University is a comprehensive public university that serves a student population of almost 17,000 and offers more than 100 undergraduate majors, twenty-seven master's degree programs, post-master's degree programs, and doctorates. Located on 557 acres within metropolitan Dayton, Wright State addresses the economic and technological development of the region through its nine colleges and schools, and off-campus research facilities. The United States Department of Education named Wright State University as one of the four outstanding colleges in the nation offering programs to students with disabilities. To assist students who are paralyzed, the buildings on the campus are connected by an elaborate underground tunnel system, which is equipped with elevators and electric doors.

Antioch College offers a distinctive liberal arts, cross-cultural, and international curriculum on its Yellow Springs campus. Antioch College

Other area colleges and universities include such institutions as the Air Force Institute of Technology, the premier Air Force graduate school for aerospace, where 21,000 Department of Defense employees complete professional continuing education programs. Antioch College in Yellow Springs in Greene County was founded in 1852 by Horace Mann, a pioneer in American public schools. Cedarville College, a privately owned college in Greene County, is approved by the General Association of Regular Baptist Churches. Wittenberg University in Clark County was ranked one of the nation's best 250 colleges by the *New York Times*.

In the Dayton region, economic development comes through education, Dayton's great technical resources and the innovative technology development programs that help the area's companies compete in a global market while providing an attractive climate for foreign investment.

The University of Dayton is the largest independent university in Ohio with more than 120 undergraduate and graduate programs in areas of study that range from the fine arts to engineering research. Jeff B. Miller/University of Dayton

EXIT

CHAPTER SIX

CULTURAL KALEIDOSCOPE

Daytonians enjoy a richly diverse kaleidoscope of cultural and recreational activities. From the fine arts to homespun festivals to professional sports, the Miami Valley offers a depth and range of activities usually found only in the largest of America's cities.

Dayton has its own opera company, ballet company, modern dance company, philharmonic orchestra and theater company. The Dayton Art Institute houses a world-famous collection of paintings and sculptures, and history is well captured in a number of museums in the area.

Known to play as hard as they work, Daytonians have created a recreational mecca. From basketball to golf to soccer, the pros keep the crowds roaring. For the amateur sports enthusiasts, a wide range of activities keep every weekend full of fun. College and high school sports are also important in the Miami Valley, giving young people plenty of time in the spotlight and a chance at the big time.

Taking advantage of the natural beauty of the region, reserves and parks provide plenty of leisure-time activities. The Miami Valley even has its own inland sandy beaches as well as the Midwest's number one water park and an amusement park with roller coasters designed to send scream-thrills through even the stoutest heart.

Setting the stage for the arts in Dayton is the landmark Victoria Theatre. Bill Swartz/BBS Images

Many of Dayton's special annual events have become world-famous, bringing people from around the globe to this city that adds so much to the quality of life by offering such a diversity of cultural events and recreational activities.

THE ARTS

The Miami Valley's grandest lady is the 127-year-old Victoria Theatre. Built as the Turner Opera House in 1866, the Victoria survived two major fires, the devastating flood of 1913, several name changes and, on more than one occasion, the wrecking ball.

When hard times fell on the city in the early 1970s, the Victoria—then called the Victory Theatre, the last of five downtown theaters—was scheduled to become a parking lot. But a grass-roots movement saved the theater and initiated a multimillion dollar project that spanned the next two decades and turned the theater into the shining star she is today. After an eighteen-month, $17.5 million renovation, the Victoria welcomed back the famous to a black-tie opening at the packed house on a warm winter night in January 1990.

The renovation paid off. Under the leadership of Executive Producer Mark Light, ticket sales tripled and the number of performances doubled within the first season alone. The Victoria Theatre Association's annual budget grew from $500,000 to $2.2 million—all within the first year after the renovation. Once host to nearly every famous actor in the world—Sarah Bernhardt, Edwin Booth, John Drew, Helen Hayes, Tallulah Bankhead, Zoe Caldwell—the Victoria once again hosts the theater world's finest.

Like all grand theaters, the Victoria even has her own ghost. As the story goes, a young actress in the early 1900s left the stage area to go upstairs to the dressing room to retrieve her fan. She didn't return and was never seen again. Her street clothes remained in the dressing room, but the fan disappeared along with the actress, still dressed in her black taffeta costume.

Over the years, those who work in the theater have reported seeing her image in mirrors and smelling whiffs of her perfume. The rustle of taffeta or the feel of someone brushing by a shoulder is more than imagination for those who have experienced the ghost of the young actress. "We've heard footsteps across the stage and on the staircase and we've heard the sound of a door opening and closing," said David Hastings, house manager. When a newcomer to the area looked through the glass doors into the Victoria's lobby one evening, she saw a young woman dressed in a black taffeta ball gown. The theater was closed and the lobby dark and empty except for the mysterious young woman. One television station even captured on audiotape a sound like that of a rustling petticoat while filming a segment for a local program.

The Victoria is anchor for the block-long Metropolitan Arts Center, which houses an educational center; the Loft, a 220-seat thrust theater; dance studios; and offices for many of Dayton's performing-arts companies and WDPR, Dayton's public radio station. In the works is a 3,000-seat concert hall.

The Human Race, Dayton's resident theater company, performs in the intimate 219-seat Loft Theatre, which is housed in the Metropolitan Arts Center. The regular season includes contemporary drama, American classics and original scripts. Musicals and comedies are produced annually at the Victoria Theatre and the outdoor Fraze Pavilion. The Human Race serves the community through programs and performances in more than 100 schools throughout the Miami Valley, reaching nearly 30,000 students every year.

Lavish, fully staged productions starring national and international luminaries are a trademark of the thirty-year-old Dayton Opera, located a few blocks away in Memorial Hall. The Dayton Opera brings to the stage spectacular fare that

Built in 1866, the newly renovated Victoria Theatre is the heart of Dayton's performing arts community. Gregory C. Sundra

ranges from traditional grand opera to Broadway musical theater. Some of the nation's most exciting young singers, currently making an impact on stages in the United States, Europe and Asia, have created roles for the Dayton Opera audience, drawn from nearly a quarter of the state.

Dayton Opera also is a statewide leader in accessibility services, bringing opera within reach of all. The company provides surtitle translations for all foreign-language productions, large-print synopses and audio description for patrons with visual impairments and audio-enhancement services and American Sign Language interpretation for opera-lovers with hearing impairments. The company brings the magic of grand opera to over 25,000 high school and university students, senior citizens and members of church and civic groups within a twenty-three-county area each year.

Complementing this program, Opera Guild of Dayton volunteers introduce opera to preschool and kindergarten audiences through the use of handcrafted "performing" marionettes. Guild members also bring creative and entertaining versions of grand opera to elementary and middle schools, where students not only take part in the "opera" itself, but also handle backstage duties in an award-winning community education effort.

Dayton's premier musical force is the Dayton Philharmonic Orchestra. Founded in 1933 by Dr. Paul Katz as a chamber orchestra, the Philharmonic evolved into an eighty-five-plus-member orchestra that offers Daytonians more than thirty concerts annually. With a season that offers two classical orchestra concert series, two pops orchestra concert series, two chamber ensemble series, two chamber music series and a summer concert band series, the Dayton Philharmonic Orchestra also performs music education programs tailored to the needs of school children.

Music lovers enjoy an afternoon of offerings by the Dayton Philharmonic Orchestra.

Andy Snow

The orchestra's Young People's Concerts are nationally recognized as one of the finest musical educational programs in the country. For more than fifty years, the Dayton Philharmonic Youth Orchestra, composed of about 150 students from around the Miami Valley, has provided a major musical opportunity for junior and senior high school musicians. In 1982 a Junior Strings Orchestra was organized for string students in grades six through twelve.

With nearly 10,000 subscribers, the Dayton Philharmonic Orchestra reaches more than 170,000 concertgoers. Many of the world's most extraordinary artists have performed with the Dayton Philharmonic, including Itzhak Perlman, Maureen Forrester, Andre Watts, Nadja Salerno-Sonnenberg, James Galway and Isaac Stern. In the pops series, the orchestra has welcomed such entertainers as Peter Nero, Roy Clark, Doc Severinsen, the Canadian Brass, Henry Mancini, Judy Collins, Mel Torme and Ben Vereen.

Music lovers also enjoy chamber music concerts. Yellow Springs hosts a series of concerts presented by distinguished chamber music ensembles. The Vanguard Concerts, another series of chamber music concerts, are held at the Dayton Art Institute.

Artists of national and international reputation perform in the Soirees Musicales concerts, also held at the Dayton Art Institute. Organized more than twenty years ago to feature piano recitals, the Soirees Musicales series brings a richness of music seldom found outside a major metropolitan area. The Dayton Bach society, a choral group of about fifty singers, has held a reputation as one of the finest groups in the Midwest throughout its nearly twenty years of performing. Annually, they perform more than five concerts of music ranging from pre-Renaissance to the twentieth century. The Bach Society also produces one of the Miami Valley's favorite holiday events, the annual Messiah Sing-In. The Gem City Chapter of the Sweet Adelines brings together women from across the Valley to sing barbershop harmony. They compete annually in worldwide competitions and the

Showcasing traditional and ethnic arts is CITYFOLK. With more than 70 events each year, entertaining groups such as the Mozowsze dancers are introduced to delighted audiences.
CITYFOLK

Gem City Chapter has won the world championship a record five times.

Jazz concerts, rhythm and blues, reggae, rock and roll, German music, Irish music—music to please the ear of every generation and every taste can be found in the region. Both at Wright State University and at the University of Dayton, concerts are held regularly by touring companies performing everything from instrumental music (the Dallas Brass) to opera (The Marriage of Figaro). In the summer, picnickers bring a blanket and lunch for a Sunday afternoon of music in the city's Dave Hall Plaza or to one of many suburban parks. Every other Friday, Courthouse Square rocks and rolls with an after-work party, complete with vendors selling hot dogs and giant hot pretzels.

The Dayton Art Institute, which will soon celebrate its seventy-fifth anniversary, houses a superb collection of painting, sculpture and graphic and decorative arts. The region's preeminent fine arts museum is itself a work of art. Its structure is one of Greater Dayton's most striking landmarks, located in the historic Grafton District. Listed on the National Register of Historic Places, the Italian Renaissance Revival building presides majestically atop a hill overlooking the city and the Great Miami River.

Every major movement in American art through the second half of the twentieth century is represented in the permanent collection and 5,000 years of cultural history are chronicled through its more than 15,000 works. Famous for its Asian art, the museum boasts an extensive assemblage of works from China, India, Japan, Kashmir, Korea, the Near East, Nepal, Southeast Asia and Tibet. Equally well known is its seventeenth-century baroque collection. The museum's contemporary collection features works by Warhol, Nevelson, Lichtenstein, Hockney, Motherwell and other avant-garde artists. The permanent collection also contains works by artists such as Claude Monet, Georgia O'Keeffe and Edward Hopper.

Visiting exhibitions include such diverse works as Japanese prints, African sculpture, Haitian painting, seventeenth-century Chinese porcelain, North American folk and visionary art, and such artists as Wassily Kandinsky, Frederic Remington and Marsden Hartley. More than 100,000 visitors from around the world visit the museum annually.

Each year in early October, the Dayton Art Institute hosts the city's fall highlight, Oktoberfest. During the three-day festival, more than 30,000 visitors enjoy the museum's collection along with good food, good music and, of course, good beer.

Dayton is also dance country. Founded in 1937 by Josephine and Hermene Schwarz, the Dayton Ballet is the second oldest regional ballet company in the nation. Nationally recognized as "the company of premieres," the Dayton Ballet has more than 225 of the world's first-time performances to its credit. At the internationally televised opening of the '87 Pan American games, 37 countries saw the Dayton Ballet perform. In 1988 the Dayton Ballet was the official U.S. representative to the Jerash Festival of Culture and Arts in Jordan.

The Dayton Contemporary Dance Company (DCDC) brought 3,000 New Yorkers to their feet in a strong ovation when the company performed a solo concert at Lincoln Center as part of its Out-Of-Doors-Concert Series. Founded in 1968 by Jeraldyne Blunden, DCDC's roots go back to 1949, when Josephine Schwarz, the ballet's "Miss Jo," felt a need to provide dance exposure to the area's black youth. Ms. Blunden, the first black to perform with the Dayton Ballet, led DCDC to national prominence with performances across the United States and Europe.

Showcase for the works of America's most talented black choreographers, DCDC brings to Dayton's Victoria stage many works rarely shown outside New York. In 1979 the company became the first black dance company to be accepted into the National Association of Regional Ballet and one of only four national companies to be designated as an "Award Company."

The Acting Company is just one of many talented theater groups that perform for Miami Valley audiences. Bill Swartz/BBS Images

CITYFOLK, a folk-arts organization, showcases blues, jazz, gospel, Irish, Polish and Celtic traditions and talents in a variety of concerts, performances and workshops. Founded in 1980 as a community-based arts project, CITYFOLK is the first professional traditional and ethnic arts organization in Ohio. Designed to stimulate greater awareness of, and appreciation for, the cultural traditions of the people who live in Dayton, CITYFOLK draws a crowd of more than 7,000 to nearly seventy events. International artists from around the world come to Dayton to bring their music and rich culture. The group Beausoleil, led by Cajun fiddler extraordinaire Michael Doucet, has performed its spicy gumbo of traditional French Louisiana music, zydeco and New Orleans rhythm and blues; Sweet Honey In the Rock has electrified audiences with singing that embraced gospel, folk, blues, jazz, rhythm and blues, African-derived field hollers and work songs.

The "blues" pack a musical punch in Dayton.
Andy Snow

Daytonians also take advantage of the many touring shows that come to Dayton regularly. From *Cats* to *Hair* to *Phantom of the Opera*, major New York companies put Dayton on their cross-country stops, adding to the area's lively diversity of arts offerings.

Community theater also thrives in the region. In everything from converted barns to post offices to park shelters, community theater offers local actors a showcase for their talent, and local audiences tickets costing about as much as a movie. Throughout the Valley are dozens of community the-

aters, mostly volunteer driven, staging everything from massive musicals to simple productions without backdrops.

Dayton's oldest community theater, at sixty-plus years, is the Dayton Theater Guild. Located in a former post office just north of downtown, the ninety-seat house wraps around the stage on three sides, adding to the intimacy of the theater. Also north of the city is the Dayton Playhouse, located in the Cultural Arts Complex at DeWeese Park. Performing began more than thirty years ago. Today they fill the 170-seat house with a dedicated audience for a five-production season of plays, special holiday performances and an annual summer festival of new plays, many written by local talent. The area's only black group, Creekside Players, performs in different auditoriums in Dayton.

In Kettering, Theater Under the Stars packs several hundred into a former junior high school auditorium. In the summer, thousands attend outdoor musicals at the Fairmont Amphitheater, making Theater Under the Stars a box-office winner. In Centerville, Playhouse South performs in the Washington Township Hall in a 358-seat auditorium with an elevated proscenium stage. The Fairborn Playhouse, founded more than twenty years ago at Wright-Patterson Air Force Base, is now in an old movie house that seats 100. Center Stage in Yellow Springs is a 100-seat house in a converted Ford dealership.

Outdoor community theater is also popular in the region. Brookville Community Theater, one of the newest organizations, performs in an enclosed shelter at the Golden Gate Park. Crossroads Community Theater in Vandalia is also one of the newer groups. Having no permanent home, their performances are held in parks.

Professional outdoor theater is at its best in Xenia, where Blue Jacket is staged every summer. Ohio's frontier story of a white man who became war chief of the Shawnee Indian Nation 200 years ago, Blue Jacket is performed on the same ground where some of the story's action historically

More than 15,000 works are on permanent display at the Dayton Art Institute, including an extensive collection of Asian art and selections from such contemporary artists as Georgia O'Keefe and Andy Warhol. Jim Baron/Image Finders

occurred. In the 1,200-seat amphitheater, fifty actors and a dozen horses depict the struggle of the Shawnee to save their homeland against the daring of frontiersmen such as Daniel Boone.

A dinner theater experience is also available at LaComedia in Springboro. Staging works from *George M* to *Fiddler on the Roof*, LaComedia adds another dimension to Dayton's diversity of live theater.

The Dayton area's newest arts facility is the Fraze Pavilion for the Performing Arts in Kettering, Ohio—the Miami Valley's summer showplace. The new $3 million outdoor amphitheater in beautiful Lincoln Park Center can accommodate 4,000 people in a relaxed, informal environment. Fraze Pavilion presents over forty performances between May and September, including visits by world-class entertainers. Dayton's resident professional performing-arts organizations enjoy a summer home at Fraze Pavilion and there are many community programs, encompassing film, dance, band, chorus and a variety of events.

Young people are an integral part of the arts scene in the Miami Valley through an innovative and unique program, the Muse Machine. Founded in 1982, the innovative program encourages secondary school students to make the arts a vital part of their lives and, in the process, develop a continuing commitment to attending and supporting the arts. The Muse Machine currently involves more than 300 dedicated teachers and 8,500 secondary student members from ninety-four schools in eleven Ohio counties. An elementary school program, the Muse Adventure, has been added; it now involves 125 teachers and nearly 3,500 students in twenty-eight elementary schools in four Ohio counties.

At Dayton-based workshops, Muse Machine teachers have studied under the likes of noted

Wright State University is often the site of seemingly impromptu concerts. William A. Holmes/Image Finders

Shakespeare director Arthur Lithgow, Peter Shaffer, the playwright of such works as *Amadeus* and *Equus*; Tony-award-winning actress Zoe Caldwell; Nat Horne, Broadway dancer and choreographer; composer Herschel Garfein; sculptor Colin Webster Watson; opera director John Sheehan; and international performance artist Ping Chone. Advanced training includes a New York seminar where teachers experience high-caliber arts workshops, performances and exhibits.

The Muse Machine couples an in-school with an out-of-school program to generate a young audience for the arts and nurture creative expression in young people. Approximately 100,000 students are exposed to local professional arts organizations through Muse Machine In-School Performances. These performances in the schools generate nearly $65,000 in revenue for the arts organizations. Students also purchase more than 10,000 tickets to area mainstage performances and exhibits each year through the Muse Machine Out-of-School Program. These ticket sales generate an additional $50,000 for the arts organizations. This added revenue enables artists-in-residence to extend their residencies, keeps local artists working in the area and fills seats that might otherwise be empty.

Although the success of the Muse Machine stems from the involvement of many committed individuals, its creation and continual wealth of new ideas flow from its founder and artistic director, Suzy Bassani, who received the 1992 Ohio Governor's Award for Arts in Education. Her commitment to the arts in Dayton and to the education of young people is exemplary, demonstrating that an individual with a passion for excellence and a commitment to a well-defined dream can make that dream a reality.

Dayton even has its own professional film

company, River City Productions, owned by Julia Reichert, a documentary filmmaker and two-time Academy Award nominee. With locally raised funds, Ms. Reichert shot her first feature-length fiction film, *Emma and Elvis*, in the city.

Film has put many a Daytonian in the Hollywood spotlight. Martin Sheen grew up here as Ramon Estevez, one of 13 children. Mr. Sheen's own sons, Emilio Estevez and Charlie Sheen, have followed in their famous father's acting footsteps. Dorian Harewood of television's "The Trials of Rosie O'Neill" grew up in Dayton, as did acting brothers Rob and Chad Lowe and producer and writer Jeff Franklin. Emmy-winner Jonathan Winters, recognized as one of the world's most talented comedians, is from Dayton, as are the Gish sisters. Daytonian Steve Martino won an Emmy for his work as a director on ABC's "World of Discovery." Although Bart Simpson of TV's "The Simpsons," may not have grown up here, his voice, Nancy Cartwright, did.

Erma Bombeck, the syndicated columnist, began her career in Dayton, as did television talk show host Phil Donahue. Pulitzer Prize-winning editorial cartoonist and creator of "Mother Goose and Grimm" Mike Peters called Dayton home for years, as did Milton Caniff, creator of "Steve Canyon" and "Terry and the Pirates." Daytonian native James Gaines is managing editor of *Life* magazine. Poet laureate of black Americans Paul Laurence Dunbar wrote most of his twenty-five books, essays and more than 100 poems from his home in Dayton. Novelist John Jakes began his writing career in Dayton, as did Dayton native Melissa Fay Greene, nominee for the 1991 National Award for Nonfiction.

Funding for the performing arts comes through a mixture of private and public sources. Major corporations, such as NCR and Mead, give generously, in excess of $1 million. But the

The Italian Renaissance Revival Dayton Art Institute commands attention at its location in the historic Grafton District, overlooking the Great Miami River. Luce Photography/ Image Finders

arts in Dayton also depend heavily on the generosity and interest of more than 400 smaller companies and countless individual donations.

Dayton's devotion to the arts has raised millions for a variety of projects. More than $17 million was raised to restore the Victoria and another $40 million is currently being raised to complete the Metropolitan Arts Center. Individual contributions of $9 million and ticket sales of nearly $3 million combine to make the arts a $12 million-a-year business that grows about 15 percent a year. Without funding, the cost of tickets would be prohibitive for many, and that is something Dayton's performing-arts groups guard against. An opera ticket would cost nearly $100 instead of around $30; the ballet would be closer to $70 instead of around $25; and the Victoria would almost double the under-$25 price of a ticket.

ARTSDAYTON, the major funding source for arts in the region, solicits money from individuals, businesses and foundations, then allocates the funds to arts groups. ARTSDAYTON has recently merged with the Miami Valley Arts Council to form a full-service art and cultural organization. ARTSDAYTON provides 16 to 20 percent of its organization's operating budgets. Serving twenty-one counties throughout Southwestern Ohio, ARTSDAYTON also provides annual funding for some forty other community cultural projects.

Montgomery County set up an Arts and Cultural District, earmarking $1 million each year for the arts from sales tax. The first countywide arts district in the state of Ohio, the Arts and Cultural District will use funds to represent the broad spectrum of the community in providing arts and cultural activities for all.

The Arts Center Foundation, a corporation of community leaders interested in the arts as they relate to community development, was responsible for raising private financing of $17.5 mil-

A Celebration of Bicycling overlooks the riders of the River Corridor Bikeway on the south side of town. Gregory C. Sundra

Women aviators are honored at the International Women's Air and Space Museum in Centerville.
Andy Snow

lion for restoration of the Victoria Theatre.

In Dayton the arts are for everyone. Affordable, versatile and available, the Dayton arts scene adds greatly to the quality of life in the region. The arts add a depth to life that can only come from watching the grace of the dancer in midair, hearing the rhymes and rhythms of music and watching the vibrancy of the colors on a great canvas. Rich with diversity, the arts impact the region economically as well as through the added quality of life. More than 1,500 people are employed in the arts. Another 2,000 volunteers help make it happen. Nearly 411,000 people attended art performances in the 1990-91 season.

Museums in the region offer a diverse tapestry of art, history and culture. Most are free to the public or charge only a nominal fee. And all have events that bring to the community a glimpse of the other side of the horizon through the expression of ethnic music and food, historic reenactments and other interesting and informative exhibits.

Riverbend Art Center, a teaching center located in the cultural Arts Complex at DeWeese Park, brings 50,000 visitors through the annual Art in the Park fair, where local artists and those from across the nation display their work. Local artists—painters, sculptors and photographers—also show their art at the High Street Gallery in the historic St. Anne's Hill District and in Artist Row, a former envelope plant in Dayton's old warehouse district. In town centers, along the riverbanks and in parks throughout the Miami Valley, artists gather on warm summer afternoons to show their work to visitors. Numerous privately owned galleries where buyers can purchase artworks for every taste and price are scattered throughout the Miami Valley.

Dayton's most spectacular museum is

Those who aspire to learn a craft or dabble in the fine arts enjoy hands-on fun at the Dayton Art Institute.
Andy Snow

the United States Air Force Museum, the oldest and largest aviation museum in the world. With more than 200 aircraft and major missiles, this ten-and-a-half-acre museum preserves the heritage of military flight. Located on the grounds of Wright-Patterson Air Force Base, the museum uses both chronological and thematic exhibits to tell the story of aviation and the role flight played in each war, including Desert Storm. Newly opened is the IMAX theater, with a sixty-by-eighty-foot screen and an image three times larger than normal film. Also on the grounds is a research facility to maintain prints, technical manuals, aircraft drawings, photographs and other USAF-related documents.

Adjacent to the museum is the United States Air Force Memorial Park, which has statuary, memorials, plaques and trees dedicated to individual organizations and military units associated with the Air Force.

Another part of aviation history can be found at the International Women's Air and Space Museum, which houses photos and memorabilia depicting women's contribution to aviation. A special exhibit on Katherine Wright displays her role in the support and encouragement she gave to her famous brothers, Orville and Wilbur. Other exhibits recognize Madame Blanchard, the woman Napoleon appointed air minister (in charge of ballooning) in 1804; Amelia Earhart, the most famous woman pilot throughout the 1920s and 1930s when women pilots were wing-walking, barnstorming and racing; Jacqueline Cochran, who helped pave the way for women to achieve military and flight status; and Valentina Tereshkova from the Soviet Union, the first woman to orbit the earth, in 1963.

The National Afro-American Museum and Cultural Center, located in Wilberforce, is hailed as a national treasure. Recording the black experience, the $4 million facility features both a permanent collection and traveling exhibits that are for the study and interpretation of African-American history and culture.

Historic homes are preserved and opened to the public in nearly every town and village throughout the region. Dayton's old courthouse is now home to the Montgomery County Historic

The annual Art in the Park fair at the Cultural Arts Complex in DeWeese Park showcases the talents of artists from across the country.
Bill Swartz/BBS Images

Society. Several United States presidents—among them Abraham Lincoln, John F. Kennedy and Richard M. Nixon—have given speeches from the courthouse steps. Built in 1850 in Ionic style, the structure is a brilliant example of Greek Revival architecture.

At Carillon Historical Park, more than fifty exhibits depict the innovation, creativity and hard work that built Dayton. Among them are the 1905 Wright Flyer III, a lock from the Miami/Erie Canal, a covered bridge, Dayton's first log cabin, a Barney and Smith wooden railroad car and Dayton-built automobiles and motorcycles. More than 145,000 visitors enjoy the park, open six months a year. They come to learn about the Miami Valley's heritage, to participate in the special events held in the park and to listen to the concerts of the 50-bell carillon. Housed in a 151-foot tower with forty-two tons of bronze bells, the landmark carillon sends music as far as a mile away during summer Sunday-afternoon concerts.

Nineteenth-century Dayton comes to life at the historic Patterson Homestead Museum.
Dan Tyrpak

The Dayton Museum of Natural History features live animals, a planetarium and the Apollo Observatory and the state-of-the-art Space Theater, one of only sixteen in the world. With the largest dome in the state, the planetarium is capable of projecting a realistic illusion of the night sky, with accurate planetary motion as viewed from Earth or from space.

The museum also built SunWatch Archaeological Park, a national landmark site where visitors can tour a restored twelfth-century village. A working archaeological excavation site as well as a living textbook, SunWatch has led to an in-depth understanding of the social and technological fabric of the prehistoric villages. Demonstrations further the understanding of Ohio's ancestors; at the annual summerfest, Native American culture is celebrated with dance, crafts and food.

History of the 1700s and 1800s comes alive when reenactments of battles from the French-Indian War and the American Civil War take place at the Piqua Heritage Festival at historic Johnston Farm. On Labor Day weekend, the 174-acre park turns into a 400-person encampment of men and women who wear deerskin hides and coonskin hats and carry black powder for their muskets, just as their ancestors did when this land was part of the Northwest Territories.

FAIRS, FESTIVALS AND FUN

The largest state fair in the United States is in Ohio, as is the largest network of historical sites. Ohio leads the nation in the number of fairs and festivals held annually. From early spring to late fall, the Dayton communities celebrate with festivals for every occasion. Each weekend, somewhere within the Miami Valley, there is a festival complete with 5 or 10K runs, craft booths and food that honors the occasion. At Troy's Strawberry Festival, among the strawberry tarts and homemade strawberry pie can be found strawberry pizza. In Waynesville, at the Ohio Sauerkraut Festival, pizza is topped with the food of the festival's celebration—sauerkraut. Sauerkraut can also be found in chocolate sauerkraut fudge and sauerkraut cream pie.

Not all the festivals serve food quite as offbeat. A few of the festivals, however, may appear a bit offbeat themselves. In Piqua, the celebration is for the Great Outdoor Underwear Festival, where an "Undy 500" Malibu car race takes place. This may sound like a laughing matter, but it is no small celebration. The likes of Bob Hope and Whoopi Goldberg autographed their "under-mentionables" for auction at the festival, which celebrates the community's heritage as a maker of undergarments. In Preble County, the Pork Festival draws craftsmasters from across the nation to show their work to thousands of visitors. Primarily a farming community, Preble County honors their livelihood through the festival, complete with pig races and hog-calling contests. In the spring, the festivals mark the end of winter and the tapping of maple syrup.

Sights and sounds of the Ohio Renaissance Festival transport you back in time to the sixteenth-century reign of King Henry VIII. Bill Swartz/BBS Images

Hot-air balloons take to the sky over the Miami Valley. Dawson Jones

In the summer, festivals celebrate everything from sweet corn to kite flying. In the autumn, festivals are held to celebrate apples, potatoes, pretzels and just about everything else the imagination can conceive. Tipp City celebrates chrysanthemums at the annual Mum Festival. In Greenville, a parade and a hot-air balloon rally kick off Annie Oakley Days to honor the town's most well-known citizen. In Kettering, thousands turn out for the annual Labor Day Holiday at Home parade and festival. Towns and townships are even reason for a festival. Old Fashion Days in Xenia and Trotwood-Madison Heritage Days are ways to bring the community together in a fun-filled weekend, complete with a pet parade, kiddie tractor pull and performances by local bands.

Food is a major part of the celebration at Dayton's annual A World A'Fair. Thirty-five countries are represented when colorful costumed participants dance the native dances of their heritage and festivalgoers feast on ethnic food and drink. Food is also a major theme of Taste of Dayton, when once a year restaurants get together so that visitors can experience a taste of this and a taste of that from a dozen different eateries.

The challenging lives of Miami Valley's early settlers are re-created during Pioneer Days at Caesar Creek State Park. Dawson Jones

Christmas is another reason for celebration in the region. With picture-postcard landscaping, complete with wild rabbits, red foxes and a plentiful deer population, the holiday season sparkles with lots to see and do. In small towns like Springboro and Waynesville, Lebanon and Bellbrook, the whole town turns out one night in November or December to herald the season. Main Street shops put out hot spiced cider and sugar cookies, carolers stroll through town, and visitors may be whisked through the candlelit village in a horse-drawn carriage. At Ludlow Falls more than 30,000 Christmas lights make up a spectacular display under, around and in the frosted waterfalls. The falls are also decorated with thousands of colorful lights at Clifton Mill, a working grist mill. Downtown Dayton is a wonderland when the public tree-lighting ceremony takes place at Courthouse Square, beginning a month-long celebration of daily programs. Throughout the month, the streets of Dayton take on the spirit of the season with strolling carolers, horse-drawn carriage rides and stores open late for shopping.

The enthusiasm of the region for fairs brings the Ohio Renaissance Festival, a twenty-acre village, which recreates the language, clothing and culture of the sixteenth century. In the village, the year is 1533. King Henry VIII has just married Queen Anne and they are traveling the countryside to introduce her to the citizens of the kingdom. The royal couple and their entourage is welcomed in grand style by the villagers of Willy Nilly by the Wash. Hundreds of craftspersons and entertainers come from across the country to sell their sixteenth-century wares and perform as jousters, fire-eaters, minstrels, jugglers, kissing wenches and actors.

The largest county fair in the state—larger than many state fairs—is the Great Darke County Fair, held at the fairgrounds in Greenville. The whole county comes alive with excitement for nine

The Fourth of July is cause for great celebration and youthful expression. Andy Snow

days in August. These are 4-H Club county fairs where winning the blue ribbon may result in thousands of dollars in prize money.

Dayton is also home to Hamvention, where an estimated 30,000 amateur radio fans meet once a year. The three-day convention is the largest of its kind in the world. Hamvention draws people from Australia, England, France, Germany, Japan, New Zealand and Russia, as well as from New York to California, and generates $11.5 million for the community. At the Hara Arena, 250 commercial and 1,100 flea market exhibitors offer amateur radio operators a chance to buy and sell radios and related equipment.

At Paramount's Kings Island Amusement Park, there's the Beast, rated number one in the country for being the biggest, baddest wooden coaster ever. For those who can still stand, there's King Cobra, America's first looping coaster ridden standing up. The Vortex loops, corkscrews and boomerangs before culminating in a 360-degree helix. Life is a little quieter at the park's Wild Animal Habitat, where more than 350 exotic animals roam in a 100-acre enclosure. The park also offers Hanna-Barbera Land, an enchanting storybook fantasy.

Spectacular Broadway-style reviews, an indoor ice show and a dolphin show are all part of the lively entertainment at Kings Island. Also in the park is Timberwolf, a 10,000-seat amphitheater for concerts of some of the country's most talented bands. For hot summer days, the park offers a twelve-acre water park, complete with a 700-foot swirling, whirling, rushing river of white-water rafting. For the adventurous soul, there's a trip up the Nile and a plunge down the Amazon Falls.

Across the street at the Beach are thirty-five acres of wild waves, sandy beaches and underground tunnel water slides. With thirty-two rides, the Beach is the Midwest's largest water park complex. Selected by *Inside Track*, the newsletter for the amusement and roller coaster enthusiast, the Beach was said to have the "smoothest, fastest and safest speed slide in the U.S.A. on which a

person can experience the thrill of airborne sliding." Beginning with Memorial Day weekend, thousands plunge down the Cliff, where brave souls or those too young to know better plummet five stories, experiencing a free-fall sky-diving feeling, wrapped in cooling, soothing water. There's also the Lazy Miami, 14,400 square feet and 300,000 gallons of water for a quieter ride that meanders along.

Plenty of dining, dancing and entertainment for a night on the town are in Dayton. From the fine dining of four-star restaurants L'Auberge and King Cole to family fare to fast food, Dayton-area restaurants offer a diversified menu. Among the region's restaurants is Ohio's oldest inn, the Golden Lamb in Lebanon, which serves Shaker Ohio pie and deep-dish cobblers. After dinner, visitors are invited to stroll through the inn, or spend the night where ten American presidents and several notables, including Mark Twain, have stayed.

More than sixty eateries are located in downtown Dayton alone. From the first warm days of spring until the final days of autumn, Courthouse Square is filled with vendor carts as office workers enjoy lunch in the sun. It's not unusual to see a volleyball game or catch a band or two in the square at noon. In season, there's even a farmer's market. It's a good place to see the mounted police patrol and a good spot to view the overhead electric trolleys.

When it comes to nightlife, downtown is jumping. From dancing to jazz and rhythm-and-blues clubs, the city's Oregon District and Neon District shake, rattle and roll with excitement. Gilly's, located in downtown's Neon District, is world-famous for the performers who come here. Greats such as Maynard Ferguson, Ahmad Jamal and Ramsey Lewis have put Dayton on the map for jazz and blues. Uptown a few blocks at Canal Street Tavern, the best folk acts from around the country come to perform at this sixties-style coffee house. Wiley's Comedy Club and Grill, in downtown Dayton's Oregon District, brings some of the biggest names in the business. The oldest stand-up comedy club in the state, Wiley's has hosted talents such as Jay Leno, Pat Paulson,

Adventure-seekers thrill to the five-story, free-fall plunge of the Cliff, just one of 32 breathtaking rides at the Beach—the Midwest's largest water park complex. C. Gatland Photography

Emo Phillips, Paula Poundstone and Judy Tenuta. Wiley's is one of three comedy clubs in the area.

For outdoor recreation, Dayton offers 35,000 acres of green space, more than any other American city its size. Within the city are nine recreation centers with ninety-six parks and playground areas, five indoor swimming pools and thirty outdoor swimming and wading pools. The city also maintains a bandshell for summer concerts, fourteen picnic shelters and more than eighty tennis courts. Each of the suburbs and small towns in the Miami Valley maintains parks and greenways as well. Kettering has won national awards for its parks and recreation areas. Three state parks are within the region, two of them with boating lakes and the third located along the Little Miami River. The National Audubon Society's regional education center is here, as are two world-class arboretums. The region even has its own cedar bog and Indian mounds that have become places for rest and relaxation as well as lessons in natural history. Most of the parks and reserves are open year-round.

The Park District of Dayton-Montgomery County, formed in 1963, provides many outdoor

A Miami Valley angler bathes in tranquillity. Bill Swartz/BBS Images

opportunities as it focuses on conservation, education and recreation in the Miami Valley. It presently manages over 8,000 acres in nine open-space facilities. Education and recreational programming is provided year-round at all nine facilities as well as along the River Corridor. Annual Park District visitation is over 3 million. Four of the Dayton-Montgomery County facilities are built around the earthen dams that were created by the Miami Valley Conservancy District after the 1913 flood. Building the dams required vision as well as innovation. As the Miami Valley Conservancy District has stated, "It should be noted that nature desires always to return an area to its original state; therefore, constant vigilance and extreme care must be maintained, else the tremendous investment is eventually lost." Today, the dams still protect the 3,900 square miles drained by the Great Miami River and its tributaries, which contain some of the region's finest recreational sites. Within these forested nature reserves visitors can canoe, picnic, horseback ride, camp, hike, fish and commune with nature.

Other Park District facilities include Possum Creek Farm and Reserve, Sugarcreek Reserve, Eastwood Park and Lake Cox Arboretum and Carriage Hill, where an 1880s farm is tended by volunteers and staff in the spirit of that time. In addition to the farm, Carriage Hill offers scenic natural areas including meadows, woodlands and ponds. Cox Arboretum is 159 acres of gardens, mature forests and meadows. Within the arboretum are nine specialty gardens, among them the nationally recognized Edible Landscape Garden and the Synoptic Shrub Garden, which displays more than 500 trees and shrubs suitable for planting in the region.

At Aullwood Audubon Center and Farm—the Audubon Society's regional education center for the seven states of the Great Lakes Audubon Region—most of the 200-acre sanctuary remains wild. Trails alive with abundant wildlife and venerable flora (including 300-year-old oak trees) wind through prairie, deep woods, pasture and sugar bush and beside marsh, ponds and streams. Exhibits at the center and its organic farm interpret natural history and humankind's relationship with nature. On land donated by Mrs. John W. Aull in 1957, Aullwood Audubon Center and Farm is a popular spot for families, especially during one of the many festivals celebrating Ohio's agricultural heritage

and the natural beauty of the region.

Greene County's Glen Helen—a 1,000-acre nature preserve owned by Antioch College in Yellow Springs—is filled with cliffs, valleys, water cascades and a mineral spring. Nearby is John Bryant State Park, a 1,000-acre wooded tract along the Little Miami River. Only a few miles east along the river is Clifton Gorge, a state preserve located in the historic village of Clifton. The gorge is a site of natural beauty and of Clifton Mill, the nation's largest operating water-powered grist mill. Just around the bend is the Indian Mound Reserve, formed around 12,000 years ago when the Wisconsin Glacier retreated from Southwestern Ohio, leaving in its wake deep river valleys and cliffs of sedimentary rock. Natural habitats that are relics of the region's past, these preserves are rich with rivers and forest, marshlands, deep gorges and waterfalls. In these spectacular retreats, hikers walk across moss-covered boulders, limestone bluffs and meadows of golden and purple wildflowers. At Indian Mound, those who choose can walk the Pollock Works, earthen enclosures constructed by the Hopewell Indians who inhabited this land between 100 B.C. and A.D 600. Most of the region's parks and reserves are open year-round. Hiking is especially beautiful during autumn when the leaves turn red and orange, yellow and gold.

Delectable treats are in store at Jay's restaurant in Dayton's historic Oregon District.
Andy Snow

Corridors of greenbelts connecting many parks and green spaces throughout the different communities are under construction. Using existing rivers, creek beds, canal routes and abandoned railroad tracks, the greenways provide travel corridors for the region's abundant wildlife as well as for bicyclers, joggers and walkers, and act as buffers to protect the streams and rivers from pollution runoff. Winding through the center city is a twenty-four-mile bike path along the Great Miami and Stillwater rivers. In Greene County an old railroad track has been turned into a bike trail that takes riders through radiant woods, past grazing horses and over wooden bridges. As additional expansion of these trails take place, riders will be able to travel much of the Miami Valley without ever leaving a scenic bike trail.

Urbanization is a concern to the region, and steps are underway to safeguard Dayton's green space. In the fall of 1988, the United States Forest System chose Greene County's Yellow Springs for the Urban-Rural Interface Project, designed to develop a model that demonstrates how a rural community can react positively to urban expansion without losing its rural feeling. In Beavercreek, a grassroots effort saved 1,000 acres of wetlands that cover ten miles along the Big Beaver Creek and into the Little Miami River. Shaped by the Wisconsin Glacier, these areas were preserved from farming and real estate development, the fate of 90 percent of the nation's wetlands. Within the wetlands are 250 species of plants, eighteen of them threatened. Significant to the entire nation, the Beaver Creek Wetlands is home to the Baltimore checker spot butterfly, blue heron, Canada geese, deer, hawks, kestrels, mink, raccoon, owls, spotted turtle and such majestic plants as the six-foot-tall queen of the prairie.

The Wegerzyn Horticultural Center adds to the city's neighborhoods through their Grow With Neighbors program. In addition to renting space for vegetable gardens at the horticultural center, Wegerzyn also reaches out into the community to help neighbors convert vacant lots into thriving, healthy vegetable gardens.

Perhaps one of the most unusual green spaces in the region is Dayton's Woodland Cemetery. Less than two miles

Mouth-watering produce can be taste-tested at the farmer's market of the Wegerzyn Horticultural Center at DeWeese Park. Bill Swartz/BBS Images

from the center city is a peaceful sanctuary, a world-class arboretum, a chronicle of Dayton's history and a tribute to the stonecutter's art. At 150 years old, Woodland is the oldest nonprofit cemetery association west of the Allegheny Mountains and one of the five oldest rural cemeteries in the United States. Revolutionary War and Civil War soldiers are buried at Woodland as well as most of the families who helped build Dayton. It is also a modern cemetery with 200 acres of wooded, rolling hills and the most interesting monuments found anywhere in the world—from angels to lions to race cars. The Wright Brothers are buried at Woodland beside their sister Katharine. So is poet Paul Laurence Dunbar, Charles Kettering and former Governor James Cox. It is a peaceful place, this cemetery in the city, and it is one more park where Dayton shows its respect for history.

SPORTS

Professional sports are big in the Miami Valley, but the amateur is not forgotten either. There's a team for everyone to root for and a sport for everyone to play. Every young star has a chance at the big time.

Professional soccer has been played in Dayton since 1988 by the Dayton Dynamo Pro Soccer Team of the National Professional Soccer League. Led by Coach Rick Schweizer, the team won the National Division Championship in the 1989-90 season. The following season they again went to the finals. Owner Jerry Butcher takes pride in using local talent for the pro team. Five of the thirteen-player team are men from the area who came to Dayton Dynamo through tough competition in the region's school soccer programs.

Pro hockey came back to town in 1991 after an eleven-year hiatus dating from the disbanding of the Dayton Gems. Now hockey fans have the Dayton Bombers, and they are hot.

Every summer the United States Powerboat

From the exciting games of the Dayton Dynamos to the fun competition of youth leagues, soccer is finding a home in the Miami Valley.
Andy Snow

Association Races are held at the Hydrobowl at the city's Eastwood Lake. Racers from across the nation meet in Dayton to compete in the country's fastest speedboats.

Professional golf is also played in Dayton, on the same courses amateurs can play daily. More than forty eighteen-hole-plus golf courses lie within the region. Two courses, the Grizzly and the Bruin, were designed by Ohio native Jack Nicklaus. The LPGA Championship is played at the Grizzly, located at the Jack Nicklaus Sports Center in Warren County. The ATP Tennis Championship is also played at the center. NCR Country Club nas played host to the U.S. Women's Open Golf Tournament and to the PGA Championship. *Golf Digest* magazine named NCR Country Club one of America's 100 Greatest Golf Courses.

What isn't offered in the way of professional sports within Dayton can be found right next door or a short distance down the interstates.

Closer than a drive across most large cities are pro baseball and pro football at their best—the Cincinnati Reds and the Cincinnati Bengals. When the Reds won the National League pen-

The Great American Trapshooting Tournament—the world's largest—is held every August in Vandalia. This 10-day event draws some 5,000 contestants from around the world. Dan Tyrpak

nant, Daytonians went wild, and when the team swept the World Series in 1990, local fans painted the town red. This is also Bengals country, and when the team went to the Super Bowl, Bengals fever covered Dayton in orange and black stripes.

America's number one sports race, the Indy 500, is only 100 miles west of Dayton in Indianapolis. South by only a couple of hours is Louisville's Churchill Downs, where the famous Kentucky Derby runs.

Riversedge Park helps connect the busy urban center of Dayton with the majesty of the Great Miami River.
Bill Swartz/BBS Images

College basketball and football play big in Dayton. The University of Dayton and Wright State University are NCAA schools that traditionally field nationally ranked basketball teams. UD Division III football has been a contender nearly every year and brought home the championship in 1989. Wittenberg hosted the finals for the NCAA Division III Basketball Tournament in both 1989 and 1990. UD's arena, which seats 13,500, is frequently the site of the annual NCAA basketball tournament and regional and state high school basketball tournaments. Dayton's Welcome Stadium, which seats 11,070, is home to UD football; high school football, soccer and track; and the Special Olympics. Wright State's basketball and volleyball teams play in the new Ervin J. Nutter Center. The Ohio State Buckeyes, frequent Big 10 champions, are next door in neighboring Columbus, state capital and home of one of the country's biggest college football powers.

Amateur sports are also strong in the region. Headquartered in Vandalia since the 1920s, the

Amateur Trapshooting Association is the governing body of the world's largest clay-target-shooting organization with more than 90,000 members. Every summer more than 5,000 trapshooters from around the world come to Dayton for the Great American Trapshooting Tournament. A ten-day event, the competition includes more than three million targets thrown from seventy-two traps on a mile-and-a-quarter-long trapline, the biggest in the world. The Great American is the largest gathering of participants in one location for a sporting event in the world, with the exception of marathon footraces. On the grounds is the Trapshooting Hall of Fame and Museum, housing one of the grandest collections of target-shooting memorabilia and artifacts under one roof. Included in the collection are personal guns of Hall of Fame honorees, Olympic Medal winners and John Philip Sousa's custom-made model.

Water sports also play an important role in amateur sports in Dayton. Canoe liveries dot the landscape along the scenic Little Miami, Stillwater and Mad rivers. At Caesar Creek and Buck Creek state parks, sailboats and skiers towed by motorboats zip across these blue-water lakes like water spiders darting here and there. Surrounded by woods, the lakes also attract fishermen, hikers and bird-watchers. Sandy beaches with "skier waves" rather than ocean riptides make these inland lakes most inviting on a hot summer's day.

Polo has been strong since 1920. Members of the United States Polo Association, the Dayton Polo Club is one of more than 200 member clubs across the nation. Horse-racing fans can

Tulips burst into color at Cox Arboretum.

Dawson Jones

The new jewel of the Miami Valley's cultural scene is the Fraze Pavilion for the Performing Arts in Kettering. A striking outdoor amphitheater hosts more than 40 summertime performances.
Bill Swartz/BBS Images

watch harness racing at the track in Lebanon. The Dayton Horse Show, one of the largest such outdoor events in the country, is held at the Dayton/ Montgomery County Fairgrounds. Horseback riding through the woods is a popular sport in the countryside that surrounds the city.

Marathon footraces can be found nearly every weekend throughout the summer somewhere within the region. In the winter, the hills and dales of Dayton make for perfect cross-country skiing. Even mountain climbers can find places to tackle in the region. With the limestone cliffs in their own backyard, many a climber finds the Dayton region a real challenge. Bird-watchers, campers, backpackers and others find plenty of sport in the Miami Valley. Dayton even has an annual fox hunt. Sponsored by the Miami Valley Hunt, hounds and hunters ride through country fields and into woods filled with autumn's splendor for a day of pageantry seldom seen in the Midwest. From fox hunts to bowling, softball to skiing, Daytonians like to play, and the diverse offering of activities for leisure time reflects the nature of the greater Dayton region.

Many a famous sports figure came out of Dayton. Mike Schmidt, the former Philadelphia Phillies all-star third baseman who hit over 500 career home runs, is a Daytonian, as is the former Los Angeles Dodgers catcher Steve Yeager. Daytonian John Paxton helped lead the Chicago Bulls to the NBA championship in 1991. Al Nels, 1988 world champion hot-air balloonist, is from Dayton, as are Edwin Moses, gold medalist in the 400-meter high hurdles at the 1976 and 1984 Olympics and 1936 silver medalist Dave Albritton. Also from Dayton is Myron

Carillon Historical Park is an oasis of history and green space in the heart of Dayton. The 151-foot tower rings out the melodious music of 50 bronze bells.
Andy Snow

E. Scott, a newspaper photographer who started the Soap Box Derby in 1933. President of The Paul Warfield Company in Dayton is the man of the same name who was inducted into the Pro Football Hall of Fame in his first year of eligibility. Drafted in the first round by the Cleveland Browns, Warfield went on to help the Miami Dolphins win two Super Bowl titles and four division championships. Dayton businessman Ernie Green is also a former Browns player, a halfback.

Dayton Offers a Diverse Quality of Life

Regardless of a person's chosen lifestyle, Dayton offers a rich kaleidoscope of amusements, everything from outdoor activities to sports and the arts.

Nearly twenty movie theaters show first- or-second-run movies and art films. Another five drive-ins fill the silver screens. For television watchers, Dayton has four network stations—WDTN-TV, Channel 2 (ABC); WHIO-TV, Channel 7 (CBS); WKEF-TV, Channel 22 (NBC); WRGT-TV, Channel 45 (Fox) and WPTD-TV, Channel 16 (PBS). Served by three cable companies, Daytonians have access to nearly fifty channels. The Dayton Daily News, Springfield News-Sun and Xenia Daily Gazette are the region's major daily newspapers. Many outlying communities also have daily and weekly newspapers. More than thirty AM and FM radio stations are in the region, playing everything from classical to Christian to jazz to pop to rock music. Dayton even has its own 24-hour news talk radio.

Within the region, there are more than 540 houses of worship, representing every major religion and more than 250 congregations of various denominations. Protestants make up the largest body of worshippers within the Miami Valley, with denominations ranging from fundamentalists to New Age. Among all denomina-

Glen Helen nature preserve in Greene County features 1,000 acres of cliffs, valleys, water cascades and a true mineral spring.
Dawson Jones

tions, Roman Catholics are in the majority, followed by Methodists, Baptists, Lutherans and Church of God. Nationally the second highest number of parishioners in the Brethren religion live in the region. Those of the Jewish faith also have a strong influence in Dayton, with five synagogues that serve orthodox, conservative and reform congregations. Whatever the religious belief, a place of worship most likely will be found in this area.

Those who follow the saying, "When the going gets tough, the tough go shopping" find the Miami Valley a paradise. With an effective buying income of over $15 billion and retail sales topping $8 billion, the Dayton area offers shoppers a variety of malls, outdoor shopping centers and specialty shops for convenient, competitive shopping. Twenty-

Colorful sails dot the waters of Eastwood Lake. Bill Swartz/BBS Images

five major shopping centers are within the region, ranging in size from 145,000 to 1,283,000 square feet. Large malls are both north and south of town, with a third under construction in the eastern suburbs. Salem Mall has 130 stores, the Dayton Mall has 160 stores and another twenty centers have at least twenty-five stores, many of them with fifty or more. Antiquing is a favorite pastime, especially in the nation's antique capital, Warren County's Waynesville. The historic Oregon District offers shops full of antiques, books and collectibles. Downtown also offers specialty shops tucked in between high-rise office towers and snack shops.

Courthouse Square in downtown Dayton rings out with the festivities of Independence Day. Andy Snow

Daytonians, who read more books than residents of any other city in the country except Seattle, require well-stocked bookstores. With two stores in particular, there is no disappointment. Books and Company is Ohio's largest book outlet and one of the country's mega-bookstores. At Wilkie's News, a reader can stop by for a book and leave with a map of Hungary, Taiwan, Cairo or Kenya as well. With more than sixty newspapers—from Los Angeles to London—in stock, Wilkie' keeps Daytonians abreast of the world.

For those who come to Dayton and the Miami Valley knowing little about it, the region is a pleasant surprise. The rolling hills and country woods of small towns and suburban areas offer a tranquil lifestyle that is close to a metropolitan area with shopping, theater, museums and a thriving nightlife. Rich in innovation, creativity and genius, Dayton and the Miami Valley offer newcomers and longtime residents unlimited economic opportunities with a Midwestern pace that values friendliness, too.

Dayton, birthplace of the airplane, is indeed flying high into the twenty-first century.

Bicycling along Dayton's pathways is a favorite way to enjoy the scenic riverside. Bill Swartz/BBS Images

Mead

CHAPTER SEVEN

PARTNERS IN EXCELLENCE

Daytonians go to work each day to a diverse array of jobs. Aerospace engineers, bankers, printers, lawyers, manufacturers, and real estate developers are just some of the people busy providing goods and services for customers around the corner—and around the world.

Some of the largest firms in the country have facilities in Dayton, yet the area also is home to a vibrant small-business community. Cutting-edge breakthroughs in industry, exciting new offerings in the service realm, and inspiring entrepreneurial success stories are taking place today throughout the Miami Valley.

While looking toward the future, Dayton businesses are mindful of their history—the blend of quality workmanship and commitment to community that has been the region's enduring hallmark. Keeping true to this tradition, Dayton's business leaders contribute a great deal of time, money, and effort to improving the places where they work and live.

Proud of their accomplishments and proud of their communities, Dayton's businesses have made publication of this book possible. The profiles that follow tell the stories of these businesses, which are so much a part of Dayton, they are its Partners in Excellence.

Many Dayton businesses make their home along the water. Dawson Jones

DAYTON AREA CHAMBER OF COMMERCE

For well over a century, there has been an organization in the Dayton area stimulating the community's economic growth and working to constantly improve the quality of life. That organization is the Dayton Area Chamber of Commerce. Known by various names in its early years, the Chamber is undergoing perhaps its most comprehensive reorganization ever to help the multi-county region compete in the ever-changing world market of the 1990s and into the 21st century.

During the mid-1990s, the Chamber is implementing the concept of a regional growth association—an overarching organization pursuing regional economic development, national/international marketing, and public affairs. The concept resulted from the Chamber's strategic planning process of the late 1980s, which included a broad-based survey of the private and public sectors in the Dayton region.

"There truly is no other organization as prepared to take on the challenge of these regional needs," says J. Bradford Tillson, 1992 chairman of the Chamber's board of trustees and publisher of the *Dayton Daily News*.

The Chamber has a long tradition of being a catalyst and coordinator for getting things done in the Dayton area. Whether assisting in the recovery from a natural disaster like the 1913 flood or pushing for the construction of a road like Interstate 675, the Chamber has consistently played key roles. During the 1980s the Chamber helped to formulate the Dayton area's economic recovery program following the loss of thousands of "smokestack" manufacturing jobs.

Today the Dayton region enjoys a healthy, diverse economy with a strong base in advanced technology/aerospace, manufacturing, and services industries. The Chamber markets the multi-county region to attract these kinds of businesses, plus those companies looking for a great location for regional offices and distribution/warehousing centers. Under the growth association these national/international marketing efforts will be greatly expanded, as will the organization's already successful lobbying program at all government levels.

Several business units are within the growth association. The Dayton Area Chamber of Commerce serves the needs of small and medium-size companies by providing a wide variety of educational and networking programs and information services. The Dayton/Montgomery County Convention & Visitors Bureau promotes

The United States Air and Trade Show is fast becoming one of the world's major aerospace expositions where companies come to do business with each other in the spacious Trade Exhibition Center at Dayton International Airport.

the area to attract meetings, conventions, trade shows, and tourists. The National Aviation Hall of Fame—the only one chartered by the U.S. Congress—celebrates the history of flight, while the United States Air and Trade Show is the world-famous event that promotes Dayton's aviation heritage and showcases the U.S. aerospace industry to an international audience.

"In all we do, our goal is to make the Dayton region a great place to work and live," says Thomas E. Heine, Chamber president. "The growth association concept enables us to be flexible and responsive to the changing needs of the region as we strive to compete in what is a continually changing world economy."

There's never a dull moment at the Chamber, according to William J. Odorizzi, who heads the chamber's economic development unit. "It's always a very exciting place to be because we are in a position to know about and be involved in so many things going on throughout the region."

"Serving the community is what it's all about," says 21-year employee Barbara Wiford, who runs the Chamber's Business Resource Center. "My great satisfaction is helping people from companies and organizations of all sizes find the information they need."

Guiding the organization's staff is a dedicated group of volunteers who represent member private and public sector organizations. These volunteers serve on a variety of committees, from the board of trustees, which sets policy, to other groups that guide the staff in meeting the needs of members and the region as a whole.

"In any organization, it is the people who make things happen," says Robert F. Chelle, 1993 chairman of the Chamber's board of trustees and president of High Voltage Maintenance Corporation. "We are fortunate to have a great group of volunteers and staff looking out for the needs of business in the Dayton region."

BenePlan Strategies

BenePlan Strategies defines productivity in terms of quality—not quantity. Each claims processor reviews an average of 65 claims a day; the industry standard is nearly 100.

Health care is a moving target. Even so, employers expect their group-benefits administrator to be in the forefront of the industry. That is why there is such a sense of urgency at BenePlan Strategies.

"To be responsive to your clients' needs, you've got to have this sense of urgency," says Ralph Zimmerman, president of BenePlan Strategies.

BenePlan understands responsiveness; it began in 1978 as a division within Dayco Corporation in response to Dayco's concern about the rising costs of its health care plan. "By bringing benefits administration in-house, we realized a 20 percent decrease in costs and a higher quality of plan administration within the first year," Zimmerman says. "Our goal today is still to reduce a company's health care costs—without reducing benefits."

BenePlan is now a wholly owned subsidiary of the M.A. Hanna Company, a *Fortune* 300 firm. At BenePlan customers get personal attention. Since each claims processor is assigned a specific group of BenePlan clients, covered employees can call and talk to the one person who processes their company's claims. This enables covered employees to build a trust and rapport with their claims processor.

To ensure quality, BenePlan audits claims in-house. As a result, the accuracy of claims processed has been 99.5 percent or higher. Audits by outside firms have shown that BenePlan consistently meets or exceeds this figure. "Our accuracy of claims processing translates to cost containment for our clients," says William C. Bligh, senior vice president.

As a third-party administrator providing services to self-insured companies, BenePlan administers group benefits including medical, dental, vision, prescription drug programs, short-term disability plans, flexible spending accounts, and cafeteria plans. The company is a leader in managed care and offers several options, including many well known PPOs, both local and national. "Assisting our clients in reducing their health care costs through effective managed care is one of BenePlan's top priorities," says Bligh.

According to Zimmerman, BenePlan's mission is providing products, services, and performance that meet or exceed client requirements. "At BenePlan," he says, "it's the client who defines our performance requirements and expectations."

BenePlan Strategies uses a fully automated state-of-the-art claims-processing system called RIMS (Resource Information Management System).

High Voltage Maintenance Corp.

A construction company had just put the finishing touches on a brand-new substation at Wright-Patterson Air Force Base in 1960 when base engineers found a major flaw. There was no one to maintain it.

The construction company responded to the problem by quickly forming a new company, High Voltage Maintenance Corp., to maintain the substation. Today HVM is one of the nation's largest independent electrical-testing and maintenance companies, with more than 2,000 industrial, commercial, governmental, and institutional customers in the Midwest.

HVM competes against such giants as General Electric and Westinghouse. There is a difference, however, between HVM and these huge corporations, says Robert Chelle, HVM president. "We have a single purpose. HVM provides quality service. We concentrate on one aspect of the electrical business rather than worry about construction, equipment installation, or equipment sales."

HVM can provide numerous different tests on equipment such as circuit breakers, cables, and transformers. For example, circuit breakers must be tested regularly to ensure they are calibrated and operational. Electrical cables, which deteriorate over time, must be checked for leakage. Since added machinery can cause overload conditions, HVM can determine when to increase transformer capacity. Lastly, in case of an electric outage, HVM needs to ensure that power will be transferred to a second source without a glitch. "Plants have to rely more on the equipment they own because damaged equipment and downtime can have a great economic impact, especially on a three-shift operation," Chelle says.

Service technicians must calibrate and test meters on an electrical power system and make necessary adjustments to ensure accuracy.

Service technicians regularly perform transformer tests, like these being conducted in a substation, to ensure reliable operation of an electrical power system.

Since HVM customizes testing and maintenance programs for each customer, the frequency of testing varies. "It depends on the duty cycles, how often certain equipment is used, and the environment in which it operates," Chelle explains. For example, electrical equipment in a foundry would be tested fairly often because of the dust, vibration, and temperature swings. Because a hospital's equipment operates under cleaner conditions, it may not need to be tested as often.

However, emergencies and accidents do happen. HVM responds to emergencies 24 hours a day, 365 days a year. As soon as a call comes in, test technicians certified by the National Electrical Testing Association (NETA) are dispatched; they meet at a HVM shop and are on their way to the site within two hours of the call.

"We normally get the plant operating again on a temporary basis until the equipment can be repaired or replaced," Chelle says. During a routine job, a crew takes field data and measurements and records test results. Back at HVM, experienced electrical engineers will review test data and make observations and appropriate recommendations before sending the engineering reports to the customer.

High Voltage Maintenance Corp. has offices in Ohio, Indiana, Wisconsin, Michigan, and Pennsylvania.

STAR BANK, DAYTON

Star Bank's roots run deep into the history of the Miami Valley, all the way back to 1866, when the H. Groby and Company banking firm was formed in Miamisburg. The bank's prime policy was to "put people first." Gregory W. Edwards, president of Star Bank, N.A. in Dayton, states that Star Bank has continued putting people first by adding convenient locations (there are 16 Greater Dayton branches), staying open longer, and offering new products and services that meet customers' needs.

"We have long been a leader in commercial banking," says Edwards. "Relationship banking is part of our business philosophy. We're very proud of the strong relationships we've developed with businesses in the many communities we serve."

At the same time, Star Bank continues its commitment to service in personal banking. Star Bank has been very aggressive in building extensive branch networks to service the consumer side of the business. "We provide a complete line of personal financial services," explains Edwards. "Our full-office automation system permits Star to respond even more quickly and effectively to the banking needs of individuals."

Star Bank's trust group has also grown steadily, offering more sophisticated money management services to a wide range of individuals and businesses. This is one of the company's fastest growing areas of business due to its emphasis on customer service, its enviable investment performance record, and state-of-the-art technological support.

Edwards attributes Star Bank's success to a variety of factors, including the strength of its employees; products and services that meet the demands of the marketplace; measured growth; cost control; and a strong policy of investing in Star's local communities.

"The individual performance of each of our 200 employees in Dayton shapes the overall financial performance of Star Bank. Superior knowledge, sales ability, teamwork, innovative thinking, and increased productivity are expected, supported, and rewarded. Beyond serving our customers in the best way we can, we also anticipate the changing needs of our customers. Star Banks have accelerated new product development and are continually evaluating existing products to identify new opportunities," Edwards says.

Star Bank supports individual communities through financing new local development, as well as by encouraging active employee participation in cultural, charitable, and civic endeavors. "Our principal focus in community outreach efforts has been to establish programs that make affordable housing available and programs that foster minority and small business development. We are committed to serving the people within our communities," concludes Edwards.

Star Bank executives celebrated the grand opening of the private banking department in May 1990 at the Talbott Tower office in downtown Dayton. Private banking services are geared toward upscale customers who want to aggressively invest funds in entrepreneurial or real estate ventures.

MILLER-VALENTINE GROUP

Miller-Valentine Group is one of the leading commercial real estate and design/build construction companies in the Midwest. Over the past 30 years the professionals at Miller-Valentine Group have developed over 30 million square feet of business space for a wide variety of clients, including many *Fortune* 500 companies.

The firm was founded as a general contractor in 1963 by Dayton civil engineer Gerry Miller. Several months later Miller-Valentine formed when Miller was joined by University of Dayton engineering alumnus Dan Valentine. Another University of Dayton alumnus, Jim Walsh, joined the firm later that same year. Thus Miller, Valentine, and Walsh are the three founding partners of the current Miller-Valentine Group.

Originally specializing in the construction of buildings, highways, bridges, and treatment plants, the young firm began with selected projects that required unique engineering or management expertise. By the late 1960s the interstate highway program had begun to slow down. Marty Miller joined the firm at that time to investigate development opportunities in the real estate investment market. What he found was an acute need for industrial space in the Dayton area.

The firm's extensive background in highway and bridge construction—concrete construction technology—led naturally to the development of a concrete tilt-up process known as the Con/Steel Building system. This high-production, efficiently engineered system of construction, co-developed with engineering firm LJB, has been utilized by Miller-Valentine and 18 licensees throughout the United States and Canada.

Miller-Valentine has developed, designed, and built a wide range of buildings, including industrial and distribution facilities, offices, office/warehouse, retail, commercial lodging facilities, medical offices, retirement housing, and nursing homes. In the Greater Dayton area, notable Miller-Vallentine projects include Wright Executive Center, Park Center, Prestige Place, and the Lincoln Park Retirement Center and Nursing Home.

The firm has also developed a number of projects in the Greater Cincinnati area and has begun expanding into the Columbus area as well as Fort Wayne, Indiana.

Miller-Vallentine Group comprises teams of professionals who actively interact with clients, vendors, and the communities in which the firm conducts its business. It does this in the interest of providing high-quality products that are also aesthetically pleasing.

Along with its development activities, the firm offers comprehensive construction services, including location and site selection and design/build construction with build-to-suit technology that meets the most specialized business facility requirements. Miller-Valentine Realty provides full-service commercial and industrial real estate leasing and property management services.

Miller-Valentine Group partners and associates are committed to providing value and full service to their clients and to providing support and involvement in the communities in which they operate.

Miller-Valentine's Dayton headquarters.

HUFFY CORPORATION

While best-known as a bicycle manufacturer, Huffy Corporation has diversified in recent years. Huffy now owns Gerry Baby Products Company, Huffy Sports Company, Huffy Service First, Washington Inventory Service, and True Temper Hardware Company.

When people think of Huffy, they naturally think of bikes. But what about baby strollers, basketball backboards, and long-handled garden rakes?

There's no doubt that Huffy has gotten serious about diversification. With the acquisition of Gerry Baby Products Company in the 1980s, Huffy expanded into car seats, infant carriers, portable cribs, and other juvenile products sold under the Gerry, Snugli, and Nu-Line brand names.

Huffy Sports Company markets and sells basketball backboards, goals, poles, and accessories while Huffy Service First assembles bicycles, lawn furniture, and other products for consumers, as well as in-store displays for retailers. The company also offers product repair/warranty and merchandising services.

Huffy's Washington Inventory Service counts, records, processes, and reports data on customer inventories and assets for retail industries, libraries, warehouses, and government agencies. In addition, with the acquisition of True Temper Hardware, Huffy now sells long-handled lawn and garden tools in the United States, Canada, and Ireland, and wheel goods and cutting tools in the United States and Canada, under the True Temper name.

Huffy's diversification strategy includes focusing on products with strong brand names, innovating products, and providing outstanding service. Perhaps the best evidence of Huffy's winning strategy is Gerry Baby Products, with sales of $17 million at acquisition. By 1991 Huffy had built Gerry into a $100 million company.

What links these six companies under the Huffy corporate logo is the fact that they either sell products to or offer services needed by volume retailers, who continue to bring Huffy success in its original business: bicycles.

"We've been in the bike business for more than 80 years," says Richard L. Molen, president and chief executive officer. "Bikes are the backbone of the corporation and our largest company."

Huffy was the first company selling bicycles at volume retailers to promote its brand name nationally, mainly through television ads in the 1970s. Soon afterward the company introduced contemporary fashion colors and graphics into the business, and the Huffy brand was suddenly propelled to the number one slot in the U.S. market. Today it stands out in the bicycle business by emphasizing quality, service, and value to the consumers of America's top selling brand of bicycle.

"We differentiate quality from just meeting specs," Molen says. "We give customers a value by producing a product that works—one that rarely, if ever, needs service."

Huffy offers more than 300 bicycle models annually. Says Molen, "Even the traditional red or blue bike with the cantilever frame and fat tires is still in the line." However, today's Huffy bikes are produced in facilities that incorporate modern manufacturing strategies such as focused factories, just-in-time production, and employee involvement teams.

"We've proven to be successful at diversifying from the bike business," says Molen. "Our corporate goal is to be a one-billion-dollar diversified consumer products and services company by the mid-1990s."

VAN DYNE-CROTTY, INC.

Creating a positive image is the number one reason companies decide to rent uniforms for their employees. Van Dyne-Crotty has built a successful business by providing customers with clean, high quality uniforms and superior service.

The company has grown rapidly in recent years, with sales increasing from $25 million in 1985 to $42 million in 1992. Sales are projected to reach nearly $50 million in 1993. Market studies confirm that Van Dyne-Crotty maintains 25 percent of the uniform rental market within its geographical areas of operation.

Van Dyne-Crotty has grown from rather humble beginnings. In 1935 Lloyd Van Dyne and Fergus Crotty borrowed $500 to open their shop-towel business. They began by selling, laundering, and supplying shop-towels to local machine shops, garages, service stations, and industrial plants. Uniforms, entrance mats, and dust control products were all eventually added to the product mix. After the founders died in 1962, the next generation expanded the business.

L. William Crotty became president that year, and saw the company extend service to four states during his 30 years as president. In 1992 his oldest son, Daniel, became president as L. William moved into the position of CEO. Today seven Crotty family members work for the company. The company reaches into six states with 700 employees, 12 district offices, and seven plants.

The company has district offices in Dayton, Delphos, Toledo, and Cleveland, Ohio; Fort Wayne, South Bend, and Indianapolis, Indiana; Louisville, Lexington, and Erlanger, Kentucky; Ann Arbor, Michigan; and Knoxville, Tennessee. The South Bend office provides service into Illinois, as well.

Dayton-based Van Dyne-Crotty has its flagship operation at 903 Brandt Street, just northeast of downtown Dayton.

Van Dyne-Crotty has built its reputation on service. Sales and service representatives are immersed in the company philosophy of service from their first day on the job. A six-week, multi-media training program includes instruction in the areas of customer communications, vehicle maintenance, safe driving, sales techniques, and product knowledge. On-the-job training is also included.

The quality of the company's service is closely monitored by a unique customer calling program called A.S.A.P. (Automated Service Assurance Program). Trained telemarketing representatives call customers regularly to conduct service audits. If a problem needs immediate attention, an electronic message is sent to the appropriate district office. Local service and account managers contact the customers immediately to resolve difficulties.

Management training is another important focus at Van Dyne-Crotty. The company's Management Development Program is a rigorous, three-year training program that teaches new managers the four areas of the business: route service, sales, production, and corporate administration.

Creative management and a strong customer focus continue to foster growth for the company.

"The company will continue to increase its holdings in the coming years. New plants and further facility upgrades are planned. In addition, we are looking at potential market opportunities and acquisitions throughout the southeast and west," says Daniel Crotty, company president.

Van Dyne-Crotty regularly reinvests in all of its operations, as well as building new facilities. The interior of the company's newest production facility is shown here.

IBM

IBM opened its first marketing and service office in Dayton in 1932. More than 60 years later, IBM Dayton continues to use advanced information technologies to provide solutions to a broad range of individual customer needs.

While best known for computers, IBM also offers professional services and consulting, office systems and related supplies and services, software solutions, telecommunications systems, and information-processing products and systems for customers of all sizes.

In Dayton, IBM's products and services help maintain inventories, conserve energy, check out groceries, handle banking transactions, provide better health care, forecast the weather, design and manufacture a host of products, and more.

Located at 33 West First Street, IBM Dayton serves customers in 11 Ohio counties and two counties in Indiana. Approximately 65 percent of its accounts are manufacturing or distribution centers. Among them are three of the area's largest entities: the United States Air Force at Wright-Patterson Air Force Base, DAYCO, and The Mead Corporation.

IBM's mission in Dayton is to create value (as defined by its customers) through the application of technology, solutions, and services. To broaden its ability to offer its customers the highest-quality solutions, IBM Dayton has formed strategic alliances and business partnerships with companies whose products and services complement those that IBM offers.

"If we don't make a solution the customer wants," explains Julie A. Walker, Business Unit Executive of IBM Dayton, "we will invite a business partner to participate in solving that customer's problem."

IBM business partners are either companies with applications expertise, software developers who purchase IBM hardware and then resell it with their own value-added software, companies providing system-design assistance, or consultants. For example, one IBM business partner in Dayton supplies software that runs IBM hardware in medical offices and is therefore, in effect, helping to install IBM equipment.

IBM Dayton has another partnership with a company that designs, builds, and installs manufacturing and production facilities and equipment. Because of this partnership, companies modernizing their production facilities can now consider the advantages of IBM computer-integrated manufacturing systems. "Such partnership help us to provide our customers with total solutions," Walker says.

Striving for quality is a way of life at IBM, and every division competes for an internal Quality Award. In 1990 IBM Dayton ranked first in the Great Lakes region for its

IBM Dayton, 33 West First Street.

superior marketing practices. IBM Dayton is continuously striving to improve the quality of its products and services.

IBM continues to be a leading corporate supporter of education, social programs, cultural activities, and charitable causes, contributing more than $126 million annually. In Dayton IBM supports these activities not just with dollars and equipment, but with its people.

IBM Dayton has a very close relationship with the communities it serves. The company's Dayton Community Action Council encourages its 170 employees to participate in community projects and charitable groups, and seeks new opportunities in which IBM can provide support, primarily through company volunteers. For example, IBM employees have collected winter necessities for the "Tuck In St. Vincent" project, which provides clothing and shelter for the area's homeless during the cold months.

Another major local effort in which IBM employees have been involved is the Kids Voting Ohio project. In 1992 about 45 IBM Dayton employees helped prepare ballots and assembled supplies at five polling places for a mock election in which area youngsters learned about the rights and responsibilities of citizenship by actually going through the voting process.

As a corporate partner in the Dayton Science Project, IBM Dayton has provided software and hardware to assist with the revitalization of the Dayton Public Schools' science curriculum. Through the company's Faculty Loan Program, IBM employees can take time off—with full pay and benefits—to lend a hand in elementary schools, high schools, colleges, and universities.

IBM has joined forces with Sinclair Community College and the University of Dayton to create an environment in which students can learn about and prepare themselves for manufacturing integration technology. IBM has given Sinclair the necessary hardware and software tools, and the system has been installed in an existing robotics lab on the Sinclair campus. Demonstrations are run at the college at least once a month.

Though its product line has evolved over the years, IBM is still in the business of helping people solve problems, and its basic values have not changed: respect the individual, provide the best customer service in the world, and pursue excellence in the accomplishment of all tasks.

"We are proud of our track record in Dayton," says Walker, "both our contributions to the community and our ability to deliver quality products and services to our customers." IBM Dayton continues to provide services, software, systems, products, and technologies that help people succeed.

AM GRAPHICS

Every once in a while Richard J. Bonnie, president of AM Graphics (an operating division of AM International, Inc.), sees a mailroom or binding machine on the market that looks all-too-similar to an AM Graphics product. Imitation, he says, is the highest form of flattery.

More than 600 employees work at AM Graphics' headquarters in Dayton.

"Other companies have copied us and have made cheaper products," explains Bonnie. "They may end up getting a sale or two, but the important thing is that we get the repeat sales."

AM Graphics is a world leader in the newspaper and publishing businesses. One of its three core businesses is newspaper mailroom systems. AM Graphics produces reliable, flexible systems that collate and insert the many advertising folders, minicatalogs, and coupons found in Sunday and daily newspapers.

A second aspect of the company is publication binding. Magazines, journals, telephone books, and other mass circulation publications are produced with AM Graphics' high-speed, high-production equipment for saddle stitching and adhesive binding. "Chances are, if you're holding a phone book, it's bound on our product," says Bonnie. The company's selective binding systems allow publications to be custom bound with specific advertisements targeting audiences based on geographic or demographic information.

A commercial range of bindery products is also manufactured by AM Graphics. Commercial and in-plant printers and trade binders use adhesive binding, saddle stitching, paper cutting, book trimming, and in-line finishing systems produced by AM Graphics. "Our commercial bindery products are designed for smaller runs, like a 12-page department store sales magazine for Sunday newspapers," Bonnie says.

The third AM Graphics business is business forms products. The company's business forms equipment is used in plants where continuous forms, credit card sets, and computer letters are produced. AM Graphics produces a complete line of web presses, collaters, and finishing equipment for business forms and promotional graphics.

According to Bonnie, AM Graphics is one of the few companies that participate in the graphic industry with as many products. "We are diverse and one of the largest," he says. "Our competitors usually specialize in only one of these businesses. We have the synergism and technology to do all three."

Richard Bonnie is committed to the amount of research and development required to keep AM Graphics on the cutting edge. "If there's a need for something new in the industry, there's an expectation that AM Graphics will develop it," he says.

Because AM Graphics has one of the most modern large-machining operations in the United States, it operates with shorter lead times. However, AM Graphics is striving to operate even faster. According to Bonnie, the goal is to reduce lead time from 12 weeks to seven or even six weeks.

AM Graphics employs more than 850 people in its state-of-the-art facilities in Dayton, Ohio, and Slough, England. More than 600 people are employed at its headquarters in Dayton.

PORTER, WRIGHT, MORRIS & ARTHUR

A lawyer's priority should be solving problems quickly and economically. That's what Porter, Wright, Morris & Arthur does best.

"A major criticism of lawyers is that they churn papers without achieving any result. We focus on the problem and take action that will get a solution—a result—most cost effectively," says R. Bruce Snyder, partner-in-charge of the Dayton presence of Porter, Wright, Morris & Arthur.

If the facts show that a case should not go to trial, Porter Wright will submit the matter for summary judgment and try to get the case dismissed. This tells the opponent that the attorney has focused on the issues in the case—and has evidence to prove the client's claims. "Consequently, the opponent will often drop or settle the claim," Snyder says.

The nationally recognized law firm, which traces its roots to 1846 in Ohio, provides services for businesses, institutions, and individuals in the areas of U.S. and foreign business, banking and insurance, construction, energy, environment, employee benefits, estate planning, federal and state regulatory work, health care, intellectual property, litigation, labor and employment, probate and trusts, real estate, transportation, federal and state taxation, and utilities. With 20 lawyers in Dayton, Porter Wright has more than 260 attorneys practicing in Dayton, Cincinnati, Cleveland, and Columbus, Ohio; Washington, D.C.; and Naples, Florida.

Since firm lawyers in other cities are resources which are drawn upon for any client, work is completed more efficiently, and clients can realize substantial savings, according to Snyder. For example, if a party in Cleveland files an action against a Dayton firm, briefs can be prepared in the Dayton office and sent via computer for filing in a Cleveland court. Rather than having Dayton lawyers go to Cleveland, trial preparation can be done by Cleveland office lawyers. Environmental or intellectual property attorneys in other offices can be brought together to resolve a client's problem in a team effort.

"This arrangement gives the client the best of all worlds," Snyder explains. "The client receives the highest-caliber services at the lowest cost."

Being a major law firm in the Miami Valley allows Porter Wright to have specialists in areas such as government contracting, intellectual property, patents, and environmental law, while a local presence permits affordable fees. "Specialists in a narrow area of the law are likely to know immediately what might take a general practitioner hours of research to find," Snyder points out.

Although a number of attorneys may be working on a case, one attorney is assigned as the client manager, responsible for ensuring the client is serviced well. Client managers advise the client about work underway by the attorney team, review completed work, send documentation, answer questions, and prepare invoices.

"It's important that the client knows there is a single person responsible, accountable, and on top of everything," says Snyder. "We want our clients to feel they can pick up the phone, talk to a lawyer, and know immediately what's going on."

According to Snyder, clients are challenging law firms to become even more cost-efficient in the rendering of legal services. With a management structure headed by a managing partner—rather than by a management committee—Porter, Wright, Morris & Arthur is positioned well to meet that challenge.

Porter, Wright, Morris & Arthur represents large and medium-size businesses, institutions, and professional individuals.

THE HARRIS-THOMAS DROP FORGE CO.

The Harris-Thomas Drop Forge Company uses rotating forge crews for forging and hot-trimming operations. © 1993 Dawson Jones, Inc.

The Harris-Thomas Drop Forge Company of Dayton, Ohio, founded in 1924, is a recognized leader in supplying net-shape and near-net-shape forged steel components to the United States auto industry in high volume on a just-in-time basis.

Harris-Thomas is noted for its technical expertise in designing dies and tooling to produce intricate forged shapes in the shortest possible time. Working closely with customers' design engineers, Harris-Thomas engineers assist in arriving at the lowest-cost, highest-strength, lightest-weight forging to meet the needs of new designs or solve problems with existing parts made with different methods of manufacture.

Currently at Harris-Thomas, parts are hot forged with air-powered closed-impression impact hammers, then cooled and cleaned, and cold worked (coined) via presses to near-net-shape or net-shape dimensions. If required, using nearby sources, Harris-Thomas can supply components that are heat treated and finish machined, ready for assembly.

Steering-arm forgings appear luminescent immediately after hot forging and trimming. © 1993 Dawson Jones, Inc.

FIFTH THIRD BANK

"The only bank you'll ever need!" It may sound like just another marketing slogan, but to generations of Daytonians, that's exactly what Fifth Third Bank has been and continues to be.

One of Ohio's oldest banks, Fifth Third opened its doors for the first time in downtown Cincinnati in 1858. It was known then as the Bank of the Ohio Valley, and its stated mission was "to grow with the city financially, commercially, and industrially."

That bank was purchased 13 years later by the Third National Bank. The organization acquired its unusual name after Third National joined with the Fifth National Bank around the turn of the century.

In 1993 Fifth Third Bank is one of 10 affiliate banks of Fifth Third Bancorp. The Bancorp, headquartered in Cincinnati, has more than $10 billion in assets and more than 260 banking centers, primarily in Ohio, Kentucky, Indiana, and Naples, Florida.

At the end of the first quarter of 1993, Fifth Third Bank has 19 banking centers in the greater Dayton area, including four in select grocery stores, which are open seven days a week.

Fountain Square, a well known symbol of Cincinnati.

Fifth Third is widely recognized by financial analysts and industry observers as one of the strongest, top-performing banks in the nation. According to First Boston, an analyst firm that follows banking trends, "The company is among the few best—if not the single best—commercial banks in the United States." The bank's continued success recently prompted *Newsweek* magazine to rank Fifth Third as one of the nation's strongest banking institutions. The bank's innovative marketing strategies were featured in a *Business Week* magazine article, which also noted that Fifth Third's rate of return on assets was one of the highest in the country for a bank its size.

The Fifth Third Bank headquarters building, located in Cincinnati, Ohio.

Along with traditional banking services, such as checking, savings, and consumer and commercial loans, Fifth Third offers its growing customer base a wide range of quality products, brokerage services, trusts and investment services, credit cards, and IRAs.

Midwest Payment Systems, Inc., Fifth Third Bancorp's data-processing subsidiary, is one of the nation's leading providers of electronic funds transfer services, serving more than 1,000 customers nationwide.

Technology, however, is only part of the reason for the bank's success. As part of its "the only bank you'll ever need" philosophy, Fifth Third has developed a relationship banking strategy in which customers receive special benefits when they take advantage of additional Fifth Third services.

Fifth Third's belief in strong, productive relationships extends to all types of interaction with the communities it serves. Through corporate sponsorships, donations, and volunteerism, the bank and its employees maintain an active commitment to the greater Dayton area.

NATIONAL CITY MORTGAGE CO.

Dayton Branch employees of National City Mortgage Co., located at 3055 South Kettering Blvd., Suite 400.

When the Peter Kuntz Company, a Dayton lumber supplier, founded North Central Mortgage Co. in 1955, it was to provide financing primarily for local home builders. After nearly 40 years and several name changes, that company, known today as National City Mortgage Co., is a full-service mortgage banking operation with 23 offices in Ohio and eight other states.

Headquartered in Miamisburg south of Dayton, National City Mortgage (NCM) is a wholly owned subsidiary of National City Corporation, a $28-billion bank holding company headquartered in Cleveland, Ohio. National City Corporation, which operates banks and other financial service subsidiaries principally in Ohio, Kentucky, and Indiana, acquired the local company in July 1989. NCM employs more than 800 people nationwide and is Ohio's largest mortgage banking firm.

National City Mortgage Co. is engaged in three distinct areas of the mortgage banking business: origination of residential mortgage loans (that is, making the loans directly to the consumer); purchasing, packaging, and selling loans in the secondary mortgage market; and servicing loans.

In the wake of the thrift crisis of the 1980s, mortgage bankers have become the leading lenders in the field of home loans. NCM, together with its sister operation, National City Bank, Dayton, is the leading provider of residential mortgage loans in the Miami Valley area. Nearly one of every five local residential loans is made by one of these two institutions.

National City Mortgage Co.'s branch offices have a current loan capacity of more than one billion dollars. The company makes both conventional loans—through the Federal National Mortgage Association (FNMA) and the Federal Home Loan Mortgage Corporation (FHLMC)—and government loans, through the Government National Mortgage Association (GNMA). The company is ranked among the top 30 residential mortgage loan originators in the United States.

As a loan servicer NCM also ranks among the top 30 nationally. Approximately $9 billion of the company's servicing portfolio is made up of loans that are "serviced for others," that is, sold to the secondary market. The remainder of the company's portfolio is serviced for and owned by National City Corporation member banks.

NCM also buys loans that are made by other brokers, banks, savings and loans, or mortgage companies, but are not serviced by those institutions. The company acquires these loans, packages them, and then sells them to the FNMA, FHLMC, and GNMA. The company continues to service the loans for a fee.

The "selling" aspect of the mortgage loan business is considered to be its most volatile due to daily interest rate fluctua-

National City Mortgage Co. customer service employees showing that no one cares more.

tion. The company has more than quadrupled its loan portfolio in the four years since it was acquired by the parent corporation. In 1989 NCM serviced 50,000 loans totaling $2.5 billion. As of this writing the company is servicing in excess of $10.6 billion in loans—that is approximately 180,000 one- to four-family residential home loans. NCM anticipates continued strong growth and expects to be servicing $15 billion by 1995.

NCM occupies two buildings on Newmark Drive totaling 107,000 square feet. To accommodate its expected growth the company added an additional 25,000 square feet to its corporate facilities in 1993.

NCM has always been one of Dayton's most active and generous corporate citizens. The company's commitment to the community can be seen in its work with neighborhood organizations and local community service agencies.

The company employs 500+ people locally and recognizes that its continued success depends on these employees. NCM's reputation as a top-quality organization rests in part on its excellent training programs, which include employee cross training, management development, and employee recognition. Mutual respect among employees and sensitivity to the needs of customers are cornerstones of quality at National City Mortgage Co. The company continues to assume an active role in the internal integration of many diverse "cultures" into one superior service-based company.

National City Mortgage Co.'s management and staff work together to develop effective service strategies. "Today the key to success in this business is service," says Leo E. Knight, Jr., National City's president and chief executive officer. "Quick approval, quick closings; it is our goal to shorten the span between the time an application is made and the loan is approved so our customers can get into their homes."

The company's employee-developed motto, "No One Cares More!" continues to be instrumental to the company's success. All National City Mortgage employees share a strong commitment to the company's goals, expressed in its Mission Statement and Statement of Values:

"National City Mortgage Company is a full-service mortgage banking company dedicated to delivering quality service to our customers, developing and retaining highly qualified personnel, while generating optimum growth and profit for our shareholders."

Left and below: National City Mortgage Co. corporate offices on Newmark Drive in Miamisburg.

THE DAYTON OFFICE OF ARTHUR ANDERSEN & CO.

Partner Les Banwart (center) discusses a new product developed by Amolé owners, Tom and Vickie Isaacs.

What sets the Dayton office of Arthur Andersen & Co. apart from other "Big Six" accounting firms in the Miami Valley is its commitment to serving privately held companies, especially family-owned enterprises. No other accounting or consulting firm in Dayton specializes in helping family-business owners solve their unique problems. No other firm has the same high level of understanding of the differences between the money problems of the entrepreneur and the corporate executive.

Arthur Andersen is the largest public accounting and consulting firm in the nation. Founded in 1913 by a college professor, the firm opened its downtown Dayton office in 1976. The office has more than doubled since that time and its client roster continues to grow.

Because it is a worldwide firm that provides comprehensive audit and tax services to large, publicly traded companies, it may be surprising to learn that more than 95 percent of the businesses served by Arthur Andersen's Dayton office are privately held. More than 80 percent of the Dayton office's clients have sales of less than $100 million, 75 percent have sales of less than $50 million, and 25 percent have sales of less than $10 million.

The Dayton office supports middle-market and family businesses with a number of services, including long-term planning; succession planning; estate planning or wealth-transfer techniques; management incentive programs to help attract and retain qualified, nonfamily key personnel; setting up and administering family partnerships and family offices; establishing outside boards; and, perhaps most important, helping family members understand and cope with the emotional issues that arise naturally in almost every family-owned business.

To help business owners transfer their businesses to the next generation or to the next management level, the Dayton office works closely with Dr. Léon Danco, the internationally acclaimed "father of family business."

The Dayton office's commitment to privately held companies is further evidenced by the "Arthur Andersen Dayton 100." Each year the firm honors the 100 largest privately held companies within an eight-county region and publicizes the impact they have had on their communities through the creation of jobs and revenues. The firm also identifies and honors an additional eight or nine "up-and-coming" companies.

Although the Miami Valley has historically produced more entrepreneurial investors than any other region in the country, the city of Dayton has traditionally focused on the larger, publicly traded entities. The Dayton office of Arthur Andersen & Co. was the first to recognize and honor the companies that provide the majority of new jobs and revenue to the area and remain loyal to the Miami Valley generation after generation.

Doug Root and Jim Dodok (right) help a client with personal financial planning.

SOUTHWESTERN PORTLAND

Southwestern Portland Cement has been manufacturing high-quality cements for more than 75 years. As part of Southdown, Inc., America's largest domestically owned cement producer, Southwestern manufactures and markets an extensive line of portland, masonry, and specialty cements at its Greene County facilities.

Cement is the essential binding ingredient in concrete, which is one of the most durable construction materials known to man. Portland cement is one of the primary constituents of ready-mixed concrete. Masonry cement is used to make mortar for laying brick, stone, and concrete masonry units.

Southwestern's Fairborn plant, which has been in continuous operation since 1924, produces nearly 600,000 tons of cement annually. Over the years many major additions and modifications to the plant have increased its production and improved the quality of its products.

The Fairborn facility's four-stage preheater kiln makes it Ohio's most modern and energy-efficient cement plant. This state-of-the-art equipment allows the company to offer a vast line of products that meet or exceed all the requirements of the American Society for Testing and Material and comply with strict federal specifications.

The Fairborn operation is concentrated primarily in three areas of Greene County. The quarry plant, where the kiln is located, is five miles east of Fairborn, on nearly 4,800 acres of property containing rock and clay resources. The "clinker"—an intermediate product in the manufacture of portland cement—made there is transported by private rail to the town plant for processing into cement and for storage and shipment. A third facility, a former cement plant also located in Fairborn, provides additional storage and shipping facilities.

To maintain its reputation as a producer of consistent, high-quality cements, the company employs a rigorous testing program. From the initial mining of raw materials to the finished grinding stage, 34 tests are performed to ensure that each load of Southwestern cement performs consistently and according to specifications.

Southwestern employs 175 highly skilled people in its Fairborn operations and has an annual payroll of more than $6.7 million. Training is a continuous, ongoing process, essential to maintaining the skill and safety of this workforce.

Southwestern employees give generously of their time and money in support of numerous local programs and projects. They are actively involved in a wide range of community, charitable, and cultural organizations.

Southwestern is also committed to protecting the environment and the health and welfare of its employees and the community. The Fairborn plant uses supplemental fuels (made from scrap tires and liquid organic waste products) and the thermal efficiency of cement kiln technology to help manage materials in an environmentally responsible manner while conserving nonrenewable fossil fuels. The plant also employs sophisticated monitoring equipment and a system of filters to ensure compliance with federal air-emissions standards.

Southwestern Portland Cement continues to play an important part in the ongoing research and development of new cements and processes that will allow taller and safer buildings to be built faster.

EMERY WORLDWIDE, A CF COMPANY

Emery's fleet carries parcels of virtually any size and weight to almost any place in the world.

Emery Worldwide is one of the foremost freight delivery operations in the world. With the hub of its integrated ground and air transport network strategically located at the Dayton International Airport, the company provides expedited service for commercial shipments throughout North America and more than 90 countries worldwide.

Emery Worldwide is the product of a merger between two highly respected shipping industry concerns. In 1989 Consolidated Freightways (CF) acquired Emery Worldwide and combined it with its existing CF AirFreight operation, expanding the domestic and international air cargo company into Emery Worldwide, a CF Company.

CF itself was founded in 1929 in Portland, Oregon, by Leland James. At first the small trucking company, then called The Consolidators, offered overnight service between Washington and Oregon within a 375-mile radius of Portland. By 1931 CF had grown into one of the largest motor carrier operations in the 11 western states.

Emery was founded in 1946 by John C. Emery and became the nation's first airfreight forwarder. By 1973 Emery was flying planes to six northeastern cities, developing individual airlines into a dedicated airlift network.

Today Emery Worldwide's integrated airfreight delivery system is capable of handling all manner of shipping needs, from one-pound industrial letters to parcels, packages, and heavy manufactured goods exceeding 10,000 pounds. The company's full range of services allow shippers to send parcels of virtually any size and weight to almost any place in the world.

From its Dayton hub, Emery planes or trucks are able to reach most major market cities in the continental U.S. in 90 minutes or less. The Dayton terminal (located at 3600 Dayton Park Drive) operates nearly 24 hours a day, processing an average of more than 100,000 packages and letters, which are carried over 125,000 air miles to 114 cities every night.

Emery Worldwide Airlines, Inc. (EWA), is the airline-certified carrier that operates and maintains aircraft for Emery Worldwide. In addition to serving Emery Worldwide's other customers, EWA is under contract with the U.S. Postal Service for delivery of Overnight Express and Priority Mail. In March 1991 the Dayton hub processed more than three million pounds of postal contract mail. During the Persian Gulf War, EWA dedicated seven aircraft to make four round-trips a week to fly supplies and mail to Saudi Arabia.

Emery Worldwide's Charter Service also operates out of the Dayton hub, offering shippers use of the company's aircraft fleet, including DC8, B-727, and DC9 jet freighters. The charter service specializes in the handling of animals and livestock. It has flown multimillion-dollar race horses, the mounts of the U.S. Equestrian Team, New Zealand deer, western lowland gorillas, and even former President Ronald Reagan's horse, Kelly.

Emery Worldwide will continue to operate as the nation's foremost airfreight forwarder, able to deliver on time any shipment, any size, anywhere.

Emery's Dayton terminal processes an average of more than 100,000 parcels and letters in a 24-hour period.

LELAND ELECTROSYSTEMS, INC.

Leland Electrosystems, Inc., is one of the country's leading suppliers of aerospace electrical power systems. The company designs, manufactures, and services a broad range of motors, generators, and electrical controls for both military and commercial applications.

The company was founded in 1921 by Dayton inventor and entrepreneur George H. Leland. His company, then called Leland Electrical Co., won acclaim in the early 1940s with the invention of the first "explosion-proof" electrical motor, which eliminated the need for hand-pumping of gasoline at filling stations. Leland also invented the rotary inverter, which converted DC battery power to AC power, for use in aircraft gyro systems.

These products, and the many others developed under the leadership of the Leland family, set a standard of innovation and excellence that continues within the company. In 1978, under its new (and current) ownership, Leland began focusing efforts on aerospace electrical systems, becoming a worldwide supplier of high-performance products for that market. In 1989 the company continued to expand its product base with the acquisition of General Electric's Aerospace Electrical Systems business.

Today the company's product line includes major electrical systems for frontline military aircraft, such as the U.S. Navy's F/A-18 fighter and the Air Force's F117 Stealth Fighter, as well as products for commercial aircraft, such as the MD11 and Boeing's new wide-body, twin-engine 777. In 1994 Leland will supply a new high-technology static inverter for the latest McDonnell Douglas twin-jet MD90.

Leland's engineers are known in the industry for their expertise in all facets of rotating and electronic power conversion design. Leland engineers have access to an on-site microfilm library of specifications and standards, computer-aided design systems, and complete drafting and reproduction facilities.

Leland exhibits at the Dayton International Trade and Air Show.

Leland employs the latest technology and manufacturing techniques in the design and production of all its products. The company's 140,000-square-foot corporate headquarters in Vandalia, Ohio (two miles from Dayton International Airport), maintains a staff of approximately 250 employees and houses all aspects of product development, manufacturing, and testing. A second facility in Erie, Pennsylvania, is dedicated to manufacturing. This plant, which employs about 125 people, complements rotary fabrication capacity at the Vandalia site.

Since 1990 Leland has aggresively pursued a modernization program of its facilities, equipment, and techniques. Its plants contain many work cells to improve product flow. Continuous improvement teams have been formed to implement employee involvement and empowerment. Leland is committed to be a leader in its marketplace.

Leland Electrosystems, Inc., is experienced and well-equipped to offer the aerospace industry complete electrical systems. The company is proud of its people, its products, and its association with the Dayton community.

Leland's headquarters in Vandalia.

NCR Corporation

When John H. Patterson first heard about a new invention that accurately recorded cash transactions by means of holes punched into a paper tape, he bought two of them, sight unseen, for his Coalton, Ohio, general store. The year was 1883, and Dayton inventor James Ritty's "Incorruptible Cashiers" made such a difference in Patterson's business that he bought stock in the company that made them. Less than a year later—despite ridicule from the local business community—Patterson acquired controlling interest in Ritty's firm and renamed it the National Cash Register Company.

Still headquartered in Dayton, NCR, an AT&T company, develops, manufactures, markets, supports, and services enterprise-wide information systems for worldwide markets.

NCR's products and services may be grouped into several general categories: industry-specific products for retail, financial, commercial, industrial, medical, educational, governmental, and other markets; small computer systems/workstations, including mobile pen-based and notebook computers, personal computers, general-purpose workstations and small servers; midrange computer systems, including workgroup servers, small, mid-size, and large departmental servers, and systems for interactive and batch processing; large computer systems for on-line transaction processing, decision support, and batch processing, and high-performance relational databases; networking systems, which include hardware and software products that enable enterprise-wide networking; imaging systems, which convert paper-based information into a more manageable electronic form, including document management systems, image-based item processing systems, and image-enhanced self-service systems; cooperative computing software systems, which integrate multivendor systems into enterprise-wide information networks; cooperative support services, which include business planning, customer education, and multi-vendor services; and synergistic products and services, including semiconductors, business forms and supplies, and data centers.

The company's worldwide marketing efforts are coordinated through four regional organizations: Europe Group, Latin America/Middle East/Africa Group, Pacific Group, and the United States Group.

NCR development takes place at 17 engineering and manufacturing centers, plus five systems-engineering sites in eight countries, including Canada, Denmark, Germany, Ireland, Japan, The Netherlands, and Scotland. NCR employs some 54,000 people, with approximately 27,500 employees in the United States.

NCR's worldwide customer-services staff comprises more than 21,000 hardware- and software-service professionals. The company provides service to its customers from more than 1,100 locations around the world, including 400 locations in the United States alone. In addition to supporting NCR products, the company provides service for more than 2,500 non-NCR products from more than 400 manufacturers.

The company's Data Services Division provides information-processing services for financial institutions through a nationwide network of data centers. The division also offers computer output microfiche, laser printing, and media conversion for all industries.

On September 19, 1991, NCR joined forces with AT&T in a merger that enhanced the strengths and expanded the resources of both companies. Though it is now a wholly owned subsidiary of AT&T, NCR's corporate structure, executive leadership, product programs, and name have remained intact.

The combined organization now offers its customers expertise in a wide range of information and interface technologies, a broad spectrum of products and services, worldwide network facilities, comprehensive support capabilities, and quality manufacturing.

AT&T's Computer Systems Organization was strategically merged into NCR, blending the best talents and resources of both operations, and resulting in complete and powerful open systems solutions—from personal computers and enterprise integration software, to the world's most comprehensive set of networking and connectivity products.

One of the most eagerly anticipated consequences of the merger is the collaboration of NCR and AT&T's Bell Laboratories, the world's premier industrial research and development establishment. Joint development projects are currently underway at NCR and Bell Labs. For example, NCR and Bell Labs are working together to apply AT&T's ISDN technology to NCR's 5682 Automated Teller Machine (ATM). Huntington Bancshares, Inc., will become the first U.S. bank to offer video teleconferencing at its ATMs—providing full-service banking to its customers at remote locations.

NCR and Bell Labs have also been working together to develop the virtual meeting room. This environment allows a group of people using the computers and phones in their offices to hold real-time discussions sharing voice, data, and images.

In February 1992 Teradata Corporation, a leader in commercial parallel processing computing, merged with NCR, becoming a wholly owned subsidiary of the company. The merger helped make NCR the leading supplier of high-performance relational database computer systems.

Applied Digital Data Systems, Inc. (ADDS), is another wholly owned subsidiary of NCR. ADDS manufactures and markets a broad line of general purpose video display terminals and multi-user business computer systems.

NCR actively participates in a number of major industry consortia, including X/Open, UNIX International, Open Software Foundation, Object Management Group, SEMATECH, and Microelectronics and Computer Technology Corporation (MCC).

NCR Corporation, along with its parent company, AT&T, is uniquely positioned to take advantage of the convergence of computers and communications—the next stage in the evolution of computerized enterprises.

NCR world headquarters in Dayton.

THE MEAD CORPORATION

Each day kids learn to read and write using school supplies from Mead and textbooks published on Mead paper.

Founded in Dayton over 140 years ago, Mead Corporation is a leader in forest products and electronic publishing, with its sights set on being number one in customer satisfaction in its chosen markets. Mead makes more than 2 million tons of paper and paperboard per year, is one of the world's foremost suppliers of paperboard packaging for the beer and soft drink industries, and has some of the nation's best-known consumer brands in school, home, and office supplies. Its electronic information services, LEXIS® and NEXIS®, are used the world over by professionals in law and accounting firms, corporations, government, medicine, and the news media.

More than a million tons of coated and uncoated paper come from Mead's mills each year to be used in commercial printing. The company is a major North American producer of coated textbook paper, carbonless paper, and greeting card stock. It also makes a variety of recycled grades and specialty papers that go into decorative laminates used in furniture and kitchen countertops.

When it comes to beverage packaging, Mead truly has a global presence, with plants in North America, Europe, and the Asia/Pacific region, as well as licensees serving 77 nations. Having developed the six-bottle basket carrier in the 1950s, Mead's packaging business has steadily grown as worldwide demand for beer and soft drinks has increased. The company is involved in every step of the packaging process: it manufactures coated paperboard used in beverage carriers, designs and manufactures carriers for its customers, and designs and builds the high speed packaging equipment used to assemble and load the carriers at a customer's plant. Mead also makes coated board for folding cartons, corrugating medium for shipping containers, and the containers themselves.

Mead is also a major force in marketing and distribution. Zellerbach, Mead's distribution company, is one of the largest paper merchants in the United States. Zellerbach also supplies packaging materials and systems and industrial products nationwide. Mead School and Office Products is the nation's largest manufacturer and distributor of school supplies. For many kids, buying their new Trapper Keeper® notebook is the first sign that school is about to start! The company also provides a wide variety of stationary products for home and office use.

As a papermaker, Mead has been involved in the expression of ideas and transfer of information for more than a century. It's no surprise that the company sensed the potential of computer-assisted information retrieval early on. Years before there were any personal computers, Mead Data Central (MDC) invented a desktop terminal for attorneys to use to access LEXIS, its online legal research service. Today, more than 350,000 users in 60 countries search MDC's LEXIS and NEXIS news and business information services.

Mead strives to be environmentally responsible, spending more than $50 million annually on operating costs for environmental safeguards. That's in addition to hundreds of millions of dollars spent to construct and maintain facilities for pollution control and solid waste disposal. By working together with its neighbors, Mead believes we can all manage our renewable resources for the future.

Logs of paper today . . . catalogs tomorrow. The nation's finest printers consume thousands of tons of Mead paper annually.

SOCIETY BANK

For more than 130 years Society Bank has been a financial leader in the Dayton area, committed to providing innovative services and banking products to its customers, and taking pride in its involvement in the communities it serves.

Society Bank's local origins date back to 1863, when the Second National Bank became the first nationally chartered bank to open its doors in Dayton. In 1925 Second National was granted trust powers and became the Third National Bank and Trust Company. As Dayton grew so did Third National, offering innovative new services, including direct auto loans, branch offices, drive-in banking, and Dayton's first automatic teller machine.

In 1984 Third National's holding company, Interstate Financial Corporation, merged with Society Corporation of Cleveland, and Society Bank was formed. Society Corporation is a fully integrated financial services company that engages in commercial banking, consumer banking, mortgage banking, and leasing, and provides investment management and trust services.

As an affiliate of one of the largest bank holding companies in the nation, Society Bank now has more than 100 banking offices in its southern region, including the Celina, Columbus, Dayton, Cincinnati, and Springfield markets.

Society Bank offers its customers a range of consumer banking services and products, including installment loans, checking and savings accounts, credit cards, and home equity lines of credit. The bank's automated teller machine network allows customers access to over 13,000 ATMs and more than 17,000 POS terminals at retailer locations nationwide. Society Bank's innovative on-line teller terminal is a sophisticated electronic data-processing system that immediately posts customer transactions.

Society Bank meets the diverse financial needs of today's corporate-banking market with high-quality professionals and a team approach to delivering a broad array of credit, corporate finance, and noncredit product solutions to public and private enterprises.

Society Bank initiates programs and keeps in touch with area citizens through "hands-on" activities like canvassing neighborhoods to introduce new banking offices and services.

Society Bank is a concerned corporate citizen committed to exploring new methods of reinvesting its time and resources into the Dayton-area communities it serves. An excellent example of this commitment is the bank's HomeAssist program. The program, which originated in Dayton in 1989, makes home ownership more affordable for low- to moderate-income individuals and families and combines a down payment grant with personalized budget planning. Society Bank has earned "outstanding" ratings—the highest possible—from the Office of the Comptroller of the Currency (OCC) for its community reinvestment performance.

Society Bank was also commended by the OCC for developing the small business seminar, "How to Borrow Money"; for designing special small-installment loans; and for offering its Value-Checking program. The bank is also involved in a number of community partnerships, including the city of Dayton's Neighborhood Lending Program, Project Homestart, Partners in Education, Habitat for Humanity, and work with the Montgomery County Community Action Agency.

NBD BANCORP

NBD Bancorp is the 16th-largest bank holding company in the U.S. Founded in 1972 and headquartered in Detroit, Michigan, the company operates banks in Michigan, Indiana, Illinois, Ohio, and Florida markets. The company also operates bank-related subsidiaries engaged in mortgage, trust, insurance, leasing, consumer credit processing, securities trading, and community economic development.

When NBD Bancorp acquired Ohio-based Mid-America Federal Savings and Loan in December 1990, it marked the first step in the company's strategic expansion into the state. NBD reorganized the ailing thrift into the full-service commercial bank, NBD Bank, with 23 branches (15 in Columbus, 8 in Dayton) that now offer commercial and consumer loans, trust, and international banking services.

John L. McCreary, president NBD Bank, Dayton region.

"Mid-America Federal was an important part of the communities it served," says John L. McCreary, president of NBD Bank's Dayton Region. "Our goal is to continue to serve those communities, doing what we do best: delivering cutting-edge services and implementing quality programs."

The affiliate of NBD Bank in Ohio, NBD Bank, N.A., in Michigan, has long been considered one of the premier corporate lending banks in the country. As part of a $40-billion bank holding company, NBD is known for its asset quality, well-performing loan portfolio, strong capital, and long record of earnings growth.

NBD's corporate cash management services give corporate customers immediate access to their financial records to improve cash flow and make informed business decisions. NBD was among the first banks to provide electronic data interchange and electronic trade payments. As one of the few banks in the Midwest with international offices, NBD has developed cash management services that accommodate the transaction and information needs of its customers who do business overseas.

NBD is, in fact, the only bank in the Midwest outside of downtown Chicago with a significant foreign presence. The company has offices in London, Frankfurt, Tokyo, Hong Kong, Toronto, and Windsor, as well as an Australian affiliate with offices in Adelaide, Melbourne, and Sydney. NBD corporate customers in Dayton are served by a bank that understands their changing needs in the growing global business environment.

The loan officer training program at NBD is well known throughout the U.S. Unlike many banks that hire lenders from other institutions, NBD recruits candidates from the nation's finest universities, then puts them through an intensive loan officer training program. The result is a highly skilled staff of lenders who apply consistent credit standards throughout the organization.

An important principle of business at all NBD banks is investment in the communities they serve. NBD Bank, N.A., the company's leading bank, was awarded an "outstanding" rating by the Office of the Comptroller of the Currency for meeting the credit needs of its communities for the most recent rating period. Besides bringing quality consumer and commercial banking services to its Dayton customers, NBD Bank is striving to do whatever it can to promote home ownership and home improvement, stimulate economic revitalization, and support Dayton businesses of all sizes.

R.L. DRAKE COMPANY

The R.L. Drake Company designs, manufactures, and markets satellite communications equipment and accessories for consumers, cable companies, and business and industry in the United States and around the globe.

Its products can be found on the grounds of hospitals and hotels, apartment buildings and condominium complexes, banks, and auto dealerships.

The company introduces rural households to cable programming and allows cable TV enthusiasts to enjoy hundreds of channels.

Drake allows physicians in California to observe a live-organ transplant in New York, and U.S. medical researchers to participate in a cancer symposium in England.

Satellite communications allow the distribution of video, audio, and data across town or across the globe. The only U.S. manufacturer of satellite receivers and accessories is the Miamisburg-based R.L. Drake Company, which celebrates its 50th anniversary in 1993.

Founded by amateur radio enthusiast and pioneer Robert Lloyd Drake, Sr., the company originally produced television interference filters and did some contract manufacturing during World War II. Drake later began building receivers and accessories for the amateur radio market. King Hussein of Jordan, Barry Goldwater, Ronnie Milsap, and other notables have used Drake gear for radio communications, said Ronald Wysong, Drake's president and chief executive officer.

In 1981, with the market for amateur radio dwindling, Drake entered the home satellite receiver market. "There are 10 to 15 million TV households in the country that do not have access to cable and never will," Wysong said. Drake equipment allows residents of these sparsely populated, rural areas with limited access to broadcast channels to receive programming from satellites.

By 1984 Drake had stopped producing amateur radio equipment and was concentrating solely on satellite equipment. A year later *Inc.* magazine recognized Drake as one of the fastest-growing private companies in the country. By 1989—with export volume soaring and home satellite television receivers being shipped to 30 some countries—Drake was named Ohio Exporter of the Year by the U.S. Small Business Administration.

One of Drake's biggest markets today is the commercial sector, which includes private cable companies (which provide linkups to apartment buildings and condominiums not served by a cable franchise), hospitals, hotels, and universities.

In 1991 Drake entered a burgeoning market by introducing its R8 Communications Receiver—a world band shortwave receiver that allows users to listen to world events on shortwave radio.

"This is not an amateur radio product," Wysong said. "This is a professional, desk-type receiver with great clarity and fidelity that allows you to listen to Radio Moscow, Radio Baghdad, and other broadcast and utility stations all over the world."

Drake has been successful in the global marketplace because it identifies markets too small, or geographic areas with needs too specialized, to interest larger manufacturers.

Drake employs more than 325 people in Ohio, Canada, and Europe. The company is still family owned, with Robert Drake's son, Peter W. Drake, serving as chairman of the board.

DEAN INVESTMENT ASSOCIATES

Dean Investment Associates is one of the country's leading privately held investment management firms. Managing assets of more than $6.5 billion, with clients ranging from multinational corporations to private individuals, Dean Investments ranks among the top one percent of U.S. money managers in performance.

A division of C.H. Dean & Associates, Inc., Dean Investments was founded in 1972 by Chauncy H. Dean, but the firm's roots can actually be traced back to 1965. At that time Dean was serving as a full professor at the graduate school of the Air Force Institute of Technology at Wright Patterson Air Force Base in Dayton. In his spare time he started a financial management firm called Dean Financial Business Management Associates. Originally a part-time professional practice, his one- and two-man operation provided comprehensive financial management services from the lower level of his home primarily to medical groups incorporating in increasing numbers in the Dayton area.

"As we served these incorporated medical groups," recalls Dean, who still serves as the firm's chairman and chief executive officer, "it became obvious to me that there was a great need for private investment management and for a firm that could bring tactical asset allocation into the investment management process—especially to bring about preservation of capital. Our first objective, then and today, is to achieve preservation of capital."

Chauncey H. Dean, chairman and chief executive officer.

Dean started his investment management division in the latter part of 1972. Unlike his financial management firm, which offered services such as estate planning, tax return preparation, and comprehensive business management, the new division specialized in the management of stocks and bonds for pension funds, endowments, universities, corporations, personal portfolios, and IRAs.

Today investment management composes nearly 95 percent of the company's business. From its downtown Dayton headquarters in the Kettering Tower, Dean Investment serves nearly 15,000 clients throughout the United States, including Alaska and Hawaii. The firm's clients include industrial corporations; colleges and universities, such as the University of San Francisco and Catholic University; municipalities, such as the City of New Orleans, the City of El Paso, and wealthy individuals, such as prominent sports figures and actors; and a variety of state worker-compensation funds and hospitals.

Dean Investment's primary objective is the preservation of capital in declining markets. In advancing markets the firm looks to enhance portfolio values through a top-down, value-oriented approach to the equity markets. The firm believes that by selecting securities that are fundamentally undervalued, the downside risk to portfolios is minimized. Furthermore, by blending together both fundamental and technical security analyses, the firm achieves consistent annual performance.

The asset allocation process the firm employs continually measures the short term (three to six months), intermediate (six months to two years), and long term (two to five years) to derive the security mix of stocks, bonds, and money markets for client accounts.

"Investment managers are typically classified as one of three types," explains Dean Investment's Robert J. Suttman II, CFA, vice president, director of consulting services, and senior institutional portfolio manager. "They are either equity fund managers, which means they manage stocks; balanced-fund managers, which means they manage stocks, bonds, and money markets all in one portfolio; or fixed-income managers. As an asset allocator, Dean Investment Associates has the ability to refine and change the mix of stocks, bonds, and money markets in an account and preserve capital in a down market."

By placing the greatest emphasis on 12- and 18-month forecasting models for making changes in the asset allocation mix of the portfolios it manages, the firm produces more favorable investment returns than could be achieved by focusing solely on the short term.

"We'd be the first to admit," says Suttman, "that for the short term your guess is as good as ours. But if you ask us where we think the market is going to be a year from now, or three or five years, based on the indicators we look at, we can give you a relatively accurate answer. We're known for this in the industry."

The Dean Investment Associates division employs 150 employees locally and publishes a quarterly financial newsletter entitled *Market & Financial Digest.* The firm began publishing the newsletter in 1984 in an effort to keep clients informed of rapidly changing market and economic conditions and to keep clients abreast of the economic outlook, interest rates, and the firm's overall stock and bond market strategies.

Dean Financial Business Management Associates is the business and personal management services division of C.H. Dean and Associates. The division provides comprehensive personal financial management services for clients, as well as tax return preparation, payroll and check preparation, management support services, and tax planning.

As the 1990s unfold, Dean Investment Associates sees a volatile future for investors—an environment in which "static" investment managers are going to be at a distinct disadvantage, and Dean investors will be ahead of the game.

"We see the coming decade as favoring our philosophy of management even more than the 1980s did," says Dean. "Prices will be moving rapidly, and in that type of environment, our tactical asset allocation system gives our clients a tremendous advantage. Yes, we're looking forward to the 1990s."

Dennis O. Dean, president and chief operations officer.

SHOOK NATIONAL CORPORATION

Shook National Corporation completed a $20-million modernization and expansion on the Ottawa Street Water Treatment Facility in 1993.

It is impossible to look at the modern face of Dayton and not see the influence of Shook National Corporation. From the Dayton International Airport to the Dayton Convention Center, from the Emery Worldwide Superhub in Vandalia to the Roesch Library at the University of Dayton, Shook has spent more than 70 years erecting some of the Miami Valley's best-known and most important structures.

Headquartered in Dayton, Shook is a full-service general contracting firm that undertakes both large and small projects for a wide range of public and private clients (about $100 million-worth annually). Shook builds educational and health care facilities; automotive plants; prisons; commercial, industrial, and retail complexes; and a wide variety of environmental projects. The company has also participated in numerous major construction management and design/build projects. Shook is consistently ranked among the top 400 contractors in the nation by *Engineering News-Record.*

The company was founded in 1922 by Dayton builder Charles H. Shook. Shook's original contracting partnership—known as Shook & Billiter—lasted about three years, after which he struck out on his own with Charles H. Shook, Inc. Over the next 40 years Shook's company would build many of Dayton's landmark structures, including the Third National Bank building and Good Samaritan Hospital. During the 1950s, in response to the growing need for pollution-control facilities, the firm began constructing water and wastewater treatment plants.

Shook built the Dayton Convention Center in the mid-1970s, and completed a $10-million, 100,000-square-foot expansion and renovation on the facility in 1989.

After Charles Shook died in 1963, management of his company passed to four key employees: Harry Gaeke, Harry Wallace, Robert Grannis, and Robert Merz. At that time the company's name was shortened to Shook, Inc.

Today the company's operations extend beyond the Miami Valley into several midwestern and eastern states. To accommodate this growth and manage its resources more effectively the company has formed several subsidiary groups under the umbrella of Shook National Corporation.

The Shook Building Group handles building projects such as hospitals, nursing facilities, athletic complexes, commercial buildings, civic centers, institutional facilities, prisons, industrial plants, and major renovation work. This group's project teams have at their disposal a fleet of equipment for excavation, concrete placement, erection, and other construction activities.

The Building Group is skilled at the "fast track" scheduling that permits clients to have their buildings up and running as rapidly as possible. For example, one of the group's crowning achievements is the Emery Air Freight Superhub Terminal at the Dayton International Airport. Completed in just six months—with 45 days lost to bad weather—this project included a 250,000-square-foot transfer building, two million square feet of cargo apron, 720,000 square feet of taxiway space, and 170 acres of site development.

The Building Group has completed such well-known local projects as the Ervin J. Nutter Center at Wright State University in Dayton, a 260,000-square-foot multipurpose

entertainment and sports facility valued at $32 million; and a $10 million renovation of the Dayton International Airport, which included a new building facade and main entry, new baggage return carousels, and complete renovation of the main terminal.

The Shook Heavy and Environmental Group builds water and wastewater treatment facilities, power plants and incinerators, and industrial and chemical treatment plants. This group maintains a fully staffed mechanical department that coordinates and expedites the installation of sophisticated process and piping systems and high-technology treatment equipment.

Some of the Environmental Group's more notable projects include a new, $15-million water treatment plant in Hershey, Pennsylvania, constructed for the American Waterworks Company; and a $20-million improvement project for the Ottawa Street Works, one of Dayton's two major water treatment plants. (This plant processes 96 million gallons of water per day and remained fully operational during construction.)

The company's other wholly owned subsidiaries include ABS General Contractors, Inc., which handles smaller commercial projects, such as churches, office buildings, and medical and long-term care facilities in southwestern Ohio. Ameritcon, Inc., concentrates on smaller environmental projects in Ohio and West Virginia. Shook also maintains an office in the Cleveland area that handles work in the northern part of the state.

Shook's work force is characterized by a wide range of ages and types of experience. The company's project managers, superintendents, and executives have an average of 19 years of field experience. Many of the company's older employees have a civil engineering or mechanical engineering backgrounds, while new hires tend to be from the construction management field. Mixing the various disciplines allows Shook employees to learn from each other and to gain valuable insights they can apply to further their job skills.

The Ervin J. Nutter Center—a multipurpose educational and sports facility—was completed by Shook in 1990 at a total cost of $28 million.

Worker safety has always been a top priority at Shook. The company's commitment to safety is underscored by its safety program, which is run by a full-time safety director who conducts weekly, monthly, and quarterly job-site inspections with project superintendents and foremen. The company also holds ongoing in-house safety training, often directed by local OSHA representatives.

The company has received numerous safety awards from the Dayton Area Chamber of Commerce and the Ohio Industrial Commission.

Shook enjoys a hard-earned reputation for honesty and quality. The company has been recognized by the construction industry for excellence with two of its most prestigious awards, the Build America Award and the Build America Merit Award sponsored by the AGC and Motorola Co.

Shook National Corporation completed the Allen Research Center in 1992. The 260,000-square-foot R&D facility, owned by Quantum Chemical's USI Division, was finished at a cost of $20 million.

The Berry Company

The Berry General Office Headquarters at 3170 Kettering Blvd., in Dayton, Ohio.

In 1910, when Loren M. Berry set out to build a company that specialized in telephone directory advertising, the 22-year-old entrepreneur chose the city of Dayton for his first office. Today the Berry Company is still headquartered in Dayton, but that original one-man office has grown into one of the largest and most influential telephone directory sales and publishing operations in the world.

Widely known as "the Yellow Pages People," the Berry Company is a pioneer in the telephone directory publishing industry. From the early days when advertising appeared in the margins of the directories' alphabetical sections to the advent of today's familiar Yellow Pages; from the publication of the first 800 number directories to the evolution of advanced information services, the Berry Company has helped to shape the modern telephone directory and make it an indispensable part of American life.

The company's growth has been impressive. It reached $50 million in sales during the 1960s, saw that amount double in the 1970s, and today is a billion-dollar industry leader. The Berry Company currently provides its services to more than 200 telephone companies in 33 states across the country.

The Berry Company's domestic operations involve nearly 2,400 employees working out of 43 offices across the United States; approximately 750 of those employees are based in Dayton.

A Berry telephone-sales representative at work.

In 1966 the Berry Company and International Telephone and Telegraph Corporation (ITT) formed a subsidiary operation called ITT-World Directories, which handles the sales and publication of telephone directories around the world. ITT-World Directories serves telephone companies in Belgium, Japan, the Netherlands, Portugal, and many other countries.

The Berry Company's sales representatives comprise one of the finest sales forces in the industry. The company is at the forefront of new technology such as a consultive, automated selling technique that utilizes laptop computers to sell Yellow Pages advertising.

Berry's core business.

This leading-edge technology enables Berry representatives to provide the latest in creative ad design and sales support, such as customer demographics, sophisticated territory mapping, and business trend information.

Berry also keeps in touch with the ever-changing needs of its advertisers/customers through Advertiser Advisory Boards.

In Dayton and around the country, the Berry Company is known for its commitment to the communities in which it operates. This commitment manifests itself in the participation and support of the performing arts and other cultural organizations, education, and youth activities. In Dayton, Berry employees act as advisors for several Junior Achievement companies. Berry has also been a United Way pacesetter.

In 1986 L.M. Berry joined forces with BellSouth and is now a wholly owned subsidiary of that company. Today the Berry Company continues to be a leading figure in the telephone directory industry.

SACHS MANAGEMENT CORPORATION

Sachs Management Corporation should not be unknown to anyone who has traveled to the Holiday Inn I-675 Conference Center or the Homewood Suites Hotel, across from Wright State University. Sachs Management—in partnership with Miller-Valentine Group—developed and manages both hotels.

Dan Sachs founded the hotel management services company in 1969. Today the Sachs team, with its corporate staff of operations and financial specialists, manages eight hotels and several restaurants throughout the Midwest .

The company is known for its expertise in site selection, design, food and beverage management, and hotel rehabilitation. According to Sachs, site-selection decisions are based on a thorough analysis of professional market studies ordered by the firm.

"We first try to identify the market where we think there's an opportunity," Sachs says. "We usually have a pretty good idea if a hotel is necessary or economically feasible. Then we take the basic information and tailor it to the market."

For example, Sachs and the Miller-Valentine Group chose to orient the I-675 Holiday Inn as a conference center because of Wright-Patterson Air Force Base and Wright State University. According to Sachs, the whole complex is designed for conferences. There is a ballroom with four functional rooms, a 100-seat amphitheater, three breakout rooms, a separate conference entrance, a built-in registration facility, and a large pre-function area for cocktail parties and other gatherings.

"When people see all this, they know we are serious about conferences," he says.

Sachs Management works closely with leading national teams of hotel architects, engineers, and interior designers. "We identify the scope of the project, tell them what size facility, the number of restaurants, and how we want to go about serving the market," Sachs says. "Then we go over design ideas with them and provide direction throughout the project."

Together with Miller-Valentine, Sachs has purchased a 217-room Ramada Inn in Cincinnati, Ohio, and the two firms are completely renovating the building.

Two ingredients help make a hotel successful: location and food and beverage, according to Sachs. Since most of Sachs' hotels have restaurants, the company has earned a national reputation for its food and beverage capabilities, which Sachs attributes to the company's food and beverage staff, who handle the planning, design, staffing, and operations of the hotel restaurants.

According to Sachs, hotels have to be refurbished every five to seven years before they get "old and stale." Since many of the company's hotels are more than 20 years old, rehabilitation has become another specialty of Sachs Management Corporation.

The I-675 Holiday Inn Conference Center attracts patrons from the Wright-Patterson Air Force Base and Wright State University, both of which are located nearby.

Homewood Suites hotels are equipped with two-room suites and kitchen areas to accommodate the extended-stay traveler. Courtesy, the Miller-Valentine Group

ROBBINS & MYERS

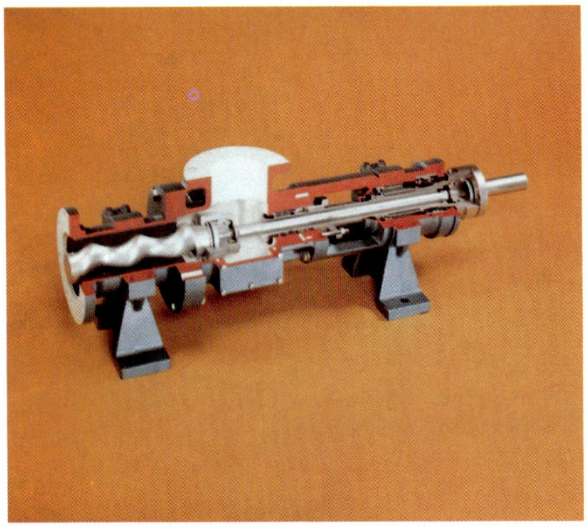

R&M progressing cavity pumps provide great versatility and dependability to a broad range of process applications.

Over the years, people have associated Robbins & Myers, the international manufacturer of pumps, valves, and mixers, with all kinds of companies and products, says Hugh Becker, director of corporate relations for Robbins & Myers. However, name recognition, he says, has not impeded the company's success.

Robbins & Myers, founded in 1878 as a supplier of castings for agricultural machines, bicycles, and later electric fans, today has annual sales that top $80 million. The former castings producer now manufactures fluids-handling equipment for wastewater treatment, pulp and paper production, chemical processing, food processing, and oil and gas recovery, as well as other environmental products.

Robbins & Myers may be most well known for its Moyno® progressing cavity pump (which looks like a giant, fattened corkscrew) designed for moving thick, viscous, abrasive, and corrosive fluids more easily through a processing or treatment plant. For example, the Moyno® pump is used to pump pulp through a paper production plant, move anything from peanut butter to maraschino cherries through a food-processing plant, and transport sludge from one part of a wastewater treatment plant to another.

"By repositioning the pump, it permits different applications," says Becker. For example, turned vertically, the Moyno® pump can be used in place of piston-type pumps for recovering oil. By reversing the direction of the rotor, this same technology can be used as a mud motor for horizontal oil-well drilling. Because the pump can withstand almost any kind of environment, Becker says, "There are very few products we can't pump with this technology."

Although an Ohio-based company since its founding in 1878, Robbins & Myers was not always based in Dayton. In 1978 the company decided to move its corporate headquarters from Springfield. Because of its strong economic environment and access to the financial community, "Dayton was selected as the headquarters site," Becker says.

The history of Robbins & Myers continues to shape its outlook and strategy today. "If you go back through history, there are two things that are consistently present," explains Becker. "We've always been innovative—that sets the tone for the next generation of products. Second, we've been devoted to quality products."

That innovation was evident from the early days, when the fledgling company launched its own line of motor-powered fans to capitalize on the growing use of electricity. Ceiling, desk, oscillating, and ventilation fans became so popular that they were the mainstay of Robbins & Myers' business. Inventors of the early 1900s—such as Charles F. Kettering (inventor of the automobile starter), Guglielmo Marconi (inventor of the wireless telegraph), and companies like Singer, Hoover, and Addressograph Multigraph—used Robbins & Myers' equipment, motors, and generator sets for their inven-

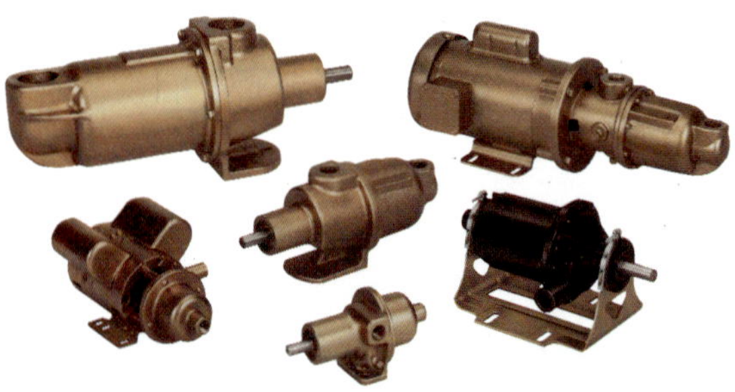

Moyno® sanitary pumps serve a wide variety of food processing, water and wastewater, pharmaceutical, and chemical process applications.

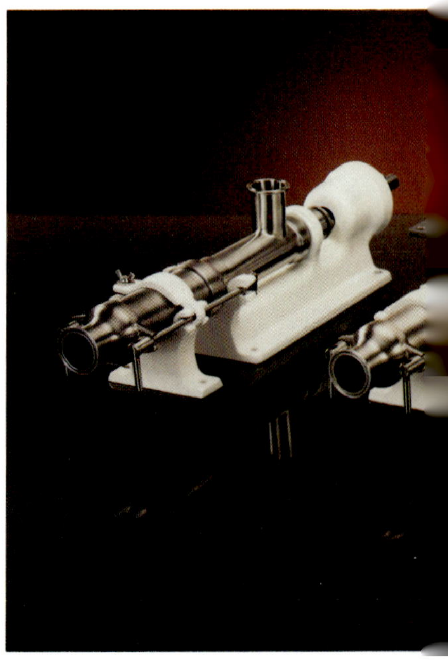

Compact and efficient, Moyno® SP pumps stand up to abrasive, viscous, corrosive, solids-laden slurries as easily as water.

tions. During World War II, the Robbins & Myers innovation was at work again producing motors that could meet the high-performance demands of delicate aircraft navigational systems.

In 1932 Rene Joseph Louis Moineau introduced progressing cavity pump technology to Robbins & Myers, which in 1936 acquired exclusive rights to manufacture and market the pump in North America.

By the late 1970s Robbins & Myers was manufacturing four principal product lines: ceiling fans, pumps, motors, and hoists and cranes. At that time, ceiling fans were half of the company's business.

By the early 1980s, however, with annual company-wide sales approaching an all-time high of $200 million, "The market for ceiling fans fell off a cliff," says Becker, with the arrival of offshore competitors selling lower-priced fans. The loss of such a lucrative market had the potential of crippling the 100-year-old company. Then came the second half of the double whammy—the weakening industrial economy.

"We had to divest of businesses and downsize to effectively turn the company around," Becker says. "It was a massive project."

The restructuring, which began in 1982, included closing plants, decreasing the work force by about three-fourths, instituting cost-reduction programs in manufacturing, and refocusing efforts on the core business (fluid management). By the second quarter of 1987, Robbins & Myers finally began turning a profit again.

The turnaround story is an important one for Robbins & Myers, says Becker. Today the company maintains three U.S. locations and others in Southhampton, England; Petit-Rechain, Belgium; Singapore, Asia; and Brampton, Ontario.

As in the past, innovation and quality will be keys that prepare the company for its leap into the next century. In the 1990s Robbins & Myers wants to expand product lines in areas that are complementary to the core businesses, make acquisitions, and enter new markets. Establishing a stronger product recognition in foreign markets is also a goal, says Becker.

"We've been in Belgium with the pump manufacturing and in the United Kingdom with a direct sales force," he says, "so we've got a base to grow on."

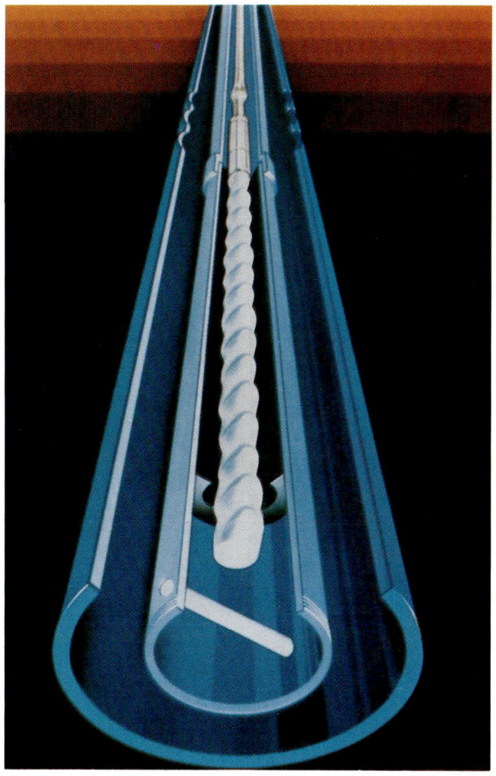

Moyno® down-hole pumps deliver advantages for the recovery of oil and gas over conventional systems with unmatched productivity and value.

Rotors, a critical component of the progressing cavity pump, reflect the leadership in quality, design and manufacturing, hallmarks of R&M.

HYDE PARK ELECTRONICS, INC.

Bill Winger, president of Hyde Park Electronics, forsees excellent growth for his company, which specializes in solving difficult sensing and control problems for container, food processing, beverage and packaging industries worldwide.

Bill Winger, president of Hyde Park Electronics, Inc., has truly worked his way up—from his own basement.

In the 1960s Winger was the sales manager at Wacline in Dayton by day. At night and on the weekends, however, Winger was hard at work building controls for machines that tested empty metal cans for air leaks. By August 1963 a brand-new company, Hyde Park Electronics, was incorporated with three equal partners. Winger was one of them, still building controls in his basement. "We got a contract, opened accounts with suppliers, got paid, paid our bills, and went from there," says Winger.

The partners did not consider themselves a full-fledged company, however, until 1967, when they moved production and engineering to a modest, 500-square-foot office in downtown Centerville. Today, with more than 40 employees and more than $4 million in annual sales, Hyde Park is known throughout the country and the world for providing "sensing and control solutions" for its customers.

Sensors, which detect objects and then relay messages to machine controls, are a critical part of the packaging process, where machines automatically fill, label, and put lids on containers, glass bottles, and metal cans. "If there's no sensor, then the machine does not know the container is there," says Winger.

Hyde Park deals in the world of high speed. On the line, up to 2,000 containers might pass per minute. Even at this speed, however, if a metal can in a chili-filling line is missing, Hyde Park sensors will tell the control system to remember the location of the missing container so that 16 ounces of chili and beans do not go splattering all over the machine. Other possible consequences of unreliable sensing include incorrect container counts, machine jams, and downtime—often several days worth.

Winger maintains that Hyde Park products are everywhere. "Most of the cans and easy-open lids made in the world are tested with Hyde Park controls," he says.

Hyde Park is one of the world leaders in ultrasonic sensing, where sound beams are used to detect the presence or absence of a container. In the past, most sensors have been photoelectric; light beams were used to detect objects. But according to Winger, photoelectric sensors are sometimes unreliable, especially if clear glass bottles must be detected. "With sonics, you detect it every time," Winger says.

Hyde Park's SUPERPROX® sensors detect objects by measuring the time it takes for a burst of energy to hit the object and bounce back to a receiver. "It's a little radar system," Winger says. Hyde Park's MICROSONIC® sensors detect objects by recording when the object blocks a sound beam. "If the beam is blocked, the sensor knows that an object is there."

According to Winger, Hyde Park's forte is solving the tough sensing and control problems and developing custom sensors and controls for specific applications. "We work best when we become an extension of a customer's engineering department," he says. "We provide the solution rather than let the customer figure it out."

Selling solutions—and not just components—is what

makes Hyde Park different from its competitors, who, says Winger, often tell their customers to pick something out of a catalog.

"When the competition can't solve a customer's problem, the customer comes to us," Winger says. "We are sometimes a last resort."

One of Hyde Park's toughest problems has been determining how to reliably detect clear glass bottles. "We didn't realize it was such a difficult physics problem to make the sensors work in plants where there was a lot of noise," Winger points out.

Although ultrasonic technology was introduced for sensing and control applications in the late 1970s, Hyde Park spent the following decade improving the technology. Now microprocessors are connected to sensing and control systems, making the sensors "smart."

"A container doesn't move by in a perfect state," Winger explains. "It's doing a lot of jiggling around. A 'dumb' sensor may not see that the container is there if it's jiggling around, and it may not be able to detect a problem."

These smarter sensing and control systems also provide additional capabilities. For example, the system can be programed to count and track containers, automatically rejecting every thousandth container for a quality inspection; detect trends, such as a series of damaged containers; or separate over-filled and under-filled containers from containers that are filled properly.

Unlike other manufacturing company presidents, who tend to promote their quality control departments, Winger proclaims openly that Hyde Park's entire staff is a quality-control department.

"Our whole company is responsible for satisfying the customer," Winger says. "If that customer is satisfied, we have the quality."

To that end, Winger ensures that the employees of Hyde Park Electronics, Inc., get to know the needs of Hyde Park customers in every possible way. Winger recently invited more than half of the company's employees—from the sales force to assembly personnel—to meet customers at a national trade show in Chicago. He believes if the employees can see what is happening with a customer, then the ultimate goal of satisfying the customer will become contagious.

"We take good care of our customers and our employees," Winger says. "The rest takes care of itself after that."

Detecting clear containers in harsh, high-speed environments is routine for the reliable SUPERPROX® Ultrasonic Proximity Sensor.

DANIS INDUSTRIES CORPORATION

Citizens Federal Centre, completed by Danis in 1990.

A company in the construction business has only one thing to live on: its reputation.

By marking its 75th year as a construction contractor in 1991, Danis Industries Corporation celebrated a long-standing reputation for integrity, quality construction, financial stability, long-term client relationships, and projects built on time and within budget. Now in its eighth decade, Danis is among the 75 largest contractors in the United States.

What does it mean to be a construction company that's more than 75 years old? "It speaks well for the quality of work we do," says Thomas Danis, a third-generation owner. "Construction companies generally don't last that long."

Danis employs more than 1,250 people in four groups: heavy construction, environmental services, real estate, and building construction. Projects span the Midwest, Mid-Atlantic, and Southeast, with offices located throughout these regions.

"How long a company stays on top depends on its creativity, aggressiveness, and willingness to change," says Danis. The company changed in the 1950s when it began building highways and bridges and initiated an environmental business. In the 1970s Danis formed a real estate company to take advantage of markets such as offices and warehouses. In the 1980s Danis acknowledged the design/build/lease-back trend and began offering those services to its clients. In the 1990s innovation, diversification, and acquisition will continue to shape the company.

Through the real estate group Danis offers complete real estate services, from site selection and construction to property management of office buildings and parks, industrial facilities, retail centers, warehouses, and distribution centers. Its three operating groups include project development, brokerage and leasing, and property management.

The construction group, which specializes in buildings and water, wastewater, and industrial treatment facilities, offers a turnkey approach to building construction, including design/build, construction management, and general contracting. To Danis' credit are ventures valued from $500,000 to $50 million, including offices, hotels, retail centers, industrial complexes, hospitals, and colleges and universities. In the Miami Valley Danis is noted for projects such as Citizens Federal Centre, Delco Products (General Motors), Emery Worldwide, Good Samaritan Hospital, Kettering Tower, Kodak, and many others. Moreover, Danis has earned national recognition for its historical renovations, including Dayton's Victoria Theatre and Trailsend Estate.

According to Danis, the key to success on any building project is the managerial talent and experience of the building team.

"For some clients, we've done four, five, or more projects a year for more than 15 years," he says. "It all boils down to people—good people who know they are responsible for building a quality building. That's what sets us apart."

Danis conducted the renovation of the Victoria Theatre in 1990.

GIDDINGS & LEWIS

Before the world adopted modern standardized measurements, items were measured using such irregular gauges as an arm, a fist, or the distance a horse could plow in an hour. Today length can be measured using an atomic clock in conjunction with light traveling in a vacuum.

"That indicates to me the revolution that's taking place in the field of measuring," says Robert Kynast, group vice president of Giddings & Lewis.

Kynast is committed to being a world leader in this revolution. In its 86-year history, Giddings & Lewis has designed and built the sophisticated machines that measure machine parts, engine blocks, pistons, crank shafts, transmission housings, gears, auto bodies, jet engine parts, air-frame components, tractor parts, compressors—even the roughest of rabbit bones.

In 1990 Giddings & Lewis became one of the first companies to incorporate lasers into its coordinate-measuring machines. Lasers produce the world's finest dimensional measuring capabilities; for some applications measurements must be accurate within four millionths of an inch.

"The name of this business, the one that ties it all together, is precision," Kynast says. Precision is something Giddings & Lewis knows all about. "We started out as a tool and die company," Kynast explains, "so we know and understand what it takes to manufacture factory parts on the factory floor."

According to Kynast, processes cannot be controlled unless parts are measured and results are relayed during production—not when the part is completely machined. While the computer revolutionized the machining process in the 1980s, it also changed the purpose of measuring.

"The automatic machine tool did everything—bores, mills, taps, and turns—so you couldn't change anything," Kynast says. Measuring was separated from the production process, performed during a quality control audit after a run of production parts.

As a result quality took a nose dive, which spelled trouble for many manufacturers, particularly U.S. automakers. According to Kynast, car parts produced in large quantities often varied from acceptable tolerances but were used anyway because they were too expensive to reproduce. In the end, consumers complained that U.S. cars simply did not last as long as imports.

Now, says Kynast, the nature of the industry is changing. The push is on for quality, low cost, and high productivity. He refuses to use the words "meet specs."

"That phrase has cost this country a lot—economically and in prestige," Kynast says. "The idea is to make a part as good as you can. We believe the people machining the parts should be the same ones running the measuring equipment."

Moving measuring machines onto the shop floor means manufacturers such as Giddings & Lewis must ensure that machines are accurate in factory environments where temperature varies and where production processes are accelerated through automation.

Giddings & Lewis is committed to leading this change in the industry. Kynast says, "We intend to be the people who provide the best answers to this need."

NATIONAL CITY BANK

Superior service . . . commitment . . . strength . . . convenience . . . dedicated local leadership. These are the characteristics that make National City Bank a formidable force in the Dayton community. With nearly 40 area offices and 60 MONEY STATION™ locations, National City Bank is conveniently located to service business and personal banking needs.

The roots of National City Bank run deep in Dayton, back to the post-Civil War era in 1871, when Merchants National Bank received its charter. After a series of mergers and acquisitions, the bank was renamed First National Bank in 1966. In 1977, First National joined National City Corporation, the strong, highly respected, Ohio-based, regional bank holding company.

The bank continued to grow, and nearly doubled in size, prior to its acquisition of the 100-year-old, Dayton-based Gem Savings in 1991. The marriage of these two well-respected financial institutions created a major banking force in the Miami Valley. In the spring of 1993, First National was renamed National City Bank, Dayton. "The strength of National City Corporation, coupled with our local decision-making, adds great depth to the ability of our local bank to serve its communities," says Fred Schantz, president of National City Bank.

With sophisticated cash management, trust, international and commercial lending services, National City Bank offers both small and mid-sized businesses superior expertise and technology to satisfy their financial needs. Likewise, consumers can choose innovative services at competitive prices. Coupled with a strong dedication to customer service, National City Bank offers customers a unique formula for dealing with their banking needs in the 1990s.

"At National City Bank, we stress the importance of personal attention and customer satisfaction to every employee. 'The customer comes first' slogan mirrors our bank's philosophy," stresses Schantz. "Many of our customers have a long tradition with our bank—their parents and grandparents still bank here. This family concept often typifies the relationships formed between customers and our employees. This warm atmosphere is an aspect of our bank that we are extremely proud of. When most of our customers deal with us for years, even generations, we must be doing something right."

National City Bank has a commitment to the Dayton area and its businesses. "If Dayton is strong, our businesses will be strong. Naturally our bank will be successful," added Schantz. Each year hundreds of bank employees take leadership roles in community projects, volunteering to serve on boards and working for other worthy causes. "People want to do business with businesses that help the community," says Schantz. "I think that says something special about the Dayton area."

With its unique design, National City Center illuminates the heart of Downtown Dayton.

ACMG, INC.

When ACMG introduced ACMG Benefits Administrators and added third-party administration (TPA) services to its long list of group-benefit-related services, it already had a leg up on its TPA competition. "ACMG has already established an excellent track record in HMO and PPO management," says Paul W. McVay, president, "which, as risk managers, includes claims adjudication as well as in-depth analysis of detailed utilization and cost reports. The transition to being a TPA gave us the opportunity to respond more thoroughly to the more demanding needs of self-insured employers for the same type of detailed reports we provide to our HMO and PPO clients." Lance D. Marshall, vice president-client relations, adds, "By maintaining our own staff of computer programmers and systems analysts, we can easily customize reports specific to the employer's needs."

TPAs process and administer claims for self-insured organizations that pay for health claims directly instead of purchasing conventional insurance. By the end of 1995 industry experts had predicted more than 70 percent of all employers would be self-insured for at least some of their group benefits. According to Marshall, this represented an opportunity for ACMG.

"The experience our managers have working in managed care can be invaluable to our TPA clients," he says. Managed care techniques including utilization review, preadmission certification, and prior approval for certain procedures were first introduced in the early 1970s with the development of HMOs. These procedures were among the forerunners of cost containment.

"There are certain procedures anticipated for certain diagnoses," McVay explains. "If the procedures aren't reasonable, based on protocol or accepted medical criteria as practiced, our computer system is programmed to catch this." ACMG's management information system operates on a large mainframe computer for claims processing and management statistical reporting. At least once a quarter (and sometimes monthly based on the need to do so), ACMG representatives meet with each of its clients to review comprehensive reports about the client's benefit program. One such report identifies the cost for each element of the client's benefit plan. ACMG helps the client determine whether actual costs are in line with projected costs. ACMG can track these costs by employee groupings such as salary and hourly, geographical locations, and others.

Because ACMG's managed health care experience is in administering HMO and PPO plans, its managers are trained to make informed decisions about utilization and reimbursement. "To continue to grow as a company, you have to make sure you interpret the client's benefit plan correctly and help ensure that cost-effective care is being rendered. Providing accurate and timely claims processing as well as access to the reporting function clients require for plan administration are paramount elements in remaining competitive in the TPA industry," Marshal says.

ACMG, Inc., employs nearly 140 professional and support personnel and maintains offices in Miamisburg, Ohio; Lexington and Frankfort, Kentucky; and Spartanburg and Columbia, South Carolina.

ACMG group-benefit managers, who have an average of 15 years' experience in managed health care, review comprehensive reports produced from the company's mainframe computer system for claims processing and management statistical reporting.

JETSTREAM INTERNATIONAL AIRLINES, INC.

Jetstream International flies Embraer-120 aircraft that are pressurized, comfortable, and fast. Jetstream is a wholly owned subsidiary of USAir Group, Inc.

In the early years of airline deregulation, Jetstream International Airlines started as a "ma and pa" operation in Latrobe, Pennsylvania, to re-establish nonstop service to major cities.

Today Jetstream International, now a wholly owned subsidiary of USAir Group, Inc., has a similar goal as a regional carrier in Dayton: to be a link between outlying areas and major cities by feeding jet traffic to USAir mainliners.

Jetstream International, also known as USAir Express, serves 30 cities and nine states—Ohio, Pennsylvania, Illinois, Tennessee, Kentucky, Indiana, Wisconsin, New York, and Michigan—plus Toronto in Ontario, Canada, feeding traffic to USAir hubs in Pittsburgh and Indianapolis. "Each day the company schedules 42 flights into and out of Dayton," says Richard Pfennig, Jetstream's president.

Jetstream relocated its corporate headquarters to Dayton in 1987 after affiliating itself with Piedmont airlines in 1985. By November 1987 USAir had acquired Piedmont, and Jetstream became a wholly owned subsidiary of USAir Group in 1988.

Pfennig says as early as 1967 USAir (then Allegheny Airlines) pioneered the concept of affiliated regional airlines by replacing flights in short-haul markets with frequent flights by regional airlines. USAir express flights are timed for convenient travel in the local markets and for easy connecting with USAir flights at hub airports. "We gather people from outlying areas like Evansville, South Bend, or Toledo," he says. It's cost effective for us as a regional carrier to fly to these cities."

The company currently operates nine Embraer-120, 30-passenger aircraft, and 24 Jetstream-31, 19-passenger aircraft. Both airplane types are pressurized, offer passenger comforts, and have the needed speed and range to serve Jetstream's route system, which now extends from Chicago in the west to Philadelphia in the east. Jetstream is well into the planning process, according to Pfennig, to replace these 33 aircraft with the newest, fastest, and most sophisticated cabin class turboprops on the market.

Although Jetstream has adopted USAir's red and blue corporate colors, Pfennig says that Jetstream, like the two other USAir subsidiaries, operates autonomously from USAir. "As an autonomous regional carrier, we can capitalize on the local market," he says. "It allows us to watch the markets in the Dayton area and work with the local chamber of commerce to get to know where people are going."

These grass roots marketing efforts let Jetstream tailor flights and connections to quickly meet the demands of the Dayton community. If there's a seasonal demand for aircraft or the need to increase departures to Indianapolis, Indiana, for example, Pfennig says Jetstream could make a schedule change in as few as 30 days.

"It's our response to the marketplace that makes the difference," he says. "Being a regional carrier, we keep the emphasis on Dayton. We want to see the local economy grow, and we want to make sure Dayton has air service to support that growth."

Instead of eliminating aircraft and departures during a recent economic downturn, Jetstream found ways to strengthen the Dayton market by establishing new departures to alternate cities that had more of a demand. "We saw an opportunity," Pfennig says. "Instead of downsizing, we entered into an expansion program in other areas."

Jetstream has plans to relocate its corporate headquarters to Dayton International Airport. "This will consolidate our flight operations, customer service, finance, accounting, training, and maintenance departments into one facility," says Pfennig. This consolidation will allow Jetstream to operate more efficiently at a lower cost.

The flight operations division establishes policies and procedures for flight control, "the heartbeat and the traffic cops for the airline," Pfennig says. Flight control is the dispatch and command control center responsible for monitoring and controlling the movement of all aircraft in Jetstream's system—to the tune of 260 departures a day.

"Our staff in flight control know the weather, release planes to fly, and are aware of any mechanical difficulties with an aircraft," Pfennig explains. "They can call on resources to respond to any type of need—from aircraft maintenance to a passenger who wants help with a wheelchair."

When people think of Jetstream, they think of USAir—at least that's the concept Pfennig tries to sell to passengers.

"We are the same as USAir Express in other cities," he says. "Like the other regional carriers in the USAir Group, we have the same product, just different equipment and a different history. Our geographic area dictates the type of equipment we fly, but the service levels on USAir Express—bags, ticket purchases, and frequent flyer benefits—are the same you would find on the mainline. Our relationship with USAir provides stability."

Pfennig says Jetstream International, Inc., remains competitive because it has aligned itself with a major airline. In fact, USAir and British Airways are now well underway toward the development of an alliance that will result in a powerful global air transportation network. Passenegers will be able to travel from Dayton to Delhi receiving the same seamless level of service. This will be the trend in the airline industry during the 1990s, and Jetstream International will play a major role in providing this fine service to the city of Dayton.

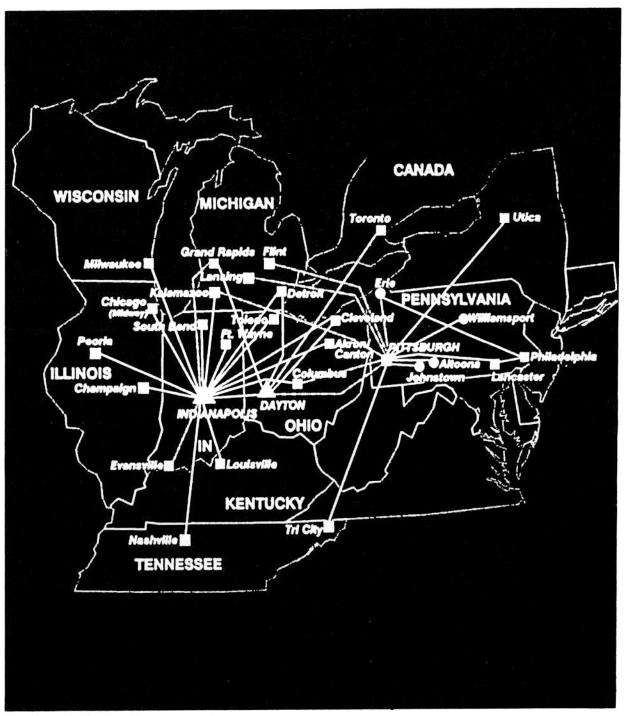

Jetstream International, also known as USAir Express, serves 22 cities and eight states.

THE IAMS COMPANY

Believe it or not, a mink—not a dog—inspired Paul Iams to create the first nutritionally complete premium dog food. Paul Iams was a self-taught animal nutritionist who had developed a food supplement for mink in the early 1950s. During a 1954 visit to a mink ranch where his supplement was being used, Iams observed the glossy coats and vitality of the dogs living there. After learning the dogs were eating the same food as the minks, he launched an intensive study of carnivore nutrition.

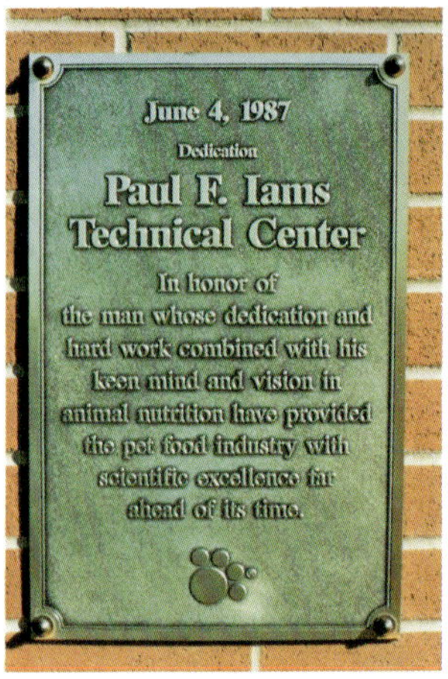

The Iams Company proudly displays this plaque at the entrance of the Paul F. Iams Technical Center and Animal Care Facility.

Iams found that dogs flourish on meat—not vegetable—protein. Dogs also need quality animal fat for energy and a healthy skin and coat, carbohydrates for quick energy, fiber for proper digestion, and vitamins and minerals to help resist disease and build healthy teeth, bones, and hair.

Armed with these findings, Iams developed a new and better dog food, forever changing the way people think about feeding their pets. "People became more interested in their own health and then expanded this interest to the health of their pets," says Clay Mathile, chairman and chief executive officer of the Iams Company. By the 1980s sales were exploding; Iams has recorded double-digit growth every year since.

Iams Pet Foods are made with the most digestible form of proteins from the highest quality ingredients. According to Mathile, a dog or cat eating Iams pet food will show marked improvement in just a few months: a soft coat, bright eyes, good muscle tone, good demeanor and attentiveness. Eukanuba Dog Food is The Iams Company premium line and is made with quality chicken meat proteins and is highly nutritious and efficient.

Iams quality food is sold by pet professionals—pet stores, veterinarians, and breeders—not through the grocery stores. "We feel our food is best sold by informed pet professionals who can explain the benefits," Mathile says. The benefits are important, since pound-for-pound Iams foods cost a little more than grocery store brands.

"But while a 40-pound dog may need to eat more than 6 cups of grocery dog food a day to get the nutrition his body needs, only about half that amount of Iams is required for complete and balanced nutrition. And because you're feeding less, it actually costs only pennies more a day to feed your pet the very best food on the market," says Mathile.

To help retailers and distributors promote the products, Iams provides national and local advertising, attractive in-store displays and promotions, informational brochures, a highly trained sales staff, and seminars on canine and feline nutrition.

The Iams Company manufactures a complete line of premium quality dog and cat foods. "When we introduce a food, it is the very best," Mathile says. "We've turned down marketing products that could have been big sellers because we felt the quality just wasn't up to our standards."

For example, the company refused to introduce a canned cat food in the 1980s, but rather waited until 1991 when scientific research allowed them to roll out a nutritious, high-quality canned cat food that tastes great. "No garlic or additives to mask the lack of good nutrition," says Mathile.

In the 1990s, the Iams Company plans to further enhance product quality, develop new products in niche markets, and expand sales abroad, Mathile says. The company employs over 600 people at its headquarters and four pet food production plants in Lewisburg, Ohio; Aurora, Nebraska; North Sioux City, South Dakota; and Henderson, North Carolina.

Eukanuba is the Iams Company premium line of dog food and is made with only the highest quality ingredients for optimal nutrition.

CHAPEL ELECTRIC COMPANY

When Fred Setzer, Sr., bought Chapel Electric in 1946, the company had just gone bankrupt.

Instead of renaming the bankrupt company Setzer Electric, he continued with the Chapel Electric name, running the business from his home on Kenmore Avenue in Belmont. Setzer had a high school education, a few years of experience as an electrician with Dayton Power & Light and McCall Publishing Corporation—and no money.

"He did no strategic planning, no marketing, and had no computerized estimating systems," says Fred Setzer, Jr., of his father. "The only thing he knew was hard work, long hours, and a belief in what he was doing."

That belief has made Chapel Electric one of Dayton's premier electrical contractors. Synonymous with "the big work" in the Miami Valley, Chapel's client project list includes such notable projects as 10 Wilmington Place, the Arcade Center, City of Dayton Wastewater Treatment Plant, Dayton's hospitals and medical centers, Eastman Kodak, Electronic Data Systems, the Kettering Recreation Complex, Mead Corporation, Mead Data Central, NCR Corporation, and the Veterans Administration Medical Center, to name a few.

For more than 45 years Chapel Electric has installed electrical systems for commercial, industrial, institutional facilities, and renovation projects, offering design/build capabilities as well as traditional hard-bid proposals. The service department is equipped to provide seven-day, round-the-clock response for emergencies, such as high-voltage equipment failures and outages resulting from tornadoes or floods, as well as general repairs, testing, and preventative maintenance.

Fred Setzer, Jr., president of Chapel Electric Company.

"We're aggressive," says Setzer. "We do 'fast-track' jobs. We don't take a back seat. If we say we're going to do something, we do it. That's where we shine."

Chapel Electric is known for its ability to plan a project by assigning a project manager, who spends time with the estimating and purchasing teams as well as the field supervision to make sure each project is laid out and then performed properly, on time, and within budget.

"Dad always took care of the customer, and he did it by having good people around him," Setzer says. His father's first two employees stayed with the company for more than 40 years and then retired. "He gave people responsibility and left them alone to do the job. He always looked for people with a drive to succeed and the desire to do more than just what was expected."

But Setzer's father also recognized the importance of team building, even in the early years. "Computers and communication systems are attainable by anyone," says Fred Setzer, Jr. "What's different about us? Our teams really function as teams to meet the client's requirements."

For more than 45 years Chapel Electric has installed electrical systems for commercial, industrial, institutional facilities, and renovation projects.

McCauley Accessory Division

The McCauley family of aircraft propellers.

Nearly 100 years ago the Wright Brothers made Dayton famous as the birthplace of aviation. Dayton inventor Ernest G. McCauley advanced American aviation with his innovative propeller designs 30 years later. Today the company he founded is still "Turning Power into Flight" with some of the most sophisticated propeller designs in the world.

Located at the Dayton International Airport, McCauley (officially known as McCauley Accessory Division) is the world's largest manufacturer of light aircraft propellers and propeller accessories. The company also manufactures turbine propellers for the regional airliner market. Cessna, the world's largest builder of general aviation aircraft, acquired McCauley in 1960, and it became a division of the company a year later. Cessna is owned by Textron, Inc.

In the early 1930s the company's founder was working at Wright-Patterson Air Force Base in the propeller division. A gifted inventor, he developed several unique controllable propeller designs, including the first hydraulic propeller. In 1935 he sold the patent for that design, among others, to finance his own enterprise, the McCauley Industrial Aviation Corporation.

During World War II the company produced more than 20,000 solid-steel propellers for the armed forces, many of which are still in service today on agricultural aircraft. After the war McCauley turned its attention to the personal and business aircraft market. Wooden propellers had almost exclusively been used on these planes before the war. McCauley changed that with the development of the Met-L-Prop, a single-piece propeller of lightweight aluminum.

By 1954 McCauley was also manufacturing the Met-L-Matic, a constant-speed, variable-blade-angle, metal propeller designed for higher-performance aircraft. McCauley's Feth-R-Matic series of constant-speed, full-feathering propellers was designed for twin-engine aircraft. In 1965 the company introduced three-blade configurations, and in 1979 began producing three-blade propellers for the latest turbine engines. By 1980 McCauley had begun producing highly advanced, four-blade "turbo-props."

Today propellers continue to be the cornerstone of McCauley's business. As Cessna's Accessories Division, the company manufactures propellers and related components, such as governors, electrical de-ice systems, and spinners. About 10 percent of the company's business is in machining operations for Cessna and others, such as the robotics industry.

All McCauley design, manufacturing, and marketing operations take place at the company's state-of-the-art,

McCauley's modern production facilities for the production of aircraft propellers.

160,000-square-foot facility at Dayton International Airport. Built in 1978, this facility includes a plant (for machining, plating, assembly, and painting operations), offices, engineering test laboratories, and a 7,000-square-foot hangar that can house three or more aircraft at once. McCauley has produced more than 340,000 propellers since starting business.

When developing a new propeller, McCauley works closely with the engine manufacturer as well as the airframer. The company prides itself on maintaining a strict confidentiality with each of its airframe customers—many of whom compete with each other.

In the early 1980s Cessna, Beech, and other airframers reduced production on all piston-engine aircraft. In fact, sales of general-aviation aircraft, which includes private, business-class, and small commuter-class planes, had been dwindling for years. By 1986 Cessna was out of the piston driven aircraft business altogether and McCauley was forced to downsize.

Since then the company has concentrated on developing products for regional commuter aircraft, presenting the market with a large number of newly designed propellers. In 1987 the company's propellers became standard equipment on the Fairchild Metro III, a 19-passenger, turbine commuter aircraft. By the end of that year, the company had formed a worldwide distribution system to sell its products and enlarge its entry into the turbine aircraft market.

In addition to creating propellers for new aircraft, McCauley has developed a new line of propellers called the "Black Mac." These propellers improve the efficiency of aircraft and help reduce noise. Many of these propellers are sold as replacements on older aircraft.

Production in the 1940s.

The company also supplies service centers throughout the world for overhaul and repair through its two distributors: Aviall's worldwide center in Dallas, Texas, and Cessna SPC in Wichita, Kansas, which maintains over 200 outlets. Deliveries from these distribution centers are made 24 hours a day, and any aircraft on the ground gets priority treatment.

In 1988 McCauley developed the first of its five-bladed propellers for the unique, all composite Beech Starship. The following year the company started a program with British Aerospace to design and develop a large, 114-inch, five-bladed propeller for the new, 29-passenger Jetstream 41, a twin-engine, regional commuter aircraft. First production propellers were shipped in 1992. This design is one of the "Black Mac" series and has unique, scimitar-shaped blades.

McCauley's newest development is the QZP (Quiet Zone Propeller) and is the forerunner of a new family of propellers McCauley is developing to meet increasingly strict aircraft noise limits in the U.S. In Europe even stricter noise limits are affecting operators of propeller-driven aircraft, which gives McCauley and its new family of QZPs an edge in overseas markets.

McCauley is concentrating its comeback from the stagnant market of the early 1980s with new efficient designs, a history of quality products and services, and a group of employees that puts quality first.

McCauley's new facility.

CITIZENS FEDERAL BANK

Citizens Federal, then a savings and loan association, opened its doors for the first time at East Third Street on August 6, 1934, at 8 a.m. sharp. A few minutes later Carl Himes of Tischer Hardware walked in, opened an account, and Citizens Federal was in business.

It was the fourth year of the Great Depression, and 10 million people remained unemployed. Opening a savings and loan—with a dedication to thrift and home ownership—was something of an act of faith. However, Citizens Federal was and has continued to be a survivor for two reasons—its conservative posture and its innovations in customer service. In 1942 the association staffed the circus-style Victory Bond Wagon in downtown Dayton to sell war bonds; customers received their bonds within minutes of making the purchase. After the war Citizens Federal granted the first GI Bill mortgage loan in Ohio. Thousands of similar loans followed.

In the 1950s Citizens Federal quickly opened branches in the suburbs as customers moved away from urban areas. The association became one of the first S&Ls with an on-line computer system in the 1960s.

In 1971 the association established Dayton Financial Services to acquire land for developing single-family residential housing. Since then, prestigious developments such as Pebble Creek, Deerwood Estates, Woodland Greens, McCray Farms, Greenleaf Village, and Timberwind have brought in tax dollars and greatly enhanced their surrounding communities.

Jerry L. Kirby, chairman of the board and president of Citizens Federal. Courtesy, Citizens Federal

In an industry faced with acquisitions and mergers prompted by the S&L crisis in the 1980s and the resulting Financial Institutions Reform, Recovery and Enforcement Act (FIRREA), created to strengthen the entire financial industry, Citizens Federal has emerged an even safer, more viable "hometown"financial institution. In 1991 Citizens Federal became a federal stock savings bank with a new name—Citizens Federal Bank, F.S.B.—owned by a holding company, CitFed Bancorp, Inc. Citizens Federal enjoys the status of being the only remaining bank to be locally owned and locally headquartered.

"The conversion gave us a means of attracting new capital into the association to support residential and other mortgage lending in the communities we serve," says Jerry L. Kirby, Citizens Federal board chairman and president. "Our depositors were the first to have the opportunity to become charter stockholders in the only major financial institution with corporate headquarters in Dayton, Ohio."

Citizens Federal is the primary tenant in the Citizens Federal Centre, a 19-story office building downtown. Citizens Federal maintains 21 branch offices in the greater Dayton area and plans to expand even further throughout the area in the1990s. Diana L. Schoenberger, vice president and director of marketing communications, says Citizens Federal is proud to have stayed headquartered locally, and that bank employees—especially senior officers, most of whom grew up in the community—have both a personal and professional interest in making Dayton grow and thrive.

"CitFed Mortgage, a wholly owned subsidiary of Citizens Federal, is one of the top lenders in the city and state, servicing more than $3.4 billion in mortgage loans annually,"says Schoenberger. "The bank, through CitFed Mortgage, is committed to residential lending and helping individuals in the community realize their dream of owning a home."

Over the years, Citizens Federal has offered creative products that give more opportunities for home ownership. Citizens Federal and CitFed Mortgage have participated in the Ohio Housing Finance Agency First-Time Homebuyers Program, special set-asides for single parents and the physically impaired, and various ongoing City of Dayton programs such as purchase rehab loans. Currently, more than 70 percent of all Citizens Federal loans are mortgage loans. The American Dream Loan, primarily designed for first-time homebuyers, waives points and closing costs to make home ownership more attainable.

"We have a low loan-delinquency ratio because we maintain high standards of underwriting," says Kirby. "This is an example of our continuing dedication to safe and sound management practices that back-up the investments of our depositors."

Education is a concern both internally and externally at Citizens Federal. The bank offers its employees a wide variety of continuing-education courses, including leadership and currency control. For banking-related courses, Citizens Federal works with the national Institute of Financial Education and Sinclair Community College, which awards degrees based on completion of an institute-approved curriculum.

Outside the bank, many Citizens Federal employees are active in adult literacy programs and in K-12 education in the Dayton community. In 1991 Citizens Federal began co-sponsoring Great Expectations, a community program to raise awareness about education and to support the development of creative and innovative educational programs. "We have a real interest in education—not only in educating our own employees—but in promoting and enhancing education in the community as a whole," says Schoenberger.

Corporate headquarters is located at One Citizens Federal Centre in the heart of downtown Dayton. Citizens Federal has 21 offices in Greater Dayton. Courtesy, Citizens Federal

Citizens Federal's commitment toward providing a high level of individual, personal service has been strengthened over the years. Outside consultants regularly conduct focus groups, interviewing customers and non-customers about banking products and services, so that Citizens Federal can continue improving its quality. "One of the most valuable things we can offer customers is access to professionals—accountants and attorneys for estate planning, and other experts specializing in trusts, IRAs and Keogh accounts, VA and FHA mortgage loans, construction loans, commercial lending, estate planning, student loans, and other areas of interest to the community," says Schoenberger.

According to Kirby, the commitment to customer service has always remained the major force behind Citizens Federal. "In the future financial world, personal service will become even more important than it is today," he says. "If one of the keys to success for a financial institution is the quality of service it offers to customers, Citizens Federal, with over a half century of innovations in customer service, will remain one of the leaders in the industry."

BANK ONE, DAYTON, NA

Bank One, Dayton headquarters—at the heart of downtown, in the Kettering Tower.

A good leader doesn't do all the talking. A good leader must be a good listener. Bank One, Dayton, the city's first and largest bank, does a lot of listening—listening that lets Bank One continue improving its programs, products, and services to better serve the community, says Donald H. Kasle, chairman and chief executive officer. "If we're going to offer products and services that are important to the community, then we have to be very community focused," he says.

Bank One's Miami Valley focus is strong. In 1992 Bank One staff interviewed nearly 1,000 organizations and individuals in the Dayton area about their banking needs and concerns. These interviews are part of the bank's annual ascertainment program, a formal system of listening, reviewing, evaluating, and responding with new products, programs, and services. In addition to its formal listening program, Bank One regularly surveys customers and noncustomers and conducts focus groups to find out how banking needs are changing.

"We're out there daily, listening to what customers need," Kasle says. For example, Sunday hours were established as a result of community input. Bank One is currently the only Dayton bank to have full-service Sunday hours.

Based on information received from citizens on the bank's community advisory council, many branches now have at least one employee trained in "signing" to service the banking needs of the more than 40,000 hearing-impaired people in the Miami Valley.

In addition, Bank One sponsors Growing Dayton, a program designed for community and neighborhood leaders, realtors, business people, clergy, and others to learn about the bank's products and services for family and neighborhood improvements. Growing Dayton programs are held in the various branches, tailored to address the financial needs and interests unique to each neighborhood.

Bank One offers private label credit cards at more than 10,000 retail locations nationwide. Customers shopping for furniture, for example, can apply for a store credit card, with credit issued and services provided through Bank One in Dayton. Card approvals take only a few minutes.

The bank has the area's oldest and largest trust division. It was also the first Miami Valley bank to establish private banking services, designed for the busy individual with special, often complicated, personal financial needs.

Bank One created the purchase rehabilitation program to serve customers who said they wanted to purchase a "fix-up" home—and still have funds to restore it. The program allows qualified persons to borrow up to 80 percent of the appraisal value of the restored home. Once the rehabilitation is complete, Bank One closes with a 15- or 30-year mortgage on the home. The bank also provides the purchase rehab loan program as part of its participation in the city's Neighborhood Lending Partnership program.

"It all came about because someone was listening when the remarks were made," Kasle says. The Dayton Neighborhood Lending Partnership is a public/private partnership created to stimulate investment and to revitalize

Creative, affordable mortgage loan products help more people realize their dreams of home ownership.

Dayton's neighborhoods. In 1988 Bank One was the first area bank to step forward in response to the mayor's plea for help in meeting the housing needs of the community. Three entities now work closely to meet housing challenges in the city: the City of Dayton, the Ohio Housing Finance Agency, and several local lenders. In 1990 the program was awarded the Housing Rehabilitation Achievement Award from the U.S. Department of Housing and Urban Development and the National Association of Housing and Redevelopment Officials.

Listening is always the first step in improving the quality of any program, service, or process at Bank One. "Quality is part of everyone's job description," says Margaret C. Kerns, vice president and chief service quality and marketing officer. "We stress quality from two points of view: our banking customers and our 'internal customers'—our co-workers."

If quality in any area of the bank needs improvement, Bank One staff—formally trained in problem solving procedures—form quality improvement teams to establish the steps needed to improve the process or service.

For example, one team was formed to improve the accuracy of customers' monthly statements. After studying the problem, the quality improvement team decided to centralize the statement and complaint system, redesign tracking forms to ensure timely follow-up with the customer, change certain procedures at the branch level, and improve communication between the bank and its regional processing center, which produces the monthly statements.

"A standard was set, and we've seen a significant improvement," Kerns says. "We are meeting quarterly to ensure that it doesn't backslide."

Dozens of Bank One employees volunteer to learn American Sign Language to better communicate with hearing-impaired customers.

Kasle says Bank One's profitability has allowed it to invest time, money, and resources back into the community. For example, Bank One staff participate on and host the Dayton Board of Education's Business Advisory Council, a forum that brings business leaders together for advice, counsel, and input to improve the quality of Dayton schools. Moreover, bank employees and managers are actively involved in almost every community organization in the area, including the United Way, Arts Dayton, the Dayton Black Cultural Festival, the Boy Scouts, and many others. Employees may even take time during the workday to serve on committees and boards of the various organizations. "There's just a culture here that suggests part of your responsibility is to be involved in the community," Kasle explains.

Perhaps the most important thing that Bank One offers is support to the community, customers, and shareholders in an era when banking is changing dramatically. "There's no single product or service that's evolutionary," Kasle states. "They're all revolutionary. It's extremely difficult to do anything but be nimble and have a culture that responds quickly to changes in the marketplace. But the fact that we've done business for 179 years suggests strongly that we're going to be here for the next 179 years."

Bank One, Dayton, with assets of nearly $3 billion, is one of the largest affiliates of BANC ONE CORPORATION, which is headquartered in Columbus, Ohio.

Growing Dayton neighborhood events bring together community activists with Bank One managers.

THOMPSON, HINE AND FLORY

Thompson, Hine and Flory may be a relatively new name in Dayton, but its roots can be traced back to 1936, and its lawyers are well known to Daytonians—some have been practicing in the area for more than 40 years.

Thompson, Hine and Flory, with other major Ohio offices in Cincinnati, Cleveland, and Columbus, opened a Dayton office in October 1989. At that time 80 lawyers from Smith & Schnacke, founded in Dayton in 1936, joined the firm. With nearly 350 lawyers, Thompson, Hine and Flory is among the nation's largest law firms and has the largest number of lawyers of any firm in Ohio. The firm's other offices include operations in Washington, D.C., Brussels, and Florida.

Thompson, Hine and Flory is the largest law firm in Ohio.

"Usually when people think of a large law firm, they think 'no access,'" says Joseph M. Rigot, partner-in- charge of the Dayton office. "But the larger the office, the better you can organize, and the better access you can give your clients. We are obsessive about being accessible."

Because Thompson, Hine and Flory lawyers practice in 20 traditional and emerging disciplines—from business and commercial litigation to intellectual property and environmental law— lawyers can call upon their colleagues in other offices as needed; and that means clients are better served. "Every one of our lawyers has a focus, and we think that in the long run, this is cost-effective," Rigot says.

Traditionally, many clients have dealt with one lawyer for all of their needs. However, Rigot says, "a lawyer is a lawyer is a lawyer" isn't true anymore. A client may come to the firm needing assistance in one area, but needs may cross over into other areas. The lead lawyer assures that those other needs are met by having lawyers in those areas focus on them.

"It's a good way to practice law, and clients are starting to prefer this approach," he says. "Often clients don't realize that they need the expertise of several different attorneys to solve their legal problems."

The firm's long-term association with The Mead Corporation and other prominent Dayton companies often influenced lawyers at Thompson, Hine and Flory to develop depth in a variety of practice areas in order to address the needs of those clients. Lawyers at the firm pride themselves on anticipating client needs and adding skills before there is a demand. "For example, we got into environmental law long before many other firms because we perceived it was a real coming need," explains Rigot.

The firm's lawyers continue to take a leadership role in community activities. Thompson, Hine and Flory helped establish the Miami Valley Research Foundation as well as the Arts Center Foundation, which provided assistance to fund the rehabilitation of the Victoria Theatre in the late 1980s. The firm's lawyers often provide pro bono legal services to community groups and serve on their boards of directors.

Says Rigot, "We're here to serve the Dayton community in any way we can."

DAYTON RELIABLE TOOL & MANUFACTURING COMPANY

It all began because someone forgot the "church key." Cans of soda and beer sat—unopened—soaking up the sun at a family picnic in 1959. Frustrated (and thirsty), Ermal (Ernie) C. Fraze tried to open a can of his favorite beverage on a car bumper and thought, "There must be a better way."

Fraze went on to invent the easy-open end, better known as the "pop top," making it possible to open cans of beer, soda, ham, herring—even tennis balls—with the flick of a thumb.

The key to Fraze's invention? Instead of being a separate piece, the "rivet" attaching the tab is formed from the parent metal of the plain end of the can end itself. The result is an attachment with a lot of strength and only the appearance of a rivet.

In spite of the pop top's convenience, companies that manufactured cans were reluctant to promote the easy-open end because it increased manufacturing costs. (Even Fraze himself predicted that the "fad" would last only one or two years.) However, the consumer drove the market, and today, the pop top is a way of life. Worldwide, Fraze's invention has created more than a half-million jobs over the years; more than $7 billion has been invested in the building of plants, aluminum-rolling mills, and manufacturing facilities for the expansion of can companies.

Fraze was always the driving force behind improvements to the pop top, which continues to evolve. Today, Dayton Reliable Tool applies the latest technology and makes innovations in the manufacturing of plain ends, E-Z open ends, and other related products for the packaging industry around the globe.

One of the many styles of conversion press systems for easy-open ends built by DRT.

Ernie Fraze, company founder and distinguished inventor.

One of the largest, most modern, high-precision machining facilities in the world, Dayton Reliable Tool employs 530 people and prides itself as a "young" company (the average age of its employees is 34). Its five Dayton plants produce the precision presses that can companies use for turning out a whopping 185 billion easy-open ends a year.

Driving the presses are sophisticated electronics and software, all developed at Dayton Reliable Tool & Mfg. Co. Standing 13 feet tall, 12 feet wide, and weighing 36 tons, the average press costs one million dollars and takes up to a year to design and manufacture. Presses are custom-designed (based on the size, shape, and type of can end to be produced) and then tested and shipped, some ready to manufacture as many as 1,800 or more easy-open ends a minute.

On the horizon are even more- sophisticated systems for producing easy-open ends and new methods for reducing the amount of material required. With material accounting for about 80 percent of the product cost, a reduction of material which saves a few pennies per thousand can save millions of dollars."

The busy DRT assembly floor.

CHEMINEER, INC.

Chemical companies, paper plants, breweries, and other fluids industries bet their production lines on the reliability of Chemineer mixers and agitators.

These companies know that front-end downtime could shut down hundreds of their other plant operations and potentially result in losses of $1 million to $2 million a week or more.

Chemineer's research and development facility includes a complete customer test lab designed to model the customer's full-scale installation.

"That's why we invest a lot of time and money into the design and manufacture of our products," says John G. Fenic, Chemineer's president. "If we can prove the reliability of our equipment to a customer, we've pretty much proven the value."

Chemineer is recognized nationally and internationally for designing and manufacturing standard and custom-designed agitators and mixers; equipment ranges in size from small mixers with a 1-gallon capacity and 10-inch shaft to large agitators with a 1-million-gallon capacity and a 50-foot shaft. Chemineer's static mixers, which provide continuous in-line mixing and processing of pumped fluids, have no moving parts and require no external power or regular maintenance. Applications of Chemineer equipment include everything from sophisticated polymerization and fermentation processes to water and wastewater treatment to simple storage operations.

"We provide answers to mixing problems," Fenic declares. Chemineer's agitation equipment may be used to create a chemical reaction in a vessel or disperse a gas into a fluid. Other applications may be in mixing penicillin batches, paint, or oil. Working closely with the customer, Chemineer recently designed, manufactured, and installed 24 of the largest and most powerful mixers ever produced—the shafts for these 1,000-horsepower mixers are 60 feet long, Fenic says.

The company's ChemScale® design procedure helps engineers select the best agitator design that economically accomplishes a desired result. Fluid viscosity, reactions required, and a combination of other variables determine how the agitator should be designed, including the type, number, and size of impellers, mixing levels, tank size, and horsepower, Fenic explains.

In its research and development (R&D) facility, Chemineer tests its designs by producing scaled-down models before manufacturing full-scale models. The R&D facility also has a laboratory that customers can use to test new applications or reevaluate old processes.

"We will change factors in the lab to find out what works best, such as a different impeller or new fluid level in the tank," Fenic says. "Once we get the right result in the lab, we can scale up and take it to the full plant level."

Chemineer prides itself on involving customers in the design, development, testing, and production of its mixing solutions. "We work with our customers—not just provide equipment," states Fenic.

Founded in 1952, Chemineer employs more than 330 people in its headquarters and manufacturing plant in Dayton and at its manufacturing facilities in North Andover, Massachusetts, and Derby, England.

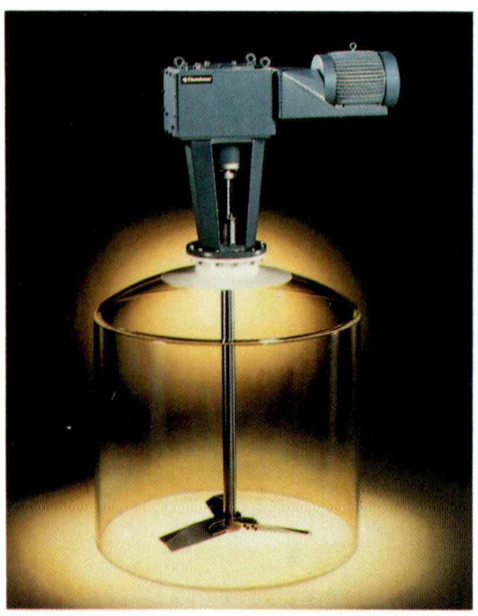

HT turbine agitators are installed worldwide in a broad range of applications, from simple storage tanks to sophisticated polymerization and fermentation processes.

MICAH SYSTEMS, INC.

Today's corporate decision-makers face a multitude of challenges in their struggle to remain competitive. They must be willing to embrace the many technological changes required to deal with the increasing complexity of modern organizations. Of these changes, information management is among the most pervasive. The combination of computers, materials, information, and enterprise management affects the way people live and do business, and the successful balance of these entities determines an organization's ability to survive and continually improve in order to thrive in the global arena.

MICAH Systems, Inc., was founded in 1983 upon this premise, when chief executive officer Doug Comstock recognized the need for efficient database design and management within the Air Force Materiel Command (AFMC). The AFMC was in the beginning stages of a massive program to modernize its logistics systems, and MICAH provided the Information Engineering (IE) methodology that was used as the basis for several of the system modernizations. This methodology was subsequently adopted as an AFMC standard.

As a systems integrator MICAH applies its IE methodology across the full spectrum of information systems lifecycle disciplines, including enterprise engineering, information systems design, software engineering, data administration, training, facilities management, system maintenance, and program management support.

MICAH recognizes data as an enterprise's most vital resource and realizes that the viability of an enterprise is determined by its ability to properly identify, store, and effectively utilize data. MICAH's IE-based development approach ensures the integration of a firm's database with the critical business applications that enable it to use its data to achieve its business goals.

Doug Comstock, founder and chief executive officer (seated), and George Duffy, president.

MICAH has more than ten years experience providing expertise in process and data modeling. MICAH has extensive experience in applying process re-engineering, facilitating Joint Applications Design (JAD) and Rapid Application Development (RAD) sessions, and applying CASE technology.

MICAH is currently providing IE services to several organizations, including the Joint Logistics Systems Center, the Defense Logistics Agency, the Defense Information Technology Systems Office, and the Air Force Materiel Command in Ohio; the Tennessee Valley Authority and Oak Ridge National Laboratory in Tennessee; and the Naval Surface Warfare Center in Virginia.

MICAH has established a solid reputation based on a commitment to technical excellence and fair business practices. Headquartered in Fairborn, the firm employs more than 80 people, with additional offices in Knoxville, Tennessee and Summersville, West Virginia.

A MICAH facilitator brings together information engineers and functional experts to create an Enterprise Model.

GENERAL MOTORS CORPORATION

Innovation:

It sparked Charles F. Kettering and his good friend Colonel Edward A. Deeds to collaborate in Deeds' barn on a more practical auto ignition. "Boss" Kettering's single-spark ignition system became standard equipment for the 1910-model Cadillac.

It caused "Boss Kett" and the Colonel to form the Dayton Engineering Laboratories Company—Delco—to manufacture this equipment.

And by 1912 it resulted in Kettering's greatest contribution—the self-starter—which revolutionized the operation of the automobile.

After several years, United Motors acquired Delco; in 1918 United joined General Motors. "It was because of Delco that General Motors came to Dayton," says F.M. McCurdy, GM's director of public affairs in Dayton. "And today GM's Dayton operations continue to be known for their innovation."

Besides the self-starter, Delco's cofounder, Kettering, invented quick-drying paint and freon, a refrigerant. "In Dayton, GM invented the disc brake, advanced the development of suspension systems, and later developed anti-lock brake systems," McCurdy says.

Workers at the North American Truck Platform Moraine Assembly Plant put the finishing touches on one of 850 sport utility vehicles assembled at the plant each day.

The first auto manufacturer to devise a Pollution Control Valve (PCV) in the mid-1970s, GM effectively limited the amount of unburned hydrocarbons that escaped from engines with a carburetor. "A 50-cent valve got rid of 90 percent of the pollution created," McCurdy says. This technology was later shared with Chrysler Corporation and Ford Motor Company.

In the late 1980s GM developed the computer-controlled ride (CCR), a suspension system allowing smoother, more comfortable traveling because it compensated for bumps in the road.

Dayton's GM operations are also credited with creating the variable-displacement air-conditioning compressor, which alternates the load on the compressor based on cooling demands. "It allows you to get more or less cooling and do it without using as much gas," McCurdy explains. "It is a more efficient use of energy."

GM is one of the biggest economic engines in town, providing employment to nearly 20,00 people in the Miami Valley. The company produces cars and trucks under the name Chevrolet, Pontiac, Oldsmobile, Buick, Cadillac, and GMC. Saturn cars, GM's new generation of high-value, expressive automobiles, were introduced in the fall of 1991. The company maintains Dayton-area operations for five of its major divisions:

- Moraine Assembly, a member of the North American Truck Platform of GM, assembles GM four-door utility vehicles. It is the only final-assembly plant in Dayton.
- Moraine Engine Plant, a member of GM Powertrain, builds the 6.2-liter and 6.5-liter diesel engines for GM vans and trucks, and some trucks designed for military applications.
- The Miami Valley operations of GM's Harrison Division are the world's largest producer of automotive air-

conditioning compressors.

• Delco Chassis Division, headquartered in Kettering, Ohio, operates five plants and a technical center in the Dayton area. The division serves the auto industry worldwide with chassis systems, modules, and components. In addition to administration and engineering activities in its headquarters and technical center, the division produces shock absorbers, strut assemblies, brake linings, anti-lock brake systems, engine and suspension mounts, and other products in the Dayton area.

• Inland Fisher Guide recently completed renovation of a new Engineering Center within its Interior Business Unit manufacturing operations in Vandalia, Ohio. This GM division is responsible for the engineering, design, and testing of instrument panels, steering wheels, and supplemental inflatable restraint systems, as well as instrument panel covers and supplemental inflatable restraints.

GM's Electronic Data Systems (EDS) employees in Dayton support the various GM plants with data processing services, staff the Dayton Information Processing Center, and service the energy, financial, health, and insurance industries.

GM in Dayton operates offices for financial services (GM Acceptance Corporation), insurance administration (Motors Insurance Corporation), defense contracting (GM Hughes), sales (GM Allison), and training.

According to McCurdy, GM has implemented a variety of innovative programs and state-of-the-art techniques to manage its operations, including employee involvement, continuous improvement, competitive assessment, and implementation of design for manufacturing/design for assembly (DFM/DFA) strategies.

"Our approach to producing high-quality cars and trucks," McCurdy says, "is to do it better through more effective involvement of the people from product design through manufacturing, sales, and service."

GM has also adopted synchronous manufacturing, which reduces production lead-time and calls for production cells, which incorporate a series of manufacturing tasks among members of a work team. The team takes responsibility for product quality, cost, and responsiveness to the customer.

"Managers are more like leaders and less like 'the boss.' They're more comfortable involving people in the decision-making process," McCurdy says.

With more and more systems responsibilities being shifted to GM's automotive component divisions, employees are more concerned than ever about their customers, who continue to want more quality, better performance, improved fuel economy—and more value.

"Today we're creatively applying a lot of innovation," McCurdy says. "Employees are motivated to look around the world for ideas to ensure the best practices are being applied here at home. The key is to stay a step ahead of the competition in the race to customer satisfaction."

GM continues to support community, cultural, and charitable organizations as well as hospitals and universities in the Miami Valley. "Our roots run deep," says McCurdy. "GM people are committed to the Dayton area and the quality of life in this region."

Transport vehicles loaded with four-door models of the Chevrolet Blazer, GMC Jimmy, and Olds Bravada prepare to leave the North American Truck Platform Moraine Assembly Plant for dealerships across the country.

ADVANCED ASSEMBLY AUTOMATION, INC.

Advanced Assembly Automation, Inc., builds special automation systems that are, in-turn, used to build automobile brake systems—and air-conditioner compressors, dishwasher doors, retractable utility knives, and a host of other products and components. As a designer and manufacturer of automated assembly and test machinery, Advanced Assembly works with product manufacturers around the world in a wide range of industries, providing practical ideas and innovative solutions to fulfill their unique manufacturing requirements.

Advanced Assembly is headquartered in Dayton, where it operates a 102,000-square-foot engineering, fabrication, and machining facility. The company is a technical organization whose background and experience enhance its objective of applying emerging technologies to the production environment.

"Our business," says company president and co-founder John Logan, "is understanding the technology that is available and applying that technology to our customers' needs." Logan has more than 25 years of experience in the assembly and test-system industry.

Every member of the company's staff of 150 highly skilled technicians and experienced engineers is a dedicated craftsman and professional. Together they possess a detailed awareness of emerging technologies, and they utilize state-of-the-art solutions in the systems they design and build, including industrial computers, robotics, and advanced vision systems.

On each project, Advanced Assembly employs a proven, methodical project management approach that involves its customers from concept to completed installation. This project management approach—coupled with the company's tough quality standards and precise manufacturing and inspection methods—is why Advanced Assembly stands out from its competitors.

"We have to manage thousands of pieces of equipment, create special machines, buy equipment from outside vendors, and then assemble all of the parts into a system that meets or exceeds all of our customers' expectations," Logan explains. "To do this successfully—and consistently—we have to manage each project with a great deal of precision."

Advanced Assembly begins each project by first seeking to clearly understand the customers' objectives and requirements. The company assigns a senior applications engineer to the project, and he or she works closely with the customer, Advanced Assembly's engineering and manufacturing managers, and outside vendors, exploring a range of alternatives and solutions.

Once a system has been designed, presented to the customer, and approved, a project assembly team is formed. That team includes a project manager, mechanical and electrical engineers, professional toolmakers, electricians, and, of course, the customer.

As the team assembles and debugs the new system, it continuously updates its documentation and closely monitors a thorough runoff procedure to be certain the system meets the client's performance criteria. Before the system is installed, the customer spends several weeks on the assembly floor in Dayton observing the working system producing the customer's product.

Finally, the team supervises the installation and start-up of the new system, supplying the customer's staff with complete instruction and maintenance manuals. The company follows up on each project with service and support.

Many of Advance Assembly's customers are manufacturers of automobile sub-assemblies and sub-components. These customers make such products as air bags, steering components, and anti-lock brake systems—all of which require elaborate safety testing.

Advanced Assembly's test systems verify that the product is assembled correctly and that it performs its intended function perfectly. Most of Advanced Assembly's test systems are integrated into the company's automated assembly solutions, although some are sold as stand-alone stations.

"Flexibility" is more than just a buzz word in many manufacturing environments. For companies requiring a high level of adaptability in their assembly automation, Advanced Assembly utilizes elements such as robots, programmable stations on adjustable X- and Y-axis tables, and quick-change fixtures. The company works with its customers to identify potential product variables up front, so that it can design and build assembly systems that accommodate the widest possible range of present and future product requirements. In addition to avoiding the acquisition of excess equipment, this approach allows the customer to meet just-in-time delivery schedules with improved product quality.

Founded in Dayton in 1984 and still privately held, Advanced Assembly is a relatively young enterprise, but it already ranks among the top operations in its industry. Its customers include manufacturers throughout the U.S., as well as Germany, the United Kingdom, Korea, and Hungary. Average projects fall in the $1-million range, though ones as large as $13 million have been successfully completed.

Advanced Assembly Automation is expected to continue its steady growth over the coming years. Its commitment to excellence and its emphasis on achieving optimum solutions for its customers almost guarantees it.

"Our future growth depends on our customers' satisfaction," says Logan. "We have to continue to put technology to work for them and strive to earn their continuing business."

The company will continue to emphasize its team approach, close customer contact, and long-term customer relationships, growing its operation one project at a time.

DIGITAL TECHNOLOGY, INC.

Digital Technology, Inc., (DTI), is one of the world's leading developers and manufacturers of test equipment for avionics and high-speed digital communications systems. The company has a long history of leadership in the industry, supplying host-based interfaces for real-time data buses and emerging high-speed buses. DTI also offers a complete line of LAN (local area network) analysis equipment for the Fiber Distributed Data Interface (FDDI).

Headquartered in Dayton, DTI was founded in 1981 during the early post-research days of the evolution of the military avionics specification, MIL-STD-1553. Avionics is the science of technology and electronics in aviation—in other words, computers in aircraft. Today's flight crews depend on computers to communicate with the many systems in modern aircraft, from cabin cooling systems to landing gear. DTI's Data Bus Subsystems Divisions manufactures the computer components used by avionics equipment manufacturers to simulate these communications protocol and test their systems.

Today DTI's products are used in all phases of avionics product development, from initial research and development in the laboratory through prototype development, production test, and installed based maintenance and support. DTI's products are used in virtually every major MIL-STD-1553 program in and out of the United States.

The company's second division has entered into the high-speed commercial digital communication test product market, placing a strong emphasis on FDDI network testing. FDDI is the high-speed, fiber optic communication "highway" that connects computer networks.

DTI's FDDI protocol support equipment, known as LANHAWK, offers a range of testing, traffic generation, and analysis solutions. The company launched the first of these products in September 1989. DTI now offers a breadth of FDDI analysis products ranging from a top-of-the-line LANHAWK FDDI network analyzer and traffic generator to a low-cost FDDI logic analyzer interface symbol generator test package.

The key to DTI's success is its overall commitment to developing innovative, high-quality products for the emerging data communications market. Members of DTI's technical staff participate in standards committees and organizations to ensure that each DTI product conforms to the most recent industry standards. The company also works closely with its customers to determine their individual needs and develop products that meet those needs.

DTI occupies more than 16,000 square feet of office, laboratory, and manufacturing space in Dayton; maintains offices in California and England; and has sales representatives and customer support personnel throughout the world. The company also manages a fully staffed customer service hotline and offers a series of product and protocol training classes.

Digital Technology, Inc., is a wholly owned subsidiary of the Dynatech Corporation of Boston, a $33-billion corporation that includes more than 50 companies serving a variety of technology markets.

BIESER, GREER & LANDIS, ATTORNEYS AT LAW

Bieser, Greer & Landis is one of Dayton's oldest and most respected law firms. Large enough to deal with sophisticated legal problems, yet small enough to be sensitive to its clients' concerns, it has been providing a wide range of legal services to the greater Dayton area for more than 135 years.

The firm was founded in 1854 by Dayton attorney Clement L. Vallandigham, a leading politician of the time. Vallandigham served in Congress; was publisher of the Empire, a Democratic newspaper; and was chief spokesman for the Peace Democrats (known as "Copperheads"), who opposed the Civil War as unjustified by the U.S. Constitution. His first law partner was his nephew, John A. McMahon, who served in Congress, and, while in his 80s, wrote the pioneering Miami Conservancy Act, which permitted formation of flood control districts in Ohio. McMahon was a leader of the Dayton bar through 69 years of active practice. In McMahon's later years he was joined by his son, J. Sprigg McMahon, as well as Robert K. Corwin, Robert K. Landis, and Samuel S. Markham. The firm's next generation of leaders were Warren Ferguson, Irvin G. Bieser, Rowan A. Greer, and Robert K. Landis, Jr.

As of this writing, the firm's partners are Charles D. Shook; Edward L. Shank; David C. Greer; Irvin G. Bieser, Jr.; Leo F. Krebs; Howard P. Krisher; Edward H. Siddens; Michael W. Krumholtz; Gregory P. Dunsky; John F. Haviland; and David P. Williamson.

Bieser, Greer & Landis is a general practice law firm, but with areas of special expertise. The firm represents clients in many different types of litigation, including business; environmental and commercial; medical and other professional malpractice; product liability; and negligence. The firm also represents clients in the financial services and health care industries and in real estate law. It represents and assists clients in a wide variety of personal matters, including estate planning, trusts, probate, and many individual legal matters.

Neither the law nor the nature of legal problems is static, and members of the firm strive to keep up with the changes and maintain top proficiency. With a client list that includes medium and small businesses, professional associations, insurance companies, foundations, and individuals, the firm's members are supported in their work by a strong staff of associates and legal assistants and by computer systems for case management and fast, accurate document processing.

Throughout its history, members of Bieser, Greer & Landis have furnished leaders of the bar and key figures in community affairs. Members of the firm continue to take pride in maintaining the highest professional standards and reputation, never forgetting their obligations to their clients, the courts, and their community.

SCITEX DIGITAL PRINTING, INC.

Situated on a 50-acre, park-like site, Scitex Digital Printing, Inc., is housed in an ultra-modern, 336,000-square-foot facility.

Scitex Digital Printing, Inc., is a world leader in the development, manufacture, and sale of computer-driven, high-speed digital printing systems based on patented inkjet imaging technology, with approximately 170 registered patents and nearly 30 years' experience in the field.

Its high speed printing systems pioneered the concept of variable-data imaging in the 1960s, and in recent years the company has introduced a continuing progression of new inkjet systems and controllers that have set the industry standard for quality and flexibility in commercial inkjet imaging.

Scitex Digital Printing, Inc., became a wholly owned subsidiary of Scitex Corporation Ltd., of Herzlia, Israel, following the acquisition by Scitex of Eastman Kodak Company's Dayton, Ohio-based inkjet imaging business on June 30, 1993.

Scitex Corporation Ltd., is a world leader in color electronic prepress systems for the graphic design, printing, and publishing markets. The company has an extensive range of products that includes creative layout and design systems, image digitizing scanners, color workstations for page assembly and retouching, digital proofers, image setters, and communication devices.

Scitex has been involved in inkjet imaging for the graphic arts market for many years. Its Iris Graphics subsidiary is recognized as a world leader in high-quality, full-color inkjet printing. Scitex also markets the Scitex Outboard printer, a giant inkjet printing system that outputs wide, high-quality, color billboard posters of practically unlimited length.

The addition of Scitex Digital Printing, Inc., has created a formidable force in inkjet imaging worldwide, with sales of computer driven inkjet printers running at a rate of more than $130 million per year. With its recent Dayton acquisition, Scitex has accelerated its drive into the field of digital filmless printing application, and has positioned itself firmly as the leading player in the fast-growing market for non-impact printing.

Dayton-based activities include sales, management and marketing, research and development, product manufacturing, ink manufacturing, and customer service and support operations. Support includes font development, custom software, technical support, sample generation, product service, and training.

The company's inkjet imagers and controllers serve the commercial printing, business forms, direct mail, direct marketing, promotional graphics, catalog, magazine, and lottery and gaming industries, as well as in-plant mailing operations.

Scitex's commercial inkjet product line includes the Ektajet 5000 Printer, Ektajet 5100 Printing System, the

Edward Durell Stone Associates, P.C., one of the country's leading architectural firms, designed the facility that houses Scitex to complement employee productivity and efficiency.

Scitex 3500 High Speed Printing System, and the Scitex 3000 High Speed Printing System. Ektajet is made by Scitex Digital Printing, Inc., under quality standards and trademark licence of Eastman Kodak Company.

The Ektajet 5000 Printer is a versatile, high-quality inkjet printer that can operate at speeds of up to 900 feet per minute, typically addressing 30,000 to 50,000 envelopes per hour.

It can be installed in-line with web presses, business forms presses, folders, and finishing equipment. It can also be set up off-line on mailing bases or conveyor equipment for addressing, individualized messaging, bar coding, and graphics.

The Ektajet 5100 Printing System is a compact, PC-based inkjet imaging system that features "automatic" operation and can easily intermix text with graphics, sequential numbers, dates, times, and bar codes anywhere within the print image area.

The system accepts data input by diskette, tape, or serial file transfer, and standard files from PC mail management, database, or word processor software can be used for production imaging on the system. The Ektajet 5100 System also can act as a controller for up to three Ektajet 5000 Printers at a single printing station.

The Scitex 3500 High Speed Printing System is a high-volume computer-driven system that has been optimized to produce letter-quality, fully variable data imaging with crisp text and high-definition graphics.

Applications for the Scitex 3500 Printing System include individualized direct mail, instant scratch-off lottery and gaming tickets, sweepstakes material, bar codes, business forms, coupons, and government mailings.

The Scitex 3000 High Speed Printing System is the world's fastest continuously variable high speed non-impact printer, permitting variable data imaging at speeds up to 1000 feet per minute.

Like the Scitex 3500 System, it also employs a powerful data station to provide full-page bit-mapped output with complete variability and real-time text rotation. However, it uses a single fluid system and accompanying 13.3-inch-wide printhead.

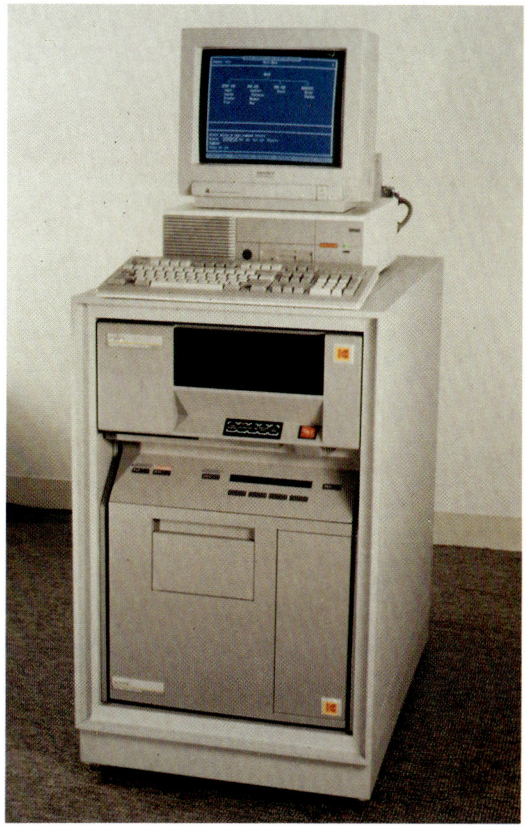

The Scitex Ektajet 5100 Printing System is a compact, PC-based ink-jet system that puts simple controls and commands at its operator's fingertips.

The Scitex 4200 Binding Line Controller is a new system designed to manage up to three inkjet printers. It can print parallel or perpendicular to the spine both inside and outside of books and can address them in either name or ZIP orientation.

The Scitex 4300 Multiple Printer Controller can drive up to eight Ektajet 500 Printers or eight Admark Printers from a single data source. Up to eight different images can be produced per printer, up to 64 images can be produced per piece, and each image can include multiple lines and/or graphics.

With its cutting-edge product line, new Dayton facility, and dedicated employees, Scitex Digital Printing, Inc., is in position to continue setting the pace in the high-speed printing industry.

The Scitex 3500 High Speed Printing System provides letter-quality, variable-data imaging for high-volume direct mail, lottery ticket applications, business forms, and other high-volume printing.

BATTELLE

Battelle is a practical company that develops, implements, and commercializes technology for the world's foremost corporations, government agencies, and trade associations. Battelle solves problems, develops and improves products and processes, provides on-site technical assistance, and manages complex technology programs in more than 20 countries.

Battelle was founded in 1929 by Ohio industrialist Gordon Battelle to provide practical solutions to the problems facing both industry and government. During the more than six decades since its founding, Battelle has grown into an international organization with an annual business volume exceeding $854 million and a staff of 8,000 scientists, engineers, and other specialists who conduct more than 5,600 projects each year.

Today, Battelle continues to "put technology to work" in essential sectors of the economy: environment, health, commercial and industrial technology, national security, technology development and transfer, and transportation.

Environmental issues have become critical to nearly every business. Battelle is addressing this critical issue by developing and applying advanced technologies and methods to protect and clean up the environment. For example, the company conducts bioventing operations to remediate soil and groundwater contamination at numerous Air Force sites.

Battelle Dayton Operations, Dayton, Ohio.

The health care industry is facing new challenges to control costs, provide universal care, and develop sophisticated systems to diagnose and cure disease. Battelle technology is meeting these needs, from reducing drug development time to providing statistical support to companies pursuing approval of over-the-counter medications.

Battelle's expertise in process development and product innovation helps businesses compete in the new global environment. From advanced biodegradable plastics to cutting-edge computer software, from manufacturing plant layout design to race car engines, Battelle gives its clients the edge they need in increasingly competitive world markets.

Battelle also applies technology to meet the defense community's rapidly changing priorities, modernizing management and systems, increasing reliability and maintainability, and demonstrating accountability for the environment.

Battelle's contract with the U.S. Department of Energy (DOE) represents a unique long-standing partnership. Battelle is the only operator of a national laboratory in the U.S. that can use the combined resources of DOE and its own facilities to provide support to both DOE and private industry. Battelle responds to the needs of energy suppliers worldwide.

The company also helps its clients to manage their technology-driven businesses and investments from a strategic business perspective. Battelle creates innovative approaches to competitive benchmarking, technology asset valuation, strategic planning, and technology transfer.

Battelle continues its long-standing commitment to enriching the many communities in which its staff members work and live. The company has contributed millions of dollars in support of a wide range of charitable organizations and programs dedicated to educational activities and community service.

SUPERVALU, OHIO VALLEY DIVISION

When two well-known Minneapolis food wholesalers, Hugh Harrison and George Newell, joined forces and merged their respective operations back in the 1870s, they did so with the hope that they would create a company that would better serve their growing list of customers.

More than a century later, the company they founded, SUPERVALU, is the nation's leading wholesale food distributor and a major food retailer. Today SUPERVALU supplies more than 5,500 retail food stores from 30 divisions operating in 44 states.

The name "SUPERVALU" didn't actually begin appearing on company trucks and storefronts for many years. Intermittent mergers and acquisitions followed the original pairing of Harrison and Newell, eventually leading to the formation of the Winston & Newell Company in 1926. Two years later Winston & Newell became one of the first wholesale food distributors in the nation to become affiliated with the Independent Grocer's Alliance (IGA).

Finally, in 1942, the SUPERVALU sign appeared on many of the company's 560 affiliated stores. The company became so closely identified with that name that Winston & Newell changed its own name to Super Valu Stores, Inc., in 1954. In 1967 SUPERVALU was listed for the first time on the New York Stock Exchange. As part of the company's 50th anniversary celebration in 1992, the corporate name was also officially changed to SUPERVALU, Inc., and a new mark was adopted—SUPERVALU.

Between 1956 and 1965 SUPERVALU grew by the acquisition of seven regional food distributors. One of those companies was the Eavey Company of Xenia, Ohio, which was acquired in 1961. Founded in 1869, the Eavey Company was one of the nation's oldest wholesale food distributors. That company is known today as the Ohio Valley Division of SUPERVALU.

SUPERVALU celebrated its 50th anniversary in 1992.

The Ohio Valley Division's 600-plus employees currently serve more than 120 retail food stores in Ohio, Kentucky, West Virginia, and Indiana, as well as eight military bases. The distribution center at 1003 Bellbrook Avenue in Xenia operates 24 hours a day, seven days a week.

Some of the services and products provided by the Ohio Valley Division include retail counseling and support, advertising, consumer research, private-label products, store design and equipment, market analysis, merchandising and accounting services, development assistance, retail training, insurance and risk planning, labor scheduling, and printing services.

Although most of the company's customers are conventional food store operations, the Ohio Valley Division also supports a number of formats, including bigg's (sic), Cub Foods, NewMarkets, and County Markets, as well as upscale and conventional food stores. This diversity in formats is a reflection of the company's and division's ability to keep pace with changes in the food industry, local competitive moves, and regional economic characteristics.

SUPERVALU's Ohio Valley Division office.

Monarch Marking Systems Company

Monarch Marking Systems is the world's leading supplier of merchandise marking, identification, and tracking systems for retail markets, and of integrated bar code applications for the logistics market. For more than 100 years Monarch Marking has been serving a broad spectrum of customers with products ranging from simple price tags and labels to advanced electronic bar-code printers and data collection systems.

Monarch Marking Systems takes pride in having been a member of the Dayton community since 1890.

The company was founded in 1890 by Dayton entrepreneur and inventor Fred Kohnle. Kohnle created a device called a pin-ticketing machine. Before the invention of this machine, merchants had to pin tags on soft goods, such as clothing, by hand, and write on hard goods, such as hand tools, with a grease pencil. Kohnle's original pin ticketer was hand operated, but at his customers' request he improved the design with the addition of a foot pedal.

Today Monarch's product line includes hand-held labelers, sophisticated electronic bar code printers, support software, and advanced data collection systems.

In 1966 the company constructed a new manufacturing facility in Dayton that still houses the company's corporate headquarters. In addition Monarch operates manufacturing and assembly plants in Canada, Mexico, Australia, England, and Singapore, serving market needs in those locations.

The company serves retailers, manufacturers, health care institutions, the transportation industry, and government. Retailers compose the majority of Monarch's customers, but because of the increasing popularity of bar coding as the method of choice for identifying merchandise and tracking inventory, manufacturers are using Monarch products in increasing numbers.

Bar coding allows retailers and manufacturers to track merchandise movement, providing critical information for just-in-time inventory management. In addition to manufacturing the equipment that makes and applies tags and labels, Monarch also makes standard off-the-shelf tags, as well as custom tags imprinted with company logos.

Monarch sells its products and services through its own sales force, as well as through distributors, brokers, and direct-mail channels. The company's field service force of about 400 people serves customers' product installation and maintenance needs. With operations in North and South America, Europe, and Asia, the company employs more than 2,000 people worldwide, with 1,300 employees in Dayton.

Since 1968 Monarch has been a subsidiary of Pitney Bowes, a $2.9-billion multinational manufacturing and marketing company. Other Pitney Bowes companies are market leaders in mailing systems, office products and supplies, management services, and lease financing.

From printers and labels to scanners and data collection systems, Monarch is a one-stop source for bar code system solutions.

RIECK MECHANICAL SERVICES, INC.

Rieck Mechanical Services, Inc., is one of Dayton's leading providers of mechanical and environmental systems for commercial, industrial, institutional, and governmental buildings. Still locally owned and operated after more than 100 years, Rieck has contributed its services and expertise to virtually every building in Dayton's skyline.

Founded by H.F. Rieck in 1893, the company was originally a furnace, roofing, and gutter installer. Through the years, the family-owned operation has passed from one generation to the next, first to B.R. Rieck and E.A. Rieck, then to B.R. Rieck's sons and grandson. The company's current name was adopted in 1969.

Seven different buildings have housed the company at various times throughout its evolution, and today the Rieck Building on Wadsworth Road comprises more than 21,000 square feet.

The Rieck staff includes 50 professionally trained technicians and engineers who provide builders and facilities managers with a wide range of professional services, including maintenance, system design, engineering, fabrication, installation, new construction, energy management, system balancing and fine tuning, and retrofit.

During the planning and design stage of a project, Rieck planners and estimators work with architects, engineers, and others to identify the parameters of the project, qualify its mechanical demands, and control the cost of construction and operation.

During the design stage, Rieck specialists consult with designers, focusing on the human needs the project's mechanical systems must satisfy. The company utilizes precise technology to analyze and predict critical system demands, providing designers with information that helps them make appropriate design decisions.

When it is time to implement a design, Rieck installs the mechanical systems with the craftsmanship and attention to detail for which it is well known.

A typical, fully-equipped Rieck Service van.

The installation of a system, however, is really only the first step in what Rieck views as a lifelong relationship. The company applies the same sophistication and attention to detail to its ongoing maintenance services, which include regular inspections and replacement and emergency services. Rieck also provides special services, such as environmental assessment, performance monitoring, and computer-based energy management and control.

In 1980 Rieck became a LINC Service representative—in fact, the company was the first LINC franchise in the world. LINC Service is a network of independent contractors providing a unique program of comprehensive, professional heating and air-conditioning services. LINC Service is represented on four continents and in every major metropolitan market in the United States.

As a LINC Service contractor, Rieck is able to provide its customers with additional services and benefits such as national purchasing power, worldwide support services, computerized maintenance scheduling, a comprehensive technical data base, expanded research and development, and ongoing professional staff training.

Rieck Mechanical Facility at 5245 Wadsworth Road in Dayton.

THE WAGNER-SMITH COMPANY

The Wagner-Smith Company is headquartered in Dayton and traces its local roots back to 1917, when the organization first began business as a pump distributor.

A diversified operation with a strong Dayton history, The Wagner-Smith Company originated in 1917, when the company was incorporated as a pump distributor. Today the organization is a third-generation enterprise providing a wide range of products and services to business, industry, and government throughout the United States and overseas.

Wagner-Smith specializes in electrical construction and maintenance services; manufacturing, sales, and rental of electrical powerline construction equipment; and sales and service of industrial pumps and systems.

In 1919 Wagner-Smith expanded into electrical contracting to build powerlines for the utility industry. The company built several hundred miles of the steel tower, high-voltage transmission lines that are still seen throughout southwestern Ohio.

Today the company's Outside Electrical Division specializes in the installation of computer-controlled coordination systems for traffic intersections. Wagner-Smith is the largest installer of traffic-signal systems in southwestern Ohio. The company performs maintenance for more than 125 government entities to provide system service and continuous, 24-hour emergency support.

This division also provides parking-lot and sports-field lighting, overhead and underground power distribution, and equipment maintenance. The company installed lighting for the world's first major league baseball night game, played at Cincinnati's Crosley Field in 1935. In Dayton Wagner-Smith participates on many area contracts, including the overhead catenary and underground power distribution for the RTA Trolley system.

Wagner-Smith's Inside Electrical Division focuses on the construction and maintenance of buildings and process systems. The company's projects range from government construction and maintenance to the installation of industrial machinery. This division's capabilities also extend to high-voltage testing, primary and secondary power distribution, energy management, emergency power sources, and fire alarm and security systems. Area projects include the Ervin J. Nutter Center and the Montgomery County Administration Building.

The Industrial Pump Division is a major stocking distributor of pumps and related equipment and systems. It services most of Ohio and part of Kentucky from offices in Dayton, Cincinnati, Columbus, and Toledo. Using its repair, rebuild, and system troubleshooting and engineering experience, Wagner-Smith's equipment recommendations are used in the industrial process and manufacturing industries.

The Powerline Construction Equipment Division was established in 1976 to rent, maintain, and sell conductor-stringing equipment to electric utilities and powerline contractors. In 1990 Wagner-Smith began to design and manufacture its own line of tension stringing equipment and related supplies and accessories. Used in the installation of electrical powerlines, telephone lines, and cable television lines, this equipment is manufactured by the company's Burleson, Texas, facility and is distributed from both Dayton and Texas.

Headquartered in Dayton, the Wagner-Smith Company employs approximately 200 people. Under the direction of the founder's grandson, Phil Wagner, the company continues to serve customers in all 50 states and internationally.

Wagner-Smith on the job during construction of a new General Motors paint facility in Moraine.

THE OLT INSURANCE COMPANY

The Olt Insurance Company is a full-line, independent insurance agency specializing in personal and commercial insurance, as well as physicians' professional liability coverage. A three-generation agency, Olt Insurance has been serving thousands of people throughout the Dayton area for more than 80 years.

The company was founded by Oscar C. Olt in 1911. A well-known area insurance man with a reputation for honesty and integrity, Olt had worked for local insurance companies for seven years before going into business for himself. His first office was located in the then-relatively-new American Building in downtown Dayton. Olt conducted his business from that office until 1916. The company moved several times during the ensuing years, but in 1976 the firm returned permanently to the American Building, which is currently listed on the National Historic Register.

Olt was active in community affairs for most of his life. He served on the Oakwood City Council, the local board of education, and was elected mayor from 1926 to 1928. Olt also served as president of the Dayton Association of Insurance Agents. He remained active in the business until his death on July 4, 1964—the day after his 80th birthday.

Olt's son, John E. Olt, joined the company shortly after graduating from Denison University in 1935. The times were tough; the country was still in the grip of the Great Depression and local insurance companies were setting very tight limits on professional liability coverage for physicians. John carved out a niche for his company by calling on doctors' offices directly and writing policies that gave them the protection they needed. Today the company is the largest writer of doctors' professional liability insurance in the region.

Still active in the business, John E. Olt served as secretary of the Dayton Association of Insurance Agents from 1937 to 1943, and later as association president.

John G. Olt, a graduate of the University of Arizona, represents the third generation to enter the family business. He is a member of the Board of the Independent Insurance Agents Association of Dayton and has served on the Public Safety Committee of the state association.

Oscar C. Olt (1884-1964), founder of The Olt Insurance Co.

The Olt Insurance Company has represented three of its major insurance carriers for a remarkable number of years. The United States Fidelity and Guaranty Company (USF&G) has been with Olt since 1912—longer than any other agency in the area; the firm has represented the Ohio Casualty Insurance Company since 1936; and the P.I.E. Mutual Insurance Company, which offers doctors' professional liability coverage, has been with Olt since 1983.

Throughout its long history, the company has maintained its independence. As a result, the Olt Insurance Company continues to give its clients a level of personal attention that is uncommon in the industry. Olt agents make it a point to get to know their clients and understand their needs. "Dependable Protection Since 1911" is more than just the company's slogan; it's the way it does business.

CIRCUIT CENTER, INC.

Circuit Center's state-of-the-art manufacturing facility.

When Ronald C. Underwood and two associates started their printed circuit board manufacturing operation in the back of a Dayton warehouse in 1973, they had about 900 square feet of space and little more in the way of equipment for their part-time venture than a Xerox camera, a manual drill, and a fish tank that they used as an etcher. Today, with 110 employees, a state-of-the-art facility, and nearly $11 million in annual sales, Circuit Center, Inc. (CCI), has become an acknowledged leader in the printed circuit board industry.

CCI, whose products range from the fabrication of single- to double-sided to complex multilayered printed circuit boards, specializes in the rapid delivery of high-quality prototypes and small-volume production orders. By incorporating into its manufacturing process some of the most advanced equipment in the industry today, CCI has become known for its on-time deliveries, exceptional technical support, and quality service at every phase of the job, from concept to design to production. In 1985 CCI was among the first companies of its size to obtain process capability for the manipulation of digital data. This process, typically referred to as data-based technology, has become requisite for those companies who look to compete in a global economy and view the world as their marketplace.

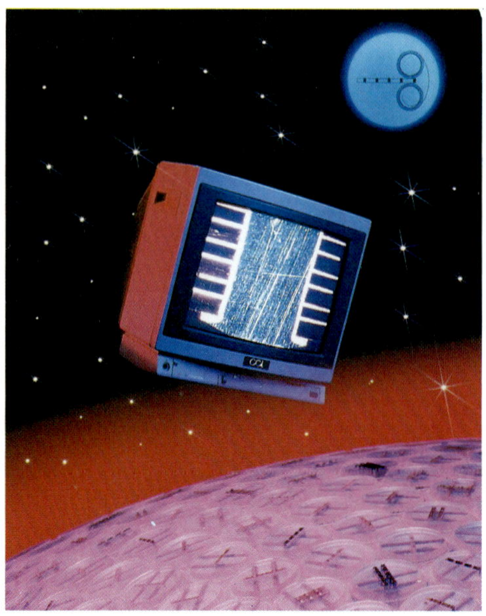

A world of microsections.

CCI's talented staff of sales personnel and engineers continually provide customers with superior technical support and service—value-added assistance that often avoids costly mistakes and missed delivery opportunities. Through utilization of the company's computerized systems, they are able to predict the impact of last-minute customer specification changes, plan for adjustments to the production schedule, and monitor available product capacity in real-time. The company's customized finite computer scheduling system optimizes production time, lowers costs, and provides customers with instantaneous information regarding the current status of their orders. Circuit Center is one of a growing number of companies uniting such state-of-the-art technology as Computer Integrated Manufacturing (CIM) with Design Rule Checking (DRC) software in order processing. Acceptance of artwork by means of magnetic tape, floppy disk, modem, and tape layout are all possible with these systems. All phototools that are a product of this operation are generated off a highly accurate and rapid laser plotter.

Surely one of the company's finest attributes remains the manufacturing facility itself. Planned and constructed over a two-year period on a six-acre lot, every aspect of the 58,000-square-foot facility was designed to optimize the circuit board manufacturing process. The building is immaculately kept, with each department segregated to minimize traffic and disruption of work flow. Temperature, lighting, and humidity are controlled to provide the optimal atmospheric conditions so vital to many of the processes used in circuit board fabrication. The building's closed-loop water system, designed for equipment cooling, helps the company maintain its established goals for environmental safety.

CCI is committed to promoting a better environment and has assumed a leadership role in research for better ways to reduce the amount of hazardous waste released through the manufacture of its products. In fact, in an unprecedented effort, the company has joined forces with the University of Dayton, the Air Force, the U.S. Environmental Protection Agency, and a consortium of industries to perfect more environmentally safe manufacturing processes. The company has dedicated space within its Dayton facility and provided significant manpower in an effort to duplicate experimental processes in real-world situations. "Promoting the protection of the environment," explains company founder and president, Ron Underwood, "is one of our most important goals."

Investing in new technologies has often been a rewarding experience for Circuit Center. Most recently the conversion of one of its most hazardous process acids, sulfuric, to a more benign one, citric, resulted in an appreciable windfall. This innovation alone accounted for a reduction of 2,600 pounds of acid from the company's yearly inventory. As a result, Ciruit Center attained a significant economic benefit, while creating a safer and much-improved working environment. Enhancements are ongoing as the company refines its operations through automation of its manufacturing process, expansion of its technical capabilities, and application of new technologies to produce the most reliable and highest quality products available.

Another innovative new process being tested at Circuit Center was developed by Sandia National Laboratories. It uses polymer coatings that are applied as a thin film from a liquid solution onto the circuit board and then air dried. Then, upon exposure to ultra-violet light, these polymers vaporize into inert gases, thus eliminating the rinsing stage, which is a major source of wastewater containing chemicals and other hazardous by-products. This new initiative promises to curb expenditures, processing time, and direct labor.

Laser technology.

CCI maintains a true "open-door" policy by encouraging visitation of its facility by private organizations, local government, and academia. "We want people to come see our facility and learn more about the complexities of circuit board fabrication," says Underwood. "At Circuit Center, every employee from sales to shipping welcomes the opportunity to have their customers experience personally the cooperative and courteous spirit that thrives within the organization."

Today Circuit Center, Inc., vies earnestly to be recognized as the Midwest's premier fabricator of prototype and low-volume printed wiring boards. The company's credo of quality, pride, service, and dependability encircle the company logo in a manifestation of its corporate convictions and values. At CCI, customer satisfaction will never be compromised, nor forsaken, for it alone is the barometer upon which CCI believes success is truly gauged.

Circuit Center is committed to excellence in quality, service, and environment.

JENKS, SURDYK & COWDREY CO., L.P.A.

The lawyers of Jenks, Surdyk & Cowdrey.

The law firm of Jenks, Surdyk & Cowdrey Co., L.P.A., was established in 1976 with local trial lawyers Thomas E. (Ted) Jenks and Robert J. Surdyk. Today the firm enjoys a well-deserved reputation for high standards in the delivery of legal services to a wide range of clients throughout central and southwestern Ohio.

Jenks, Surdyk & Cowdrey is primarily engaged in a civil trial practice that includes business, personal injury, casualty, and products and professional liability claims. The firm represents a diversity of clients including medical and legal professionals, businesses, governmental entities, insurance companies, and risk management consortiums throughout the state. Included among its clientele are national retail chains for which the firm is local counsel, governmental entities throughout southwestern Ohio, manufacturing concerns, and local businesses.

The firm has adopted a policy of careful, controlled growth since its founding and now includes 10 capable and experienced trial lawyers who are admitted to practice before all courts of record in the State of Ohio and the U.S. District Court for the Southern District of Ohio. Some are admitted before the Third and Sixth Circuit Courts of Appeal and the United States Supreme Court, as well as various state and federal courts in New York and Pennsylvania.

Lawyers from Jenks, Surdyk & Cowdrey have successfully litigated precedent-setting cases in the Ohio Supreme Court. The firm has been consistently recognized with the highest rating for legal ability by *Martindale-Hubbell*, a professional publication that evaluates both lawyers and law firms. All of the firm's lawyers are members of the Dayton, Ohio State, and American bar associations, as well as the Ohio Association of Civil Trial Attorneys. Jenks and Surdyk are long-time members of the International Association of Defense Counsel. Both are fellows of the Ohio Bar Foundation.

Jenks, a past president of the Dayton Bar Association and former member of the American Bar Association's House of Delegates, is also a fellow of both the American College of Trial Lawyers and the American Bar Foundation. He is named in *The Best Lawyers in America* and *Who's Who in America*. Surdyk and Cowdrey are both diplomats of the Court Practice Institute.

The firm and its lawyers are active participants in numerous service organizations and are frequently involved in community projects. The firm's professional staff is supported by paralegals, clerks, and other personnel utilizing state-of-the-art equipment for case management, research, and word processing. Its computers have direct access to the Montgomery County Common Pleas Court case files so that its lawyers may acquire, use, and provide instantaneous information on the status of every civil case before that court at minimum cost.

The firm's newly remodeled, two-story offices are located across from Memorial Hall in downtown Dayton. To better serve clients, a second office is maintained in downtown Cincinnati.

Jenks, Surdyk & Cowdrey's lawyers consider competent and ethical service to be the foundation of an aggressive trial practice. The firm's founding philosophy of dedication to its clients, its profession, and its community continues to guide its practice.

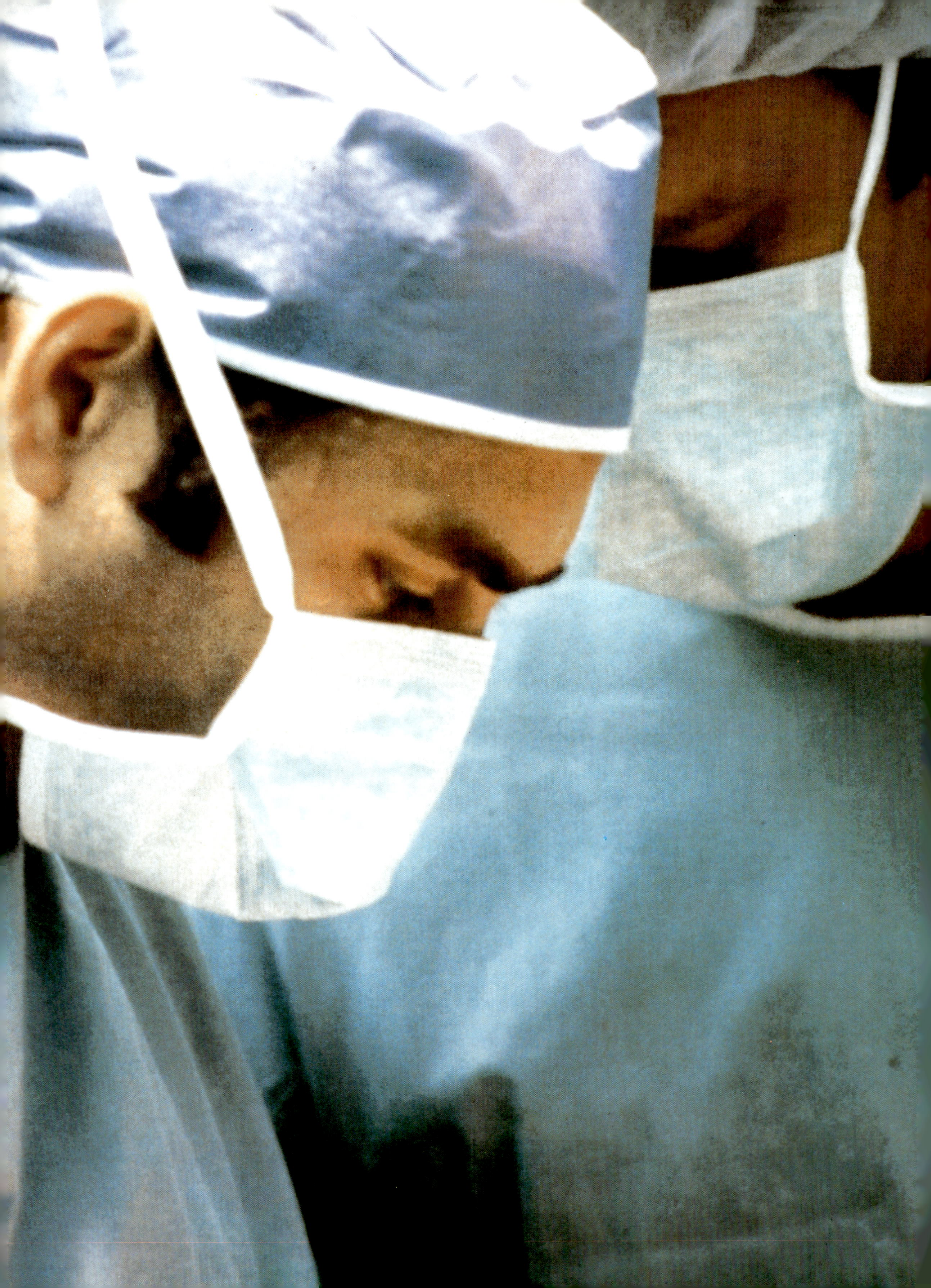

Chapter Eight

Commitment to Progress

Dayton boasts an impressive collection of world-renowned medical centers, highly respected schools and colleges, popular TV and radio stations, and first-class entertainment venues. By being the best at what they do, these institutions provide local residents with a quality of life all can be proud of.

Dayton's medical centers are equipped with the latest in technology and are staffed by the best-trained personnel. Patients in every stage of life are assured of receiving the very best medical attention. Area hospitals employ specialists from every discipline so that everyone—no matter their problem—can be provided with the care they need.

Schools and colleges busily prepare their students to face the challenges that await them at graduation. Working closely with area employers, educators ensure that lessons taught in the classroom can be applied in the workplace.

For information or entertainment, the people of Dayton need not go far. TV and radio stations fill the air with quality programming around the clock. Local newspapers report the latest developments at home and abroad. Museums and theaters offer patrons a world of culture—right in their own backyard.

Behind all of these institutions are the unique stories of their successes, their plans for the future, and their Commitment to Progress.

Dayton boasts one of the best hospital systems in the country. Greene Memorial Hospital

Previous page: High-tech industry has found a home in Dayton. Center for Artificial Intelligence Applications

THE CHILDREN'S MEDICAL CENTER

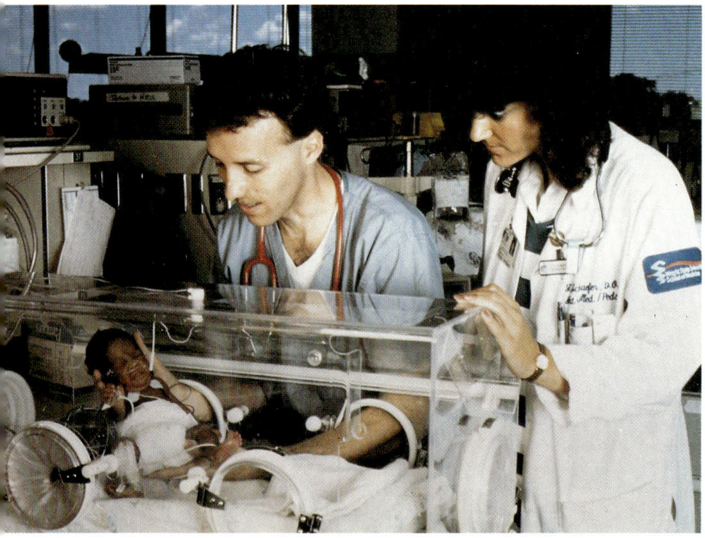

The Neonatal Intensive Care Unit at The Children's Medical Center.

Children are not miniature adults. Their bodies are different—not just smaller—and they react differently to injury or illness. A child experiencing shock, for example, may exhibit symptoms that are nothing like those of an adult. Children have "different-sized" emotions, too. Dealing with the way a child feels about being sick is as much a part of effective pediatric care as prescriptions and procedures.

At The Children's Medical Center (CMC) in Dayton, children are recognized for what they are: special people with special needs. Caring for young patients, from newborns to adolescents, CMC provides the type of care that treats the emotional as well as the physical needs of the child. That makes CMC a special place for kids of all ages.

One of only 56 full-service children's medical centers in the United States, CMC is a not-for-profit, 155-bed, regional pediatric hospital serving a 20-county area in southwestern Ohio, eastern Indiana, and northern Kentucky.

CMC is staffed with more than 1,300 employees, including nurses, technicians, therapists, and developmental experts trained in pediatric care and dedicated to the needs of children. Together with CMC's doctors, these caring, hard-working people help make a child's stay at CMC as pleasant as a hospital stay can be.

More than 175 physicians and residents provide special care and treatment to young patients at CMC. The center's medical staff includes a number of specialists who have helped the hospital become recognized around the country and the world in the vital field of pediatric medicine.

CMC's facilities are specially designed to provide for the needs of young patients at every age. In CMC's Neonatal Intensive Care Unit (NICU), seriously ill and premature infants, from newborn to 28 days old, are cared for in one of the most sophisticated facilities of its type in the area. Under the medical direction of board-certified neonatologists, the NICU staff provides care to these fragile patients and also deals with the emotional needs of new parents.

CMC's fourth-floor, Duke/Robinson Patient Care Area is dedicated to the special needs of infants and toddlers. Soft colors, child-oriented wallpaper, and lots of windows create a cheerful, homelike environment for little ones.

The third-floor, school-age-patient unit also features cozy, comfortable surroundings. A full-time schoolteacher is available for children who require a lengthy stay in the hospital and need to continue with their studies.

Not quite children and not yet adults, teenagers are recognized as special people at CMC; they have a special place called the Young Adult Unit. Specifically designed for adolescent care, this modern, colorful, 17-bed unit gives teenage patients many choices and much freedom, recognizing their need for independence. Teenaged patients are encouraged to wear street clothes, to be up and around, and to socialize in a fully equipped recreation room.

CMC's commitment to pediatric medicine allows everyone to focus exclusively on the complex medical and emotional needs of children. A good example of this is the center's child life department. Trained in

The Children's Medical Center is known for the intensity of the care provided.

child development or related fields, child life specialists provide therapeutic and entertaining games and activities to ease the anxiety of hospitalization.

Most surgeries performed today at CMC are done on an outpatient basis. Young patients in the center's day surgery program spend the nights before and after surgery at home. The nonthreatening atmosphere allows for close parent contact immediately before and after surgery. A presurgical tour for children and parents helps reduce anxiety. The tour includes a visit to the operating room, where patients and parents examine some of the equipment, and a lively educational show starring the center's friendly mascot, Wally B. Bear.

The department of surgical services provides the special pediatric touch for both inpatients and outpatients needing surgery. The staff of anesthesiologists, surgeons, and nurses have the special skills required to care for CMC's pediatric patients. The department is divided into preoperative and postoperative areas and has seven operating rooms designed especially with kids in mind. CMC recently opened the Almost Home unit, which is a short-stay/observation unit for children who do not require the intensity of care given during a traditional hospital stay. A typical visit in the Almost Home unit is less than 24 hours, and parents are encouraged to stay with their children.

CMC's emergency department is one of the few in the country staffed on a full-time basis by board-certified pediatricians who specialize in emergency medicine. The department uses equipment designed exclusively for children, and just as important, employs the know-how needed to help children through an emergency situation.

An integral part of CMC's emergency department is the Pediatric Trauma Center, which specializes in treating seriously injured children. The center's staff of pediatric specialists includes surgeons, radiologists, and anesthesiologists who are on call 24 hours a day.

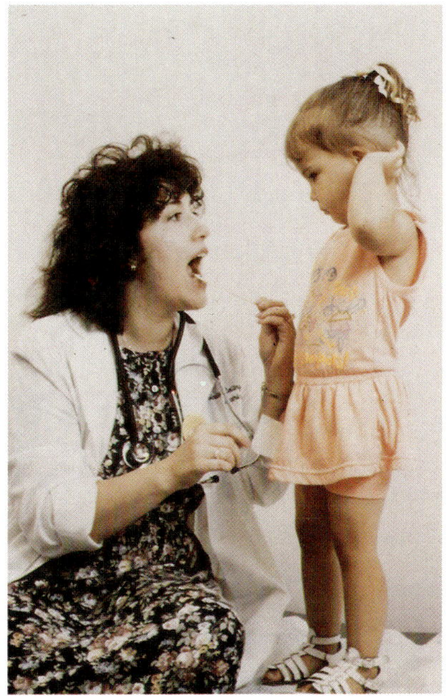

The Children's Medical Center offers 34 specialty clinics with a goal of providing the best care available.

More than 100 CMC professionals make up one of the most highly sophisticated emergency medical treatment systems anywhere in the United States. The system includes three transport vehicles, designed by the center's hospital staff exclusively for children. Equipped to handle nearly any emergency or trauma situation, the vehicles are used to transfer infants or children from other hospitals to specialized care at CMC.

Children's Urgent Care is the only urgent care facility in the Dayton area devoted exclusively to children. Pediatricians from CMC's emergency department provide care for minor medical problems, including fever, lacerations, earaches, and sports injuries. Children's Urgent Care also offers laboratory and X-ray services. The center is located south of town on Far Hills Avenue in Lamplighter Square.

CMC also operates 35 specialty clinics and a general pediatric clinic, providing both routine check-ups for healthy children and appropriate treatment for the ill.

The primary mission of The Children's Medical Center is to provide the highest quality patient care to infants, children, and adolescents at all care levels. As the hospital approaches the year 2000, that mission remains unchanged, and with the continued support of the community, CMC will continue to provide top-quality health care for all children.

CEDARVILLE COLLEGE

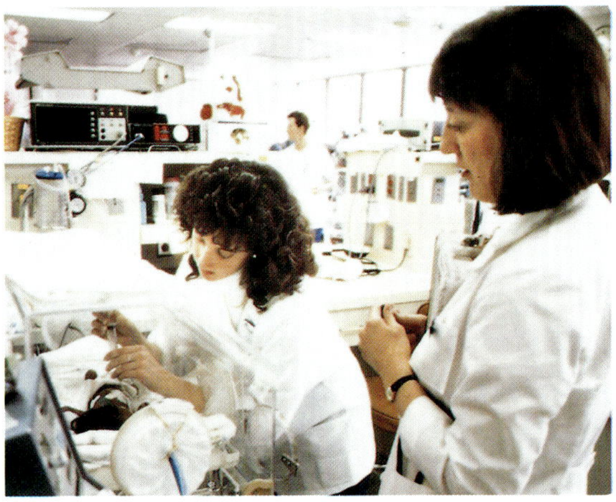

Cedarville offers programs in accounting, business administration, engineering, education, nursing, psychology, the sciences, and mathematics.

Cedarville College has become synonymous with Christian education of the highest quality. Combining faith and learning was once the province of many colleges. It is a process that still thrives at Cedarville. It does so on a modern, well-equipped campus in rigorous academic programs that produce graduates who are in demand.

Located 25 minutes east of downtown Dayton, on a 160-acre campus, Cedarville is a Baptist college of arts, sciences, and professional programs. It offers more than 75 areas of study to 2,200 students from more than 45 states and several nations. Its students, some of whom have some of the highest ACT scores in the nation, are admitted from the top 25 percent of college-bound students. Cedarville offers the programs most in demand by students and employers, including accounting, business administration, engineering, education, nursing, psychology, the sciences, and mathematics.

Major accounting firms, corporate giants, and many regional firms visit campus annually to recruit Cedarville students. Scores of schools, hospitals, and other agencies also interview seniors. The college has one of the best records of its graduates being accepted into medical and law schools, as well as into other graduate programs. Cedarville is fully accredited by the North Central Association of Colleges and Schools.

Cedarville is a Christian college, and students and faculty attend a daily chapel service. Every degree program includes the equivalent of an academic minor in Bible. Students may also select a major in Bible to prepare for a variety of ministry careers. The college emphasizes the development of a Christian world and life view, and professors integrate biblical principles with other subject matter of their disciplines.

Volunteerism is an important ingredient of the Cedarville experience. At any given time, approximately 80 percent of the students are involved in ongoing volunteer activities in a variety of settings—churches, jails, hospitals, nursing homes, and social agencies throughout the Miami Valley. This spirit of volunteerism extends to more than a dozen other nations each summer as Cedarville students engage in transcultural ministries.

Another hallmark of Cedarville is its commitment to free enterprise, both in its instruction and in its operation, which is independent of direct government funding.

The college radio station, WCDR-FM (90.3), serves Dayton and almost all of southwestern Ohio with its unique blend of news and information, Bible teaching, and inspirational music.

Attractive new academic buildings, residence halls, and athletic facilities attest to Cedarville's steady growth. With a record of high-quality undergraduate instruction, the college has cultivated a growing national reputation and constituency and enjoys a distinctive niche in higher education.

Cedarville College is located 25 minutes east of downtown Dayton, on a 160-acre campus.

GREENE COUNTY

Greene County, Ohio, is located in the southwestern part of the state, nestled comfortably among the major metropolitan areas of Dayton, Columbus, and Cincinnati. The 140,000 people who call it home enjoy both the luxury of quick access to significant urban areas and the ability to retreat afterwards to a country and bucolic setting.

Greene County is very fortunate to have a very diverse and strong economy. The County has in place a formal economic development program designed to maintain and encourage the steady and gradual growth it has been experiencing for many years. This economic growth has resulted in more than one billion dollars in investments in Greene County over the past seven years.

The County is home to Wright Patterson Air Force Base, Ohio's single-largest, one site employer. More than 200 research and development firms are also based in the County. By starting to diversify and to apply their research to non-defense areas, these firms have assisted the region in maintaining its strong economic base.

Though aerospace is a very significant part of the local economy, agriculture still ranks as a major industry in the community. These two areas are enhanced by the presence of automotive, distribution, and software industries that have assisted the County in maintaining and developing an even stronger trade base.

Greene County, during the 1980s, was the fifth-fastest-growing county in the state, with the creation of more than 11,000 new jobs. That trend continues as the County moves into the 1990s.

Greene County is unique for providing the educational opportunities that it does. County residents place great emphasis on quality education for a quality future. The training of the County's most important assets, the people who comprise its future labor force, is paramount, from prekindergarten programs through the college and university levels. The County is fortunate to have school districts that rank as leaders in the state on K-12 achievement tests; to boast a certified vocational school with a close working relationship with industry; and to be the home of five colleges/universities, and three branch universities at Wright Patterson Air Force Base. In addition, there are nearly 20 universities within a one-hour commute. Courses are available at all levels, from baccalaureate to doctorate, with subjects ranging from computer science and engineering to medicine and zoology. Superior education is a trademark of the Greene County community.

Aerospace represents a major ingredient in the economic mix of Greene County.

Greene County is a good place to not only work and live, but also to play. Taking time to relax is important. No matter the season, in and around the County one will find exciting choices for leisure-time activities. Though there has been rapid expansion in the County, more than two-thirds of its land is still undeveloped and/or agricultural. More than 10,000 acres of natural preserve, wetlands, and parks have been set aside for permanent protection and for use by Greene County residents. The area is also home to the U.S. Air Force Museum, the National Afro-American Museum, and an exciting epic outdoor drama depicting the life of the Shawnee Indians.

Greene County recently opened a 13-mile bike/hike path that will be even further enhanced by similar trails crossing the County, north to south and east to west.

Swimming, tennis, basketball, racquetball, soccer, fishing, hunting, golfing, ballooning, and horseback riding are all activities that are available in the County. Whether for spectating or participating there is always something fun to do in Greene County.

The many farms of Greene County attest to the important role agriculture still plays in the community.

KETTERING MEDICAL CENTER

Charles F. Kettering Memorial Hospital, named in honor of the esteemed inventor.

The polio epidemic that struck Chicago during the hot summer of 1948 seriously affected hundreds of Chicago youngsters. It also made a lasting impression in Dayton, Ohio.

"The epidemic nearly overwhelmed that area's health care facilities," says Robert L. Willett, president and chief executive officer of Kettering Medical Center. "And among the citizens who answered the call to assist during the polio siege were Eugene and Virginia Kettering."

The Ketterings lived in Hinsdale, Illinois, at the time. As volunteers, they watched the physicians and staff work at the Hinsdale Sanitarium and were impressed with the compassionate, quality care provided during those dark days by the Seventh-Day Adventist health facility.

In 1958, following the death of Eugene's father—the esteemed inventor Charles Franklin Kettering—Eugene and Virginia Kettering began searching for an appropriate memorial to "Boss Ket."

"They decided a hospital would be a fitting tribute to Charles Kettering's interest in and involvement with medicine," says Willett. "And they remembered the special medical care they had witnessed at the Seventh-Day Adventist facility in Hinsdale. They decided that the hospital must exceed the norm, just as the noted inventor had throughout his life."

As an inventor, manufacturer, former director and vice president of General Motors Corporation, and former head of GM's Research Laboratories, Charles Kettering was second only to Thomas A. Edison in the number of patents he held. Among Charles Kettering's many inventions are the automobile self-starter, anti-knock gasoline, safety glass, quick-drying paint for cars, the lightweight diesel engine, and safe coolant for refrigerators and air conditioning systems.

On March 3, 1964, the hospital conceived and supported by Eugene and Virginia Kettering as a living memorial to Charles F. Kettering opened its doors to serve the community. Following Boss Ket's tradition of excellence and innovation, the hospital named in his honor has been on the cutting edge of medical technology throughout its history.

"Kettering was the first in the area to offer computerized axial tomography (CT), the first to install a magnetic resonance (MR) imager, and the first to use a positron emission tomography (PET) scanner for research and diagnosis," explains Willett.

Kettering Medical Center is recognized as one of the leading heart centers in Ohio, earning it the reputation as

Kettering Medical Center combines state-of-the-art technology with the Seventh-day Adventist tradition of healing in all aspects of human life—physical, mental, and spiritual.

the "heart specialist." A pacesetter in cardiac surgery, KMC's top-rated team of cardiothoracic and vascular surgeons performs approximately 800 open-heart procedures annually. These specialists are backed by KMC's comprehensive range of diagnostic, treatment, and rehabilitative services.

The first non-military hyperbaric oxygen chamber, used to encourage healing in reimplanted fingers or toes and to treat carbon-monoxide poisoning and stubborn infections, was installed at Kettering in 1985.

Another KMC milestone was the opening of an affiliate institution to serve the southern Montgomery County and northern Warren County area. Sycamore Hospital, located in Miamisburg, opened its doors in 1978. Together, Sycamore and Kettering Memorial Hospitals now serve nearly 100,000 patients each year.

Daniel Goronzy is executive vice president and chief operating officer. "We're proud of Kettering's mission to restore and promote the health of our neighbors and friends," he says. "We continually strive to provide health care that combines the highest professional and scientific quality with Christian compassion.

"Through the Kettering College of Medical Arts, we offer future health care professionals a wide variety of undergraduate allied health programs. Kettering is also helping educate tomorrow's physicians through graduate medical education programs," Goronzy adds.

In addition, KMC's continuum of medical care includes services and programs that extend Kettering medical Center care to homes and businesses throughout the Miami Valley area. "The Kettering Breast Evaluation Center offers women safe, low-dose mammograms at two convenient area locations," says Goronzy. "Kettering Workers' Care, our newest service to the community, provides a comprehensive center of services designed to get injured workers fit and back on the job as soon as possible."

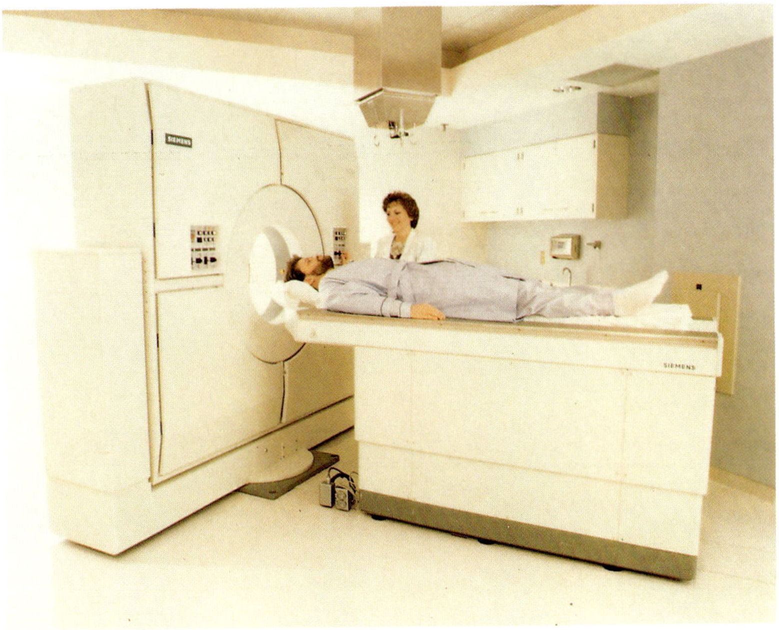

KMC's cardiac and oncology programs are backed by some of the most advanced technology for diagnosis of heart disease and cancer.

Kettering Affiliated Health Services provides patients and their families with quality health care and support services in the comfort of their own home. A wide variety of services, from high-tech nursing care to chemotherapy and blood transfusions, a full line of home care supplies and durable medical equipment, are available through Affiliated Health Services.

"Quality medical care is the cornerstone upon which Charles F. Kettering Memorial Hospital was established," says Willett. "It remains the foundation upon which Kettering Medical Center stands."

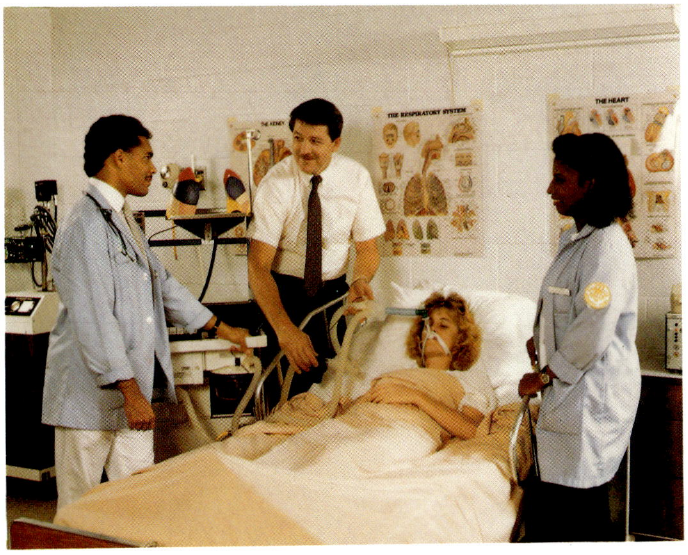

Kettering College of Medical Arts offers two-year programs in a variety of health-related professions. In training for a health career, KCMA students put their knowledge to work by assisting with day-to-day patient care at the medical center's hospitals.

UPPER VALLEY MEDICAL CENTERS

Located in a peaceful, wooded, country setting, Dettmer Hospital is one of the largest, most comprehensive providers of behavioral medicine services in the state.

Focused on the growing need for accessible, quality, cost-efficient services, Upper Valley Medical Centers (UVMC) is committed to responsive health care planning. UVMC is a not-for-profit, 920-bed health care system comprising two acute-care hospitals, a specialty hospital, four long-term care facilities, and 16 outpatient centers. The organization was founded in 1986 with the merger of Miami County's three hospitals: Stouder Memorial Hospital and Dettmer Hospital in Troy, and Piqua Memorial Medical Center in Piqua. As health care changed, the hospitals realized they could serve the community better if they worked as a unit instead of as three separate entities. This combination made it possible to both cut down on duplication of services and to bring more advanced medical treatment to the Miami Valley.

Dettmer Hospital is growing to be one of the largest, most comprehensive providers of behavioral medicine services in the state. Located in a peaceful, wooded, country setting, this 160-bed facility offers treatment programs for adult and adolescent chemical dependency, as well as adult, adolescent, and child psychiatry services.

Creative problem solving resulted in the formation of Dettmer's residential services, bridging the gap between traditional inpatient and outpatient treatment. These specialized programs provide recovery programs for those who do not (or no longer) need outpatient care, but do need a structured living and treatment environment.

Adult residents live and receive treatment in the Jacob Dettmer Residence, a 32-bed living facility where men and women return to normal lifestyles with the best chance of recovery and optimum cost-effectiveness. Younger people, ages 12 through 17, occupy the Adolescent Residential Center, which offers close-to-home treatment for teenagers, previously available only outside the greater Miami Valley area.

SpringMeade, Tipp City, was thoughtfully designed for the moment when a resident can no longer manage to live at home, but is not ready to reside in a highly institutional environment.

Jacob Dettmer Residence offers men and women the opportunity to return to normal lifestyles with the best chance of recovery and optimum cost-effectiveness.

Another example of creative problem solving and an important joint venture is Systems (Miami Valley Labor Management Health Care Delivery Systems). A 26-bed treatment center located in Dayton, Systems is a cooperative effort between Dettmer, UVMC, and IUE 775 (International Union of Electronic, Salaried Machine, and Furniture Workers). An alternative to inpatient care, Systems is a unique set of residential, transitional, and outpatient treatment services for alcoholism, drug addiction, and other behavioral problems.

UVMC also reaches out to a multi-state area with a number of highly specialized programs. Rebound is a national system that develops and manages programs for patients with a wide range of neurological injuries and conditions, including traumatic brain injury, stroke, spinal cord injury, brain tumors, and others. The Rebound Unit at Piqua serves traumatic brain injury patients during the coma stages of their recovery. A Rebound second-stage rehabilitation unit for traumatic brain injury/coma patients is located at Dettmer Hospital.

For children with ongoing medical and therapeutic needs, UVMC offers love, support, and specialized care in an enhanced pediatric department at Piqua, enlisting the management expertise of Dayton's Children's Medical Center. Children's also joined in partnership with UVMC to develop the children's rehabilitation unit at Stouder, designed to care for infants, children, and adolescents with ongoing therapeutic and medical needs. The expanded capabilities of care afforded by both units serve as an important convenience for Miami Valley families by keeping their children close to home for the special care they need.

As the staff at the Children's Rehabilitation Unit will tell you, there is no greater reward than that which comes from helping children.

Systems offers a unique set of residential, transitional, and outpatient treatment services for alcoholism, drug addiction, and other behavioral problems.

The Midwest Center for Head Pain Management is also housed at Stouder, providing inpatient and outpatient treatment for chronic migraine and other severe head pain. The treatment combines physical, occupational, and speech therapy with innovative use of music and creative arts.

Because every individual in each stage of life deserves quality care that is cost-effective and convenient, Upper Valley Medical Centers also sets the standards in caring for older adults. Four long-term facilities, Covington Community Care Center, Covington; Koester Pavilion, Troy; Sunny Acres Care Center, Sidney; and SpringMeade, Tipp City, comprise 430 beds. A variety of options are available from two-bedroom coach homes to suites in a more traditional health center. Whatever the choice, residents can move into a stimulating life stage of physical, social, and emotional well-being.

For additional information on any of Upper Valley Medical Centers' programs, call The Professionals at 1-800-432-UVMC or 339-8377 in Troy.

ST. ELIZABETH MEDICAL CENTER

In 1878 two Franciscan Sisters of the Poor, following a mission to serve their community, founded Dayton's first hospital: St. Elizabeth Medical Center. Located a few blocks from downtown Dayton, St. Elizabeth is a Catholic, not-for-profit, community health care center. The 631-bed facility is a member of the Franciscan Health System of Dayton and its national system, the Franciscan Sisters of the Poor* Health System, Inc.

The rehabilitation process is highly effective at St. Elizabeth Medical Center.

St. Elizabeth enjoys a well-earned reputation for leading-edge, progressive medicine and a broad range of services.

The St. Elizabeth HeartCare Center was the first cardiology program in the area to offer advanced bi-plane cardiac catheterization diagnosis and treatment for heart disease. Its cardiac rehabilitation program offers one of the most progressive recuperation options available.

The St. Elizabeth Regional Cancer Center began working closely with national researchers in 1992 to offer area cancer patients the latest in clinical treatments. The opening of the Advanced Cancer Treatment Program marked the beginning of new regional advances in cancer therapy.

The St. Elizabeth Rehabilitation Center—an accredited provider of physical, occupational, and vocational therapies—offers many specialized services, including a computer-assisted communication program, a rehabilitative driving school, and the Regional Pain Program for people who suffer from chronic pain.

Cardiac rehabilitation at St. Elizabeth Medical Center allows patients to recover significantly.

A leader in sports injury evaluation and treatment for more than a decade, the medical center expanded its services in 1991 with a 25,000-square-foot facility. In addition to a comprehensive physical therapy and treatment area, the center offers a 20-meter lap pool, a therapeutic pool, X-ray and cast facilities, patient evaluation areas, and satellite facilities.

The St. Elizabeth Breast Center, which opened in 1992, is the region's first comprehensive breast program. In addition to mammography, the center offers stereotactic biopsy, consultation with a variety of specialty physicians, and individualized counseling support and materials.

The medical center also offers educational programs for women through its Women's Health Services. Its Mother/Baby Unit was the area's first maternity program to offer the birthing room option and remains a leader in family-centered maternity care.

Psychiatric Services include both adult and adolescent programs which emphasize individualized care through innovative treatment options.

The Digestive Disorders Center at St. Elizabeth is the area's only dedicated center for the diagnosis of digestive ailments.

One of the fastest-growing services available through St. Elizabeth is Home Care. Upon leaving the medical center, patients in need of continuing medical observation or treatment can, upon referral, receive in-home service with individual monitoring by staff nurses.

St. Elizabeth Medical Center continues its more than 115-year commitment to the people and communities of the Dayton area.

THE DAYTON ART INSTITUTE

The Italian Renaissance building that houses the Dayton Art Institute was a contribution to the community from Mrs. Julia Carnell.

The Dayton Art Institute was founded in 1919 as a museum and art school. Its mission was to educate the local community about the visual arts and to give the people of Dayton an opportunity to experience the work of great artists firsthand.

Today, with a growing membership of more than 4,000 people, the Institute boasts a collection of more than 10,000 works, from the art of ancient Asian cultures to the modern work of Andy Warhol.

Located in downtown Dayton at the corner of Forest and Riverview avenues, the Institute resides in a stately building of Italian Renaissance villa architecture, with cloisters and courtyards off its 30 galleries. The Institute is a showplace of fine art treasures.

Its Asian Wing displays a collection of historical and modern pieces from the East. Its American Wing houses a collection of antiques and pre-modern American oil paintings, as well as the Ponderosa Collection of contemporary American art. European oil paintings, sculptures, and tapestries are found upstairs in the European Wing.

The Special Exhibition Gallery hosts special exhibits, such as the 1992 Kandinsky show and the 1993 Eyes on Fire exhibit, and also showcases the work of talented local artists.

Other important works are displayed throughout the Institute: large sculptures, African and pre-Columbian art in the Lower Court; and part of the institute's modern art collection in the Great Hall. The innovative Experiencenter is an interactive gallery in which patrons get real hands-on experience with other cultures.

Nearly 30,000 volumes about art and architecture are available to the public in the institution's library. The Museum Store offers an assortment of books, gifts, cards, and collectibles for visitors. The Museum Frame Service helps patrons present and preserve their personal art treasures.

VICTORIA THEATRE ASSOCIATION

For more than 125 years Dayton has enjoyed a rich heritage of live theater. That heritage is embodied by the limestone-and-brick building with the distinctive mansard roof, standing at the corner of Main and First streets: the Victoria Theatre.

The Victoria first opened its doors in 1866 as the Turner Opera House. In succeeding years the theatre saw it all, from legitimate theater to burlesque, from vaudeville shows to symphony orchestras, from dance recitals to Disney movies.

Despite damage from fires and floods, economic depression, and the threat of the wrecking ball, the Victoria has survived and flourished to become Ohio's highest-subscribed-to theatre. Today the theatre continues to preserve the best of tradition in grand theatrical style, while continually adapting to the changing needs of its audiences.

The Victoria Theatre Association annually presents a broad program of quality productions, including a Mainstage Theatre Season of six productions; a six-production, family-oriented season called Theatre for the Young at Heart; the DISCOVERY! Season, an educational outreach program that brings more than 50,000 school children to the theater each year; and the JUBILEE! Season, which features outstanding African-American performers.

Scores of patrons also pour through the Victoria's doors for performances by many of Dayton's finest art organizations.

A community treasure.

SINCLAIR COMMUNITY COLLEGE

Students in the Engineering & Industrial Technologies Division at Sinclair Community College have access to state-of-the-art CAD/CAM equipment and other technologies. Sinclair's modern training facilities help meet the Miami Valley's ever-expanding high-technology needs.

Find the need and endeavor to meet it. With that simple philosophy, the Dayton YMCA opened a night school for men in 1887 and established what would become Sinclair Community College.

David A. Sinclair, the college's founder, believed in fostering a close relationship with the business community the YMCA school served—a conviction held by Sinclair's current president, David H. Ponitz.

"Our connection to the community includes broad partnerships between the college, schools, industry, business, social agencies, policy groups, and senior colleges," Ponitz says. "We also have an obligation to build partnerships that are not only local and national, but global too."

Today Sinclair is one of the nation's leading two-year public colleges, serving more than 40,000 credit and noncredit students each year. On its downtown campus and through more than three dozen college centers in and around Montgomery County, Sinclair offers 2,500 courses in seven academic divisions: allied health technologies, business technologies, engineering and industrial technologies, extended learning and human services, fine and performing arts, liberal arts and sciences, and continuing education. In addition to traditional classroom offerings, Sinclair provides a myriad of award-winning programs to serve the needs of adult learners.

The corporate and community services division, with headquarters in the modern David H. Ponitz Sinclair Center, continues the college's tradition of responding to the training needs of business, government, and nonprofit organizations in the Miami Valley. Equipped with the latest in satellite, video, and computer capabilities, the 200,000-square-foot facility offers 35 meeting rooms, a full-service catering staff, and experienced training professionals to support the most ambitious meeting and training needs. This successful college-community relationship is a tribute to Sinclair's 1,000-plus full- and part-time faculty, who are distinguished in both the classroom and the community.

Fully accredited by the North Central Association of Colleges and Schools, Sinclair is a member of the prestigious League for Innovation in the Community College and is a frequent recipient of the State of Ohio's coveted Program Excellence Award.

However, Sinclair, which has one of the lowest tuition rates in Ohio, is known for its affordability as well as its high quality. Because it is affordable, the college has a diverse student body of all ages, ethnic backgrounds, and academic histories. According to Ponitz, "A community college has a special obligation to break down separation based on age, race, and ethnic background." Sinclair Community College truly serves the community.

The David H. Ponitz Sinclair Center has become the premier corporate and community center in the Miami Valley. The center hosts a wide variety of credit and noncredit training programs for hundreds of Ohio's corporate, government, and nonprofit organizations.

WHIO-TV

Dayton's leading television station is also the Miami Valley's oldest television station. WHIO-TV signed on the air for the first time from its south Dayton Studios on January 26, 1949, and has held the number-one spot ever since.

WHIO serves roughly a half-million homes in Dayton and the Miami Valley. A CBS affiliate since its founding, the station's initial market dominance was derived primarily from high-quality network programming. Today it is WHIO's comprehensive local news and information broadcasts that keep it ahead of the competition.

Widely known as the area's news source with "Coverage You Can Count On," WHIO commands literally twice as many viewers as other stations in the area in many key news time periods. The station broadcasts three and a half hours of regularly scheduled local newscasts daily, Monday through Friday. It is the only television station in the area with a two-hour Saturday morning newscast, the only station with daily noon newscasts seven days a week, and the first to expand its Monday-through-Friday-evening newscasts to 5:00 p.m.

In addition to its regularly scheduled news and information programming, WHIO produces a number of prime-time news specials throughout the year. Target Seven, for example, is a popular one-hour special that focuses on a single issue affecting local viewers.

WHIO is also known for its coverage of sports and special events. As the area's Cincinnati Reds baseball station, WHIO broadcasts more than 50 games every season. The station also carries University of Dayton basketball live.

David Lippoff, vice president and general manager of WHIO-TV.

As the official television station for the United States Air and Trade Show and The Dayton Airshow, WHIO broadcasts five hours of continuous live coverage of these events every year, and then produces syndicated one-hour specials, which are aired in more than 200 markets around the country.

WHIO has demonstrated its commitment to the local community with a broad range of public affairs programming. For 11 years the station has televised the Children's Miracle Network Telethon, the proceeds from which benefit Children's Medical Center in Dayton. For 17 years the station has sponsored the United Negro College Fund telethon. WHIO also sponsors the annual March of Dimes Walk America, the Boy Scouts' Scouting For Food program, Ruth Lyons' Christmas Fun, and the Easter Seals telethon.

WHIO also sponsors the Don Wayne Scholarship fund, which provides college scholarships to high school students interested in pursuing careers in communications studies.

One of WHIO's strengths has always been its people. The station continues to encourage all of its 120 employees to participate in local community activities, social action groups, and schools.

WHIO-TV is owned by Cox Enterprises, Inc. Founded in Dayton by the former governor of Ohio, Cox is a communications company with interests in a number of media. In the Dayton area Cox also owns the *Dayton Daily News*, WHIO-AM Radio, WHKO-FM Radio, and the *Springfield Daily News*.

Jim Baldridge and Cheryl McHenry.

THE CITY OF KETTERING

Charles F. Kettering was surely one of the world's most gifted inventive geniuses. His nearly 200 patents include the electric cash register; the automobile starting, lighting, and ignition system; and anti-knock gasoline. Yet his most enduring legacy may not be his inventions, but a proud southwestern Ohio community named after him.

Located in Montgomery County, just 15 minutes south of downtown Dayton, the City of Kettering is a community with a national reputation for excellence. Over the years, Kettering has received numerous national awards for its parks and recreation programs, its volunteerism, its sister city program, and its many beautification efforts. A visitor coming to Kettering will find a quality of life that is hard to find elsewhere.

For nearly a decade after its incorporation in 1955, Kettering was Ohio's fastest growing city. Today, with a population of more than 60,000, Kettering is the state's 14th-largest city, and it continues to attract new people and businesses looking for a special community.

The education system in Kettering is among the best in the state. Kettering schools excel in every category, from kindergarten basics through high school academics and sports. The city's extensive adult education programs provide more than 165 classes to help people sharpen their skills, express their creativity, and learn more about the world around them.

Kettering is the home of the Cox Heart Institute School of Medicine and Kettering Medical Center. Both facilities are on the cutting edge of medical technology and ensure area residents of the finest in health care services.

WaterRave's, Kettering's water park, features a zero-depth pool, water slides and falls, a sand volleyball court, and more.

Because of the city's central location (within about an hour's drive of Dayton, Cincinnati, and Columbus) and its supportive business climate, Kettering's business community is second to none, and includes both large and small companies. The city's unique new focal point for business and community activities is the Lincoln Park Center. Located on a picturesque, 100-acre site, Lincoln Park combines a public commons with areas set aside for commercial and residential use. Also located within Lincoln Park is the Miami Valley's summer showplace, the Fraze Pavilion. A 4,500-seat outdoor amphitheater, the Fraze features national entertainers and is the summer home of the area's regional performing arts groups.

Kettering's Miami Valley Research Park, a hub for some of the country's most brilliant minds, helps to develop new technologies for a broad range of applications.

Kettering's close proximity to Ohio's major metropolitan areas gives its residents the best of both small-town and big-city life. But residents don't have to leave the area to enjoy a rich variety of amenities. Kettering has 23 park sites—totaling 400 acres—located within the city; 33 public tennis courts; 38 baseball/softball diamonds; 16 football/soccer fields; and 8 self-guided fitness trails and BMX tracks. More than 800 recreational and cultural activities are conducted in Kettering yearly.

Fraze Pavilion, Kettering's 4,500-seat amphitheater, has hosted numerous national entertainers, including Harry Connick, Jr., Ray Charles, Yanni, and Dolly Parton.

GREAT TRAILS BROADCASTING COMPANY

In 1975 WING relocated to this studio located on East David Road in Kettering.

Stanley M. Krohn, Jr., was a businessman with a problem. The year was 1925 and Krohn owned a retail radio store in Dayton. He had a knowledge of electronics and a fine selection of the latest products; unfortunately there were no radio stations broadcasting in the area.

To support his retail business, Krohn secured a broadcast license and started his own station. Broadcasting from the front window of the radio store itself, WDBS (Watch Dayton Broadcasting Station) went on the air with five watts of power. Krohn later moved the small station to the four- story Gibbons Arcade Building on West Third Street, and changed its call letters to WSMK (for his own initials).

WSMK was Dayton's first radio station and was the first station to be acquired by Charles Sawyer, founder of Great Trails Broadcasting. Headquartered in Dayton, Great Trails is a privately owned corporation that owns or operates radio stations WING (AM) in Dayton, WGTZ (FM) in Eaton, WAZU (FM) in Springfield, and WCOL (AM and FM) in Columbus. The company also owns television stations WHAG-TV in Hagerstown, Maryland, and WFFT-TV in Fort Wayne, Indiana.

Sawyer was a prominent Cincinnati attorney with a distinguished career in public service; he served as U.S. Ambassador to Belgium, Minister to Luxembourg, and U.S. Secretary of Commerce under President Harry S. Truman. He acquired WSMK in 1939 and changed its call letters to WING, more closely identifying the station with Dayton, the birthplace of aviation and home of the Wright Brothers.

Shortly after he acquired the station, Sawyer moved WING's broadcast studios to the Loew's Theater building in downtown Dayton. In 1944 he constructed a new tower and transmitter building on East David Road, south of the city. Operations were conducted from the Loew's Theater location until 1960, when the station moved to new quarters in the Talbott Tower on First Street.

Today WING broadcasts 24 hours a day from its studios and transmitter on East David Road. Ohio's 11th-oldest continuously licensed broadcasting station, it operates on 1410 kHz with a power of 5,000 watts. WING is an affiliate of CBS Broadcasting Network and was one of the first stations in the area to carry CNN Headline News.

WING has been responsible for a number of other firsts, as well. It was the first local station to broadcast the Two-Worlds Monza Race, direct from Milan, Italy. It was the first Dayton station to broadcast the athletic activities of the University of Dayton, Wright State Raiders basketball, and Cincinnati Bengals games. And it was the first station in the city to broadcast rock music.

WING continues to carry local news in both the lifestyle and traditional formats, plus sports and weather.

Charles Sawyer died in 1979 at the age of 92. He was succeeded by his grandson, Alexander J. Williams, who currently serves as company president.

WING's First Street studio, pictured here in 1963.

DAYTON NEWSPAPERS, INC.

Publisher Brad Tillson is a past chairman of the Dayton Area Chamber of Commerce.

The *Dayton Daily News* leads the way in excellence in reporting and innovative news gathering and has broken new ground in computer-assisted reporting techniques. It boasts an award-winning editorial staff, including Pulitzer Prize winning cartoonist Mike Peters. News bureaus are maintained in Columbus, Ohio and Washington, D.C.

The staff is committed to continuous improvement of the paper's format and development of new sections to better satisfy the needs of its readers. In recent years the paper has introduced several new sections, including GO! for entertainment and SmartMoney for personal finance. The *Dayton Daily News* also publishes a weekly tabloid-sized publication, the *Downtowner.*

In addition to publishing the *Dayton Daily News*, Dayton Newspapers, Inc., has developed a number of related services.

The company's telemarketing services evolved from its own subscription sales operation. Since 1992 the company has provided its telemarketing expertise to other publishers, selling subscriptions throughout the Dayton area, Cleveland, Springfield, and Texas.

Recently the company also began publishing "niche" books and other types of specialty publications, such as *Go! The Magazine*, *Active Times* and souvenir and trade programs for the Dayton-based U.S. Air and Trade Show. The company also operates Miami Valley Distribution Systems (MVDS). MVDS delivers product samples and monthly consumer magazines, such as *Sports Illustrated*, *Redbook*, *Seventeen*, and about 20 other titles throughout greater Dayton.

The company's voice information services provide access to news and information to anyone with a touch-tone telephone. Through the service investors can track stock prices, sports fans can learn the latest scores, and callers can check their horoscope, get information about their favorite soaps, or play games. There are also local news and weather categories. Voice information typifies the new communication technologies that DNI is embracing to meet consumers' and businesses' changing needs.

A strong supporter of community projects, the *Dayton Daily News* is involved with the sponsorship of numerous arts and educational programs, including the Excellence in Teaching, Ten Top Women, and Entrepreneur of the Year awards. *Dayton Daily News* Valley Food Relief annually raises more than $200,000 for the Red Cross Emergency Food Bank.

Dayton Newspapers, Inc., is a diversified media and communications company. Formerly called the *Dayton Evening News*, the newspaper was purchased and renamed in 1898 by James Cox, an ambitious reporter and former teacher. Over the years, Cox—who eventually served three terms as governor of Ohio, served in Congress, and made an unsuccessful run for the presidency — built his newspaper's circulation and acquired other local and regional papers. Today, with more than half a million readers, the *Dayton Daily News* is the largest metropolitan newspaper in the greater Dayton area. With 1,100 employees, it is one of downtown Dayton's largest employers.

Dayton Newspapers, Inc., is part of Cox Enterprises, Inc., which owns the *Atlanta Journal and Constitution*, the *West Palm Beach Post*, and the *Springfield (Ohio) Sun*, among other respected newspapers. The company also owns a number of radio and television stations, including Dayton's WHIO-WHKO Radio and WHIO-TV.

MIX 107.7, WMMX-FM

WMMX-FM, better known locally as Mix 107.7, is one of the most popular radio stations in the Dayton area. Broadcasting 24 hours a day from its studio at 101 Pine Street in Dayton's Oregon District, WMMX reaches some 60,000 loyal listeners every day.

WMMX's format is adult contemporary—popular music from the '70s, '80s, and '90s. Previously called WWSN, the station's call letters were changed in 1993 to the more descriptive WMMX to better reflect the programming "mix."

Well known for its half-hour music sets, where 30 minutes of uninterrupted music frequently runs longer, WMMX boasts some of the more popular on-air personalities in the Dayton area. With Bob Sweeney hosting the Mix Morning Show, Dean Taylor in the midday slot, Dan Edwards at the mike in the afternoon, and Fred Tomlinson on the night watch, the station's on-air staff has accumulated more than 60 years in the local market. And their popularity is anything but waning.

The station also provides its listeners with a comprehensive morning news program, news and traffic reports in the afternoon, and weather reports from the area's only licensed meteorologists, the weather staff from WDTN-TV Channel 2.

Known to its listeners as a lifestyle station, WMMX regularly gives away some of the most generous prizes in radio. In a recent promotion, for example, $1,000 was given away every day to listeners who called in to the station's Song of the Day contest.

Over the years, WMMX has consistently remained among the leading FM stations in the Miami Valley. One of the forces behind the station's success has been its strong and committed sales organization.

Also integral to its success is the station's long history of community service. More than just entertainment, WMMX is a real community-oriented radio station and a tireless supporter of local organizations and events. Through live remote broadcasts and other promotions, the station has raised money for local charities, nonprofit groups, and community causes. WMMX has worked hard to help the homeless, fight crippling diseases, and address issues of concern to the local community.

WMMX is one of a trio of local stations owned by Stoner Broadcasting, the 26-year-old communications company. Along with WMMX, Stoner owns and operates Dayton's WONE-AM and WTUE-FM. All three consistently top-ranked stations broadcast from new studios located in the Pine Street facility, commanding significant shares of their respective markets.

MARIA-JOSEPH LIVING CARE CENTER

It is hard to miss the life-size watercolor mural on the ground floor of the Maria-Joseph Living Care Center.

The tree of life—with its embedded roots, solid trunk, and delicate branches reaching out toward the sky—is the care center's logo, denoting consistency, growth, proliferation, and generative and regenerative processes. The tree represents inexhaustible life.

"That mural was painted by one of our residents, who is in her 70s," says Cheryl Frazier, vice president of public relations. "It took her a whole year to complete it."

The tree of life is a fitting symbol for Maria-Joseph, a 440-bed nursing care and retirement community for older adults and chronically ill persons, dedicated to dignity and quality of life. "Underlying all we do here is our continuing responsibility to enable our residents to experience the most desirable quality of life possible," says Bonnie Langdon, president and chief executive officer.

To carry out its mission, Maria-Joseph offers seven levels of care: independent living, supervised and assisted living, intermediate and skilled nursing care, a geriatric rehabilitation unit, and an Alzheimer's unit. Maria-Joseph is considering adding independent living cottages, either on or off campus.

Intergenerational programming is one of the many opportunities available to residents of the Maria-Joseph Living Care Center.

Choices are what Maria-Joseph is all about; regardless of how a person's needs might change, a continuum of care is available. One resident was admitted to Maria-Joseph's geriatric rehabilitation unit, having been confined to a wheelchair for three years after an automobile accident, which had left her unconscious for 12 months. The rehabilitation team, along with other professionals, helped her regain lost skills.

"Through concentrated efforts, she resides in one of our independent living quarters and often travels with family and friends," states Frazier. The geriatric rehabilitation unit has been recognized as a model facility nationwide.

Along with the comprehensiveness of its on campus services, Maria-Joseph provides a full-range of outpatient services through its home health program which includes both certified and private duty services. Personal emergency response services are also available to community residents through the services of Lifeline.

Back on campus, Maria-Joseph sponsors the Early Childhood Center, one of the first preschools in the nation to receive accreditation from the National Academy of Education for Young Children. Preschoolers have the opportunity to frequently interact with the older adults at the care center.

The Maria-Joseph Living Care Center is accredited by the Joint Commission on Accreditation of Healthcare Organizations, a distinction awarded to only 5 percent of care centers throughout the country. Maria-Joseph Living Care Center is a member of the Samaritan Health Resources network, a subsidiary of the Sisters of Charity Health Care Systems, Cincinnati.

WDTN-TV

In 1949 there were only 92 television stations in America, and 11 were based in the state of Ohio. WLWD, owned by the Crosley Broadcasting Corporation and licensed by the FCC in 1947, was the first station to be licensed in Dayton, Ohio. The station's first broadcast in 1949 was the premiere of Texaco Star Theatre featuring Mr. Television himself, Milton Berle.

WLWD was later sold to Avco Broadcasting. In 1976 the station was purchased by Grinnell Communications Corporation, a profit-making arm of a liberal arts college in Iowa, making it one of the few commercial stations ever to be purchased by an educational institution. After 27 years of broadcasting, WLWD became WDTN Channel 2.

Hearst Broadcasting, a division of the Hearst Corporation, acquired WDTN-TV in 1981. Hearst Broadcasting includes six television stations, which collectively reach almost seven percent of the nation's viewers.

A national leader in the broadcasting business, WDTN now reaches hundreds of thousands of viewers with a wide variety of quality local and network programming, in-depth news coverage, sports, and community service programs.

WDTN has been responsible for a number of industry firsts. It was the first station in the country to sign a color telecasting agreement with NBC, broadcasting Dayton's first colorcast—the Rose Bowl Parade of 1954. The station was also among the first in the country to use radar for weather reporting. One of America's most popular television shows originated on WDTN; Phil Donahue made his talk-show debut on the station in 1967.

WDTN was among the first television stations to expand its local evening news broadcast to a full hour. The station was also among the first to adopt a "LIVE newsroom" format. Today WDTN uses state-of-the-art ENG equipment and advanced microwave technology to bring viewers live, up-to-the-minute news reports.

The team to turn to for news that hits home.

WDTN was one of the first stations in the world to carry sports events staged in a television studio before a studio audience: live studio wrestling. It was the first in the area to broadcast University of Dayton basketball, live bowling, and nighttime baseball, and among the first in the country to broadcast live automobile racing.

Committed to the community, WDTN has a long tradition of involvement in local affairs. With projects like "Coats For Kids," "Food For Friends," "Drugbusters," "Family Works," and "Great Expectations," Channel 2 has established a reputation of leadership when it comes to serving community needs.

Providing the best in news, information, and entertainment programming, WDTN will continue to be the station Dayton and the Miami Valley turn to, today and into the twenty-first century, for "News and Help That Hits Home!"

Phil Donahue talks to Jane Fonda (in the early days) at WDTN Channel 2.

MIAMI VALLEY REGIONAL TRANSIT AUTHORITY (RTA)

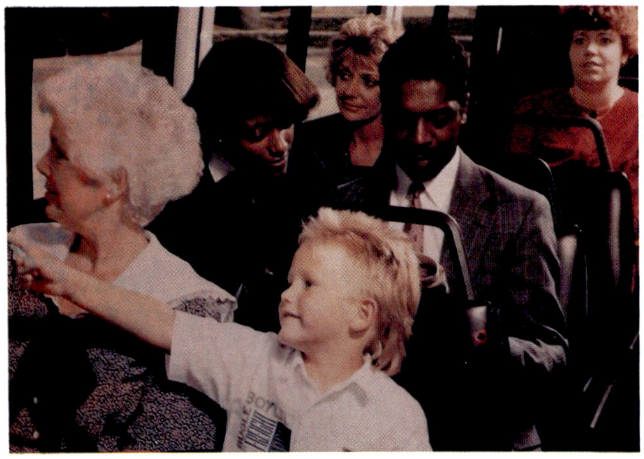

Miami Valley residents enjoy the comfort and convenience of RTA service.

The Miami Valley Regional Transit Authority (RTA) is a publicly owned, non-partisan agency that operates the public transit system of Montgomery county. For more than 20 years, the RTA has been providing quality transportation services to county residents.

Prior to 1972, a private operator, the City Transit Company, provided transit services under a franchising agreement between the cities of Dayton, Kettering, and Oakwood. For 17 years City Transit enjoyed excellent growth, sparked during the war years by the public's need for low-cost transportation. City Transit's ridership began to decline with the post-World War II popularity of the automobile. Ridership losses eventually forced City Transit to increase fares and dramatically cut service.

Facing continued fare increases and service cuts, the cities of Dayton, Kettering, and Oakwood joined forces and proposed emergency ordinances to create a regional transit authority. In 1971 the ordinances were overwhelmingly approved by area residents, and the Miami Valley Regional Transit Authority was created. On October 4, 1972, RTA bought the rolling stock of City Transit, and RTA began operations on November 5 of that year.

At first RTA was governed by a board of trustees and managed by the ATE Management and Service Company, Inc. RTA continuously expanded and developed the transportation services available to the local community, and served approximately 250,000 people in a 50-square-mile area. There were 16 scheduled bus routes in operation seven days a week from 5:00 a.m. to midnight. The RTA fleet included 45 diesel buses and 75 electric trolley buses.

In 1979 the Board of Trustees elected not to renew a contract with the ATE Management and Services Company, deciding instead to hire an in-house general manager.

In 1980, after placing a measure in front of voters, a ½-percent sales tax was approved by Montgomery County residents, and RTA began operating county-wide service on July 4th. As a result, RTA's fleet doubled in size to meet the demands of the increased service area, and RTA's board of trustees grew to eight members with representation from across the county. Eventually an additional board member was added to make the nine-member board of trustees that is in place today.

Countywide service was accomplished with a two-phase expansion plan. Phase I of the expansion included new routes that connected suburban areas with downtown Dayton and new express routes serving downtown Dayton, Wright Patterson Air Force Base, and Wright State University.

Six months later, Phase II of the plan was implemented. This expansion represented dramatic growth for the system, with additional routes into downtown from outlying areas and routes between and within suburban communities connecting to radial routes serving the downtown central business district.

RTA's transit system now operates 28 regular routes and 10 express routes across all of Montgomery County and parts of Greene County, serving more than 465 square miles and nearly 600,000 people. Today RTA employs more than 600 people, including bus

Approximately 90 percent of Montgomery County residents live within a half-mile of an RTA bus stop.

operators, maintenance employees, and a professional staff.

In 1990 a special committee was created to help RTA develop and maintain an appropriate and attainable vision for the role of the public transit through the year 2000. The "RTA in 2000 Committee," composed of broad-based community representatives, focused on developing a consensus for RTA in the areas of finance, service, and governance. The committee's long range strategic vision was shaped by extensive fact finding on broad issues impacting transit and shared with the RTA board of trustees in the Spring of 1992.

RTA's commitment to meeting local public transportation needs in a revitalized, cost-effective manner has allowed for many innovations within the present transit system. Routes have been modified and improved to meet the changing needs of the region.

RTA continues to play a major role in bringing about positive changes in the communities it serves by developing and supporting programs that benefit everyone throughout the region. For example, in addition to maintaining a fleet that is 100-percent wheelchair-lift-equipped, RTA has taken an active role in developing a paratransit plan that serves to meet the Americans with Disabilities Act legislation.

The RTA is also committed to strengthening the communities it serves through support of revitalization and development. For example, RTA has worked with the City of Dayton, Montgomery County, the Ohio Department of Transportation, and others on the Main Street Project, reestablishing downtown Dayton as the center of the community with a transit system that serves everyone in the area.

RTA is concerned about the environment and dependency on foreign oil. In 1991 the RTA Board of Trustees reversed its 1988 decision to phase out electric trolley buses, opting instead to develop a plan to refurbish the overhead and substation infrastructure and to develop a renovation and service implementation plan. Efforts to preserve the environment continue at RTA through recycling of antifreeze, wash water, and the reclamation of freon. RTA has been honored with Montgomery County's Government Award for developing and maintaining an effective waste-reduction program.

The Miami Valley Regional Transit Authority is committed to providing a flexible, broad-based public transportation system for the Miami Valley that is cost effective, integrated with the region's economic and mobility needs in a manner sensitive to special populations, and governed by a structure that is accountable to the people of the community.

Dayton is one of only five cities in the United States that continue to operate electric trolley buses.

The old bus barn, used to house the RTA fleet on Western Avenue, was in operation until 1978.

GOOD SAMARITAN HOSPITAL AND HEALTH CENTER

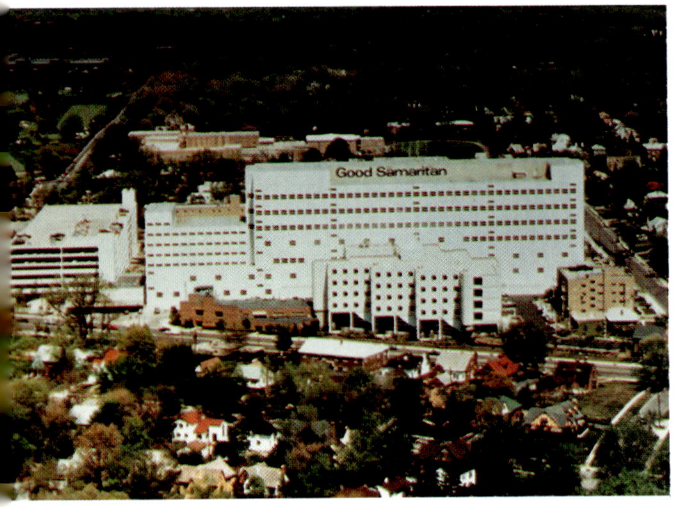

Good Samaritan Hospital is a 560-bed tertiary care facility known for its extensive regional heart center. In the past six years, it has treated more heart patients than any other Dayton-area hospital. Its counseling and treatment centers offer a rare blend of inpatient and outpatient mental health programs tailored to the unique needs of each individual.

The health care industry is experiencing an era of change, and Good Samaritan Hospital's strategy for surviving it is teamwork.

"Our hospital has a dual mission," says K. Douglas Deck, president and chief executive officer. "We are first of all in the healing business, and to heal we must adopt sound business practices. Change creates an opportunity for Good Samaritan Hospital to be creative."

Good Samaritan's management style is progressive. In many departments, the hospital has discarded the hierarchy management mindset in favor of a team approach. Teams of employees now take on responsibilities traditionally reserved for managers—a step that takes advantage of the skills and knowledge of the people closest to the work. Team members are free to suggest ideas about better ways to get the job done. Because teams tend to make decisions more quickly, actions can be taken more quickly. The result is better patient service and care. "Teams are showing the way to high performance," states Deck.

Over the years, Good Samaritan has evolved structurally and functionally to meet the needs of its patients. This philosophy has resulted in many innovative and outreach services unrivaled in the Dayton area. For example, at the Dayton Laser Center at Good Samaritan, many long hospital stays have been turned into brief outpatient stays. (Deck recalls one busy executive who was recently admitted to the Dayton Laser Center and had surgery on Thursday, went home on Friday, and returned to work on Monday.) More and more patients are discovering the benefits of less invasive surgery; in many cases there is less blood loss and a quicker recovery when compared with conventional surgery.

The Dayton Laser Center has more than 90 specially-trained physicians in 14 specialty areas. Using lasers and a laparoscope (an instrument that lets surgeons see inside the body without a large incision), a less-invasive alternative is often available for gynecological operations, ophthalmology procedures, gallbladder removals, hernia repairs, and prostate surgery.

Cardiac care is another center of excellence at Good Samaritan, which has long been recognized as a pioneer in the diagnosis and treatment of heart-related illnesses. In 1959 Good Samaritan performed Dayton's first open-heart surgery; today the hospital does more than 900 open-heart surgeries a year. In 1966 Good Samaritan was the first Dayton-area hospital to establish a coronary care unit, and in 1981 it performed the area's first balloon angioplasty. In the past six years, Good Samaritan has treated more heart patients than any other Dayton hospital.

Since 1986, the Family Birthing Center has provided complete birthing suites that are a mother's home away

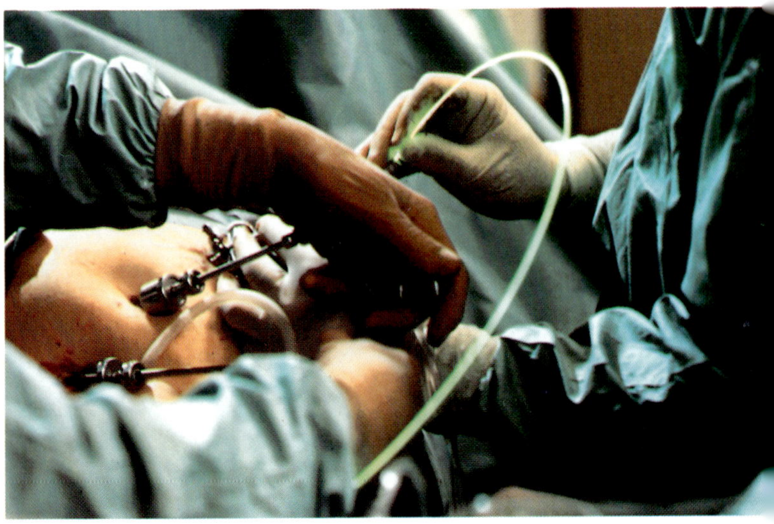

Surgeons at the Dayton Laser Center at Good Samaritan use the precision of less-invasive surgery in a variety of procedures. It is the most comprehensive laser surgery program in the region.

from home. With family members at her side, a mother can enjoy an atmosphere of support and comfort in the privacy of a beautifully decorated birthing room. Each suite has many of the comforts of home: a rocking chair, private shower, and even a sleeper sofa for dad. Patients are cared for by physicians and nurses skilled in every aspect of newborn care. As a model facility, the center, which was the first all-suite birthing unit in the state of Ohio, is being imitated by hospitals all across the United States and Canada.

A fourth center of excellence is the Good Samaritan Counseling and Treatment Centers, which provide state-of-the-art facilities. Founded in 1968 as an eight-bed psychiatric unit, the mental health program expanded in 1969 to offer a comprehensive array of outpatient services. In 1980 the department further expanded to offer chemical-dependency treatment services.

Teams of physicians, nurses, therapists, technicians, and administrators ensure that patients receive confidential and individualized service so patients can begin the healing process, cope with stress, and lead fuller lives. The staff uses a variety of therapeutic approaches, including individual and group psychotherapy and a supportive environment.

"Good Samaritan Hospital's excellence in laser surgery, cardiac care, women's services, and mental health is redefining outstanding performance through a team approach to vision, strategy, operations, and improvement—all in the interest of patient satisfaction," Deck states.

Another important mission of the hospital is providing health care for those who cannot afford it. At the Robert Vogel Health Center and Charles Drew Health Center in West Dayton, Good Samaritan has provided health care services for the less fortunate for more than 12 years. Other outreach services include providing substance-abuse and child-safety programs in conjunction with local school districts; encouraging revitalization and development in north Dayton through membership in the Upper Salem Business Association; and offering services such as support groups, stop smoking programs, cholesterol screenings, and risk assessments for heart attacks.

"By taking charge of our own future, we can tackle head-on the changing business of healing," Deck says. "And by understanding the changes we face, we can maintain our commitment to all Dayton communities that we will be here when you need us."

Good Samaritan Hospital, established in 1932 by the Sisters of Charity of Cincinnati, has 560 beds and a staff of 500 physicians, 2,200 professionals, and more than 300 volunteers. It operates as a secondary and tertiary full-service hospital and a major teaching facility for Wright State University.

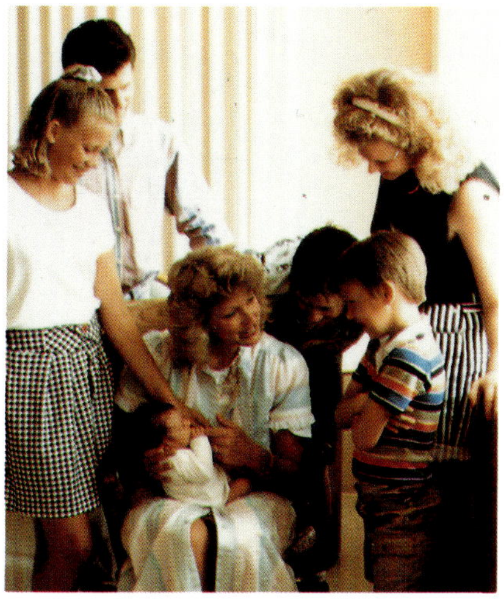

The Family Birthing Center was Dayton's first complete unit of private birthing suites. Since 1986 more than 11,000 mothers have experienced the birth of their baby in an intimate environment.

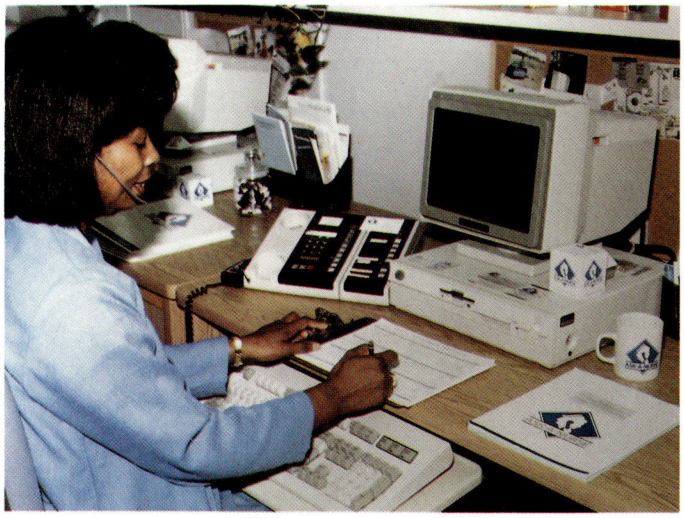

The hospital's 24-hour telephone health information and referral service, called ASK-A-NURSE, puts a nurse as near as the phone. In the last year, the service has helped more than 120,000 callers.

MIAMI VALLEY HOSPITAL

An artist's rendering of Miami Valley Hospital circa 1890.

Leadership is born of high ideals and far-sighted visions translated into action. For more than 100 years, Miami Valley Hospital, "The Region's Leader," has earned its reputation for excellence by offering the broadest range of high-quality services delivered by a compassionate and experienced staff of employees and physicians. And every day, Miami Valley Hospital looks for ways to do things even better.

"We go to great lengths to enforce the notion of customer service, augmenting our clinical care and competence by treating patients and their families with dignity and respect," says Thomas G. Breitenbach, president and chief executive officer. "Our consumers and the medical community consistently rate Miami Valley Hospital as highest in quality."

The largest, most comprehensive hospital in the region, MVH also ranks among the nation's top 100 hospitals in size, with 772 beds and a staff of more than 1,000 physicians representing 34 medical and surgical specialties. Many of Miami Valley Hospital's health professionals are instructors for the Wright State University (WSU) School of Medicine, the WSU/Miami Valley School of Nursing, and other health care programs.

According to Breitenbach, MVH has been at the forefront of medical innovation by introducing new services that meet the community's needs and by enhancing existing programs.

MVH provides the region's most comprehensive maternity program in a 17-county area of west-central Ohio, offering both high-risk maternity and neonatal care. The Berry Women's Health Pavilion, which opened in 1990, features 24 private rooms for family-centered birthing; high-risk antepartum rooms for women experiencing complications during pregnancy; an expanded, nationally recognized neonatal intensive care unit; and classrooms for birth and family education. More than one of every three babies born in Montgomery County—more than 5,000 births a year—gets a start at MVH.

"Birthing mothers have no reason to go anywhere else for maternity care," Breitenbach says. "Miami Valley Hospital's maternity facility is recognized as one of the finest maternity facilities in the state of Ohio for comprehensive services and quality patient care."

In 1985 MVH was the region's first hospital to offer in vitro fertilization (IVF). "Based on the number of successful pregnancies, we can proudly say we've been able to help many childless couples enjoy childbirth," Breitenbach says. In addition to in vitro fertilization, the Fertility Center offers gamete intra-fallopian transfer (GIFT) and a wide range of andrology services.

With the establishment of CareFlight in 1983, MVH became the region's only hospital offering a 24-hour air ambulance service serving critically ill and injured patients within a 150-mile radius.

MVH operates Dayton's only Regional Emergency and Trauma Center, staffed with physicians and nurses specially trained in emergency medicine. An in-house trauma team, which provides surgery, anesthesia, nursing, and ancillary services, is available 24 hours a day; also available are the services of specialists in orthopaedics, internal med-

CareFlight, Miami Valley Hospital's air ambulance service, provides advanced life support and skilled nursing care to critically ill and injured patients within a 150-mile radius.

icine, obstetrics and gynecology, and dentistry.

Miami Valley Hospital also leads the region in maternity care, cancer treatment, and physical rehabilitation by serving more patients than any other hospital in the area, Breitenbach states.

Other recognized regional services include the Regional Adult Burn Unit and the Regional Chronic Kidney Dialysis and Transplant Center.

At Miami Valley Hospital, nurses form the backbone of a treatment philosophy emphasizing care of the whole person. "Nurses are truly a part of the professional team, and patients acknowledge this," Breitenbach says. Through the primary nurse concept, MVH nurses accept total responsibility for nursing care of a group of patients and work closely with physicians to plan and implement that care.

"Another way we've been innovative is by providing patients an appropriate level of care in an appropriate setting," he says. For example, more services are being performed on an outpatient basis. In the 1990s, Breitenbach predicts, more care will be delivered at alternative sites: homes, satellite clinics, and satellite diagnostic centers.

"Cataract surgery, for example, can now be performed on an outpatient basis for 20 to 30 percent of the cost of a hospital stay," he says. "It's important that hospitals be cost-conscious as well as quality-conscious."

Part of MVH's mission is assuring access to health services for all persons with a life-threatening or incapacitating condition, regardless of the ability to pay. "Our role in charity care has been larger because Dayton, unlike most cities its size, does not have a county hospital specifically charged with responsibility for indigent care," Breitenbach points out.

In 1990 Miami Valley Hospital provided $5.9 million of uncompensated charity care for the uninsured. As society continues cutbacks in health care financing, Breitenbach is concerned about the most vulnerable: working poor, single parents and the indigent.

"The tragedy of the uninsured is real; the answers are difficult," Breitenbach says. "All hospitals, including Miami Valley Hospital, must continue their mission of providing charity care to those who need it, while finding ways to reduce the costs of all care."

Among the outreach programs sponsored by MVH is the East Dayton Health Center, a neighborhood medical facility staffed by three MVH physicians and operated in cooperation with the Combined Health District of Montgomery County and the city of Dayton. The Born Free Program, a community perinatal substance-abuse program based at MVH, works to reduce cocaine and crack abuse among pregnant women and the effects substance abuse has on both mother and infant.

Miami Valley Hospital is one of three subsidiaries of MedAmerica Health Systems Corporation. Other entities include the Miami Valley Health Foundation, which handles fund-raising, and Fidelity Prescriptions and Complete Home Care, which operate comprehensive home health services and a group of retail pharmacies.

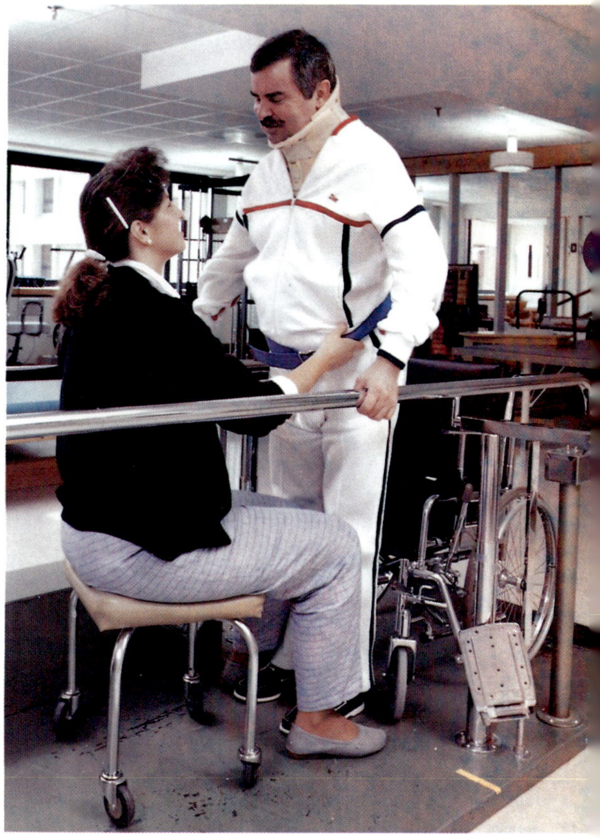

The Rehabilitation Institute of Ohio at Miami Valley Hospital provides area and regional patients with state-of-the-art inpatient and outpatient services to assist them throughout all stages of rehabilitation.

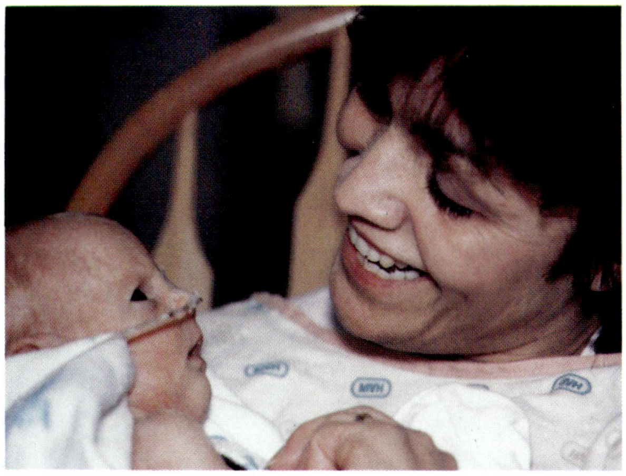

More than one of every three babies born in Montgomery County—more than 5,000 births each year—gets a start at Miami Valley Hospital. The hospital, noted for its high-risk maternity and newborn care, serves patients from 17 counties.

CONTINENTAL CABLEVISION

Continental Cablevision, Inc., signed up its first customers in Tiffin, Ohio, in 1964. Today Continental is the nation's third largest multiple system operator, with annual revenues in excess of one billion dollars, 8,000 employees serving 650 communities, and nearly 3 million subscribers.

"Cable in the Classroom" demonstrates the resources offered by cable television for educators.

The company was founded in 1963 by two young Harvard Business School graduates, Amos B. Hostetter, Jr., and H.I. Grousbeck. The pair formed a small company that offered 10 channels of cable television brought to Tiffin-area residents through a single, 520-foot antenna tower.

The company currently serves nearly 300,000 subscribers in 150 communities across the state. Ohio is both the oldest and one of the largest of Continental's operating regions, and has been a pioneer in the interconnection of neighboring cable systems. In fact, greater Dayton ranks as one of the largest cable interconnects in the nation and was the first major advertising interconnect in the state.

Continental is highly decentralized, with each of its nine operating regions functioning autonomously. In addition to its Ohio systems, the company owns and operates cable systems in California, Connecticut, Florida, Illinois, Iowa, Maine, Massachusetts, Michigan, Minnesota, Missouri, New Hampshire, Nevada, and Virginia. The company's corporate offices are located in Boston.

Continental Cablevision of Greater Dayton currently operates a cable system with the capacity to provide their customers 80 or more channels. To provide this unprecedented variety, Continental was one of the first cable companies to install high-capacity fiber optic transmission systems. As a founding member of CableLabs—a cable television research and development cooperative—Continental continues to explore advanced television technologies.

Over the years Continental has been instrumental in the development of several satellite-delivered cable networks. Continental helped found C-SPAN, which provides live coverage of the U.S. Senate and House of Representatives. In addition, Continental was a co-founder of Viewers Choice, a leading national pay-per-view service, and E!, Entertainment Television.

Continental Cablevision is an industry leader in Ohio. Company co-founder Amos Hostetter, Jr., served as the first president of the Ohio Cable Television Association, and company personnel have held a variety of leadership positions in that organization over the years.

The company has won every major performance award the cable industry bestows, including *CableVision* magazine's Operator of the Year award, which the company received three years in a row. Forbes magazine has called Continental's efforts, " . . . the best in the cable business." The company has received more national ACE awards over the last two decades than any other cable company.

A Continental customer service representative assists a customer.

VETERANS AFFAIRS MEDICAL CENTER

The Department of Veterans Affairs Medical Center had a lot to celebrate in 1992. In the year marking its 125th anniversary, the facility moved most of its patients into a sparkling new state-of-the-art patient tower while also preparing to host the 12th National Veterans Wheelchair Games.

The 10-story patient tower completes a series of modernizations that began in 1980. It features all private and semiprivate rooms; the latest in sophisticated medical care equipment; and spacious, well-equipped, intensive care capacity. It is complemented by the earlier clinic addition, which provides ambulatory care, laboratory, and surgical space. "The resulting complex represents a quantum leap in medical care capability for our veterans," says Ed Thorsland, Jr., VA Medical Center director.

Located on a 382-acre tract in west Dayton, the medical center offers comprehensive programs of primary, secondary, and most levels of tertiary care in medicine, surgery, neurology, psychiatry, rehabilitation medicine, and dentistry. The Medical Center consists of a 456-bed hospital, a 284-bed nursing home, and a 545-bed domiciliary.

With the number of older veterans expected to increase rapidly, demand for VA services will rise, Thorsland says. "By the year 2000, the number of veterans over age 65 will be 9 million—or approximately 35 percent of the total veteran population. As our older veteran population expands, there will be an even greater need to expand our already existing hospital-based home care and adult day health care programs." To meet the needs of an aging veteran population, the medical center is also replacing its 284-bed nursing home facilities (circa 1945) with a new 360-bed facility. Construction is expected to start in 1995.

Dayton's VA Medical Center is the third-oldest and one of the largest in the country. An active participant in the local health care community, the medical center is a member of the Greater Dayton Area Hospital Association and the Ohio Hospital Association. It is part of a four-hospital consortium operating a Magnetic Resonance Imaging (MRI) Center for the Miami Valley. It also shares health care resources with the United States Air Force Medical Center (USAFMC) at Wright-Patterson Air Force Base and with Wright State University (WSU). A primary teaching facility for the WSU School of Medicine, the medical center provides about 50 percent of the undergraduate clinical training requirement.

The medical center offers the latest technology in cardiac catheterization, computerized tomography (CT) scanning, and radiation therapy. Through its Department of Defense sharing agreement, the VA Medical Center has become a national referral center for hyperbaric oxygen therapy.

The medical center's primary service area consists of 28 counties in Ohio and one in Indiana that serve as home to 382,000 veterans. With its 2,200-plus employees, residents, physicians, and dentists, the facility treats 7,700 inpatients and 190,000 outpatients per year. In fiscal year 1992, the medical center had an overall budget of $106,000,000 with a projected payroll of $75,000,000.

Dayton's VA Medical Center is the third oldest and one of the largest in the country.

Miami Valley Career and Technology Center

Miami Valley Career and Technology Center. Photo by Oldham/Roach

A renaissance is taking place in vocational education, and the Miami Valley Career and Technology Center is leading the way. In fact, this leadership has made the Center so popular that it has grown to become Ohio's largest career center. Each year more than 15,000 adults and 1,700 high school students utilize the most modern, hands-on training facility of its kind in Ohio. The Center offers over 50 different career programs, ranging from FAA-licensed aircraft mechanics to restaurant and hospitality management. The Center is accredited by the North Central Association of Colleges and Schools and has been designated as an Adult Full Service Center by the Ohio Department of Education. The school's 200-acre main campus is located in northwest Montgomery County, just six miles west of the Dayton International Airport.

The schools's mission is growing in importance each day. With the number of jobs for technicians expected to grow 38 percent by the year 2000—faster than any other major occupational group—today's vocational students are becoming highly prized. Industries are finding they can save training time and money by hiring graduates of quality vocational schools.

"Vocational education prepares students for 70 percent of all jobs; not just as mechanics and plumbers," says Dr. Dale Baughman, Superintendent of the Miami Valley Career and Technology Center, which serves 27 school districts within Darke, Miami, Montgomery, Preble, and Warren counties. The mission of the vocational and career education system is to prepare youths and adults to make informed career choices—and be able to enter, compete, and advance in a changing work world.

The Center is part of a special statewide plan for modernizing vocational education. Called Ohio's Future at Work, this plan ensures that vocational graduates will be prepared to enter the global workforce of today and tomorrow. "The modernization plan is reinventing our whole enterprise," Baughman says.

At Miami Valley Career Technology Center the vocational education renaissance is in full bloom:

• The school has become market-driven, and contacts with business and industry are close and frequent. "We have developed an educational program that teaches employer-verified skills, and we provide the facilities and equipment to back it all up," Baughman says.

Business and industry representatives visit the school regularly to report on the basic and newest skills needed by various specialists; in turn, the Center's faculty go off-campus to visit dozens of businesses and industries to remain current as to employers' requirements and expectations. Says Baughman, "We listen to the people who hire."

• Tech Prep programs in place at the Center combine high school and college technical education. "Tech Prep moves education from the abstract and theoretical to the applied and relevant, which results in increased comprehension and higher test scores," Baughman explains. The Center plans to continue providing "hands-on and heads-engaged education" that combines academic foundations with career preparation.

• The Center has been recognized for its model pro-

Miami Valley Career and Technology Center offers an FAA-licensed aircraft mechanics program. Photo by Oldham/Roach

gram of applied academics. The applied academic approach relies on teacher teams—a math teacher and a trade teacher in electronics, for example. "Math is taught in a context that matters," Baughman says. "It's practical, yet retains academic integrity."

Students can then take what they have learned in the classroom and apply it in the lab. "If a resistor blows, electronics students will be able to use algebra to calculate the load," Baughman continues. "They're working to solve real problems." Many distinguished visitors, including vocational educators from many states and several foreign countries, have been to the Center to see the applied program in action. The Center has been included in numerous research studies by the National Center for Research in Vocational Education and was mentioned in a recent *Fortune* article about how academics are made relevant at the school.

• Computer literacy is required of all students. Besides computer literacy, a strong emphasis is placed on basic skills, assistance for the handicapped, a positive attitude, applied math, and applied communications.

• The Center encourages education after high school. At the Center, students can prepare for a job and for college. "It's not an either-or question anymore," Baughman says. Ohio vocational graduates meet the same academic requirements for graduation as students enrolled in a college prep curriculum; plus, they meet entry-level job requirements in their vocational field. National studies by the Ohio State University have shown that 60 percent of joint vocational school and comprehensive high school vocational graduates go on to either four-year colleges, community colleges, or technical colleges. Baughman adds, "At Miami Valley Career Technology Center, students with good grades can earn college credit for courses required by Edison State Community College, Sinclair Community College, and Clark State Technical College."

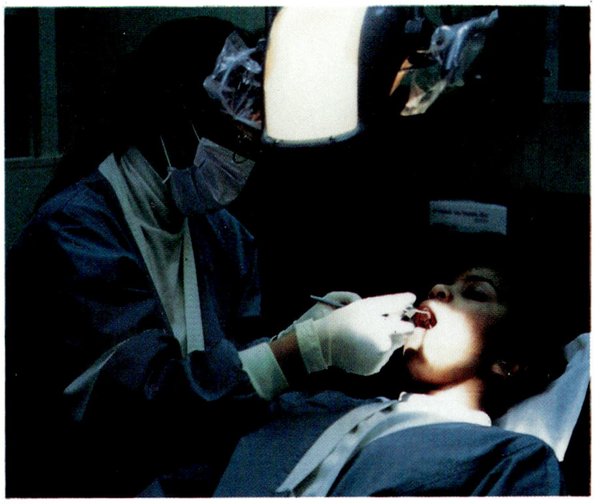

Students have the opportunity to work in their vocational area for pay through a co-op experience during the last semester of their senior year. Photo by Oldham/Roach

• The Center "guarantees" its graduates to employers. Each graduate earns a certificate of completion and a detailed skills profile related to the graduate's training. "Within two years, if an employer believes one of our graduates cannot perform at the competency levels indicated on the certificate, we will retrain that student and get the individual back on-line at no cost to the employer," Baughman explains. He notes that the guarantee has become an incentive for students.

Students also have the opportunity for paid work experience in their vocational area through a co-op experience during the last semester of their senior year. The co-op job frequently leads to a full-time position after graduation. "It smooths the transition from learning to earning," Baughman concludes.

The Center provides the most modern, up-to-date, hands-on training facility of its kind and offers individualized educational programs in more than 50 careers. Photo by Oldham/Roach

LUTHERAN SOCIAL SERVICES OF THE MIAMI VALLEY

The Homestead at Bethany Lutheran Village offers a secure, attractive environment.

Lutheran Social Services of the Miami Valley (LSS) is a nonprofit organization that provides social ministry on behalf of congregations of the Evangelical Lutheran Church in America and the Lutheran Church-Missouri Synod. Incorporated in 1926, LSS has long been recognized for its consistent efforts to improve the quality of life in the communities it serves through a variety of ministries. The caring ministry of LSS reaches many people in southwest Ohio, southeast Indiana, and northern Kentucky.

LSS serves persons at various points of need through four primary ministries: Bethany Lutheran Village, Community Services, Manors of the Valley, and We Care Homes.

Bethany Lutheran Village is a continuing care retirement community that has adhered to a mandate of excellence since its founding in 1946. Today more than 730 people call this unique community home.

Bethany is designed to meet the current and future needs of its elderly residents through its five levels of care, ranging from independent living to skilled nursing care. Bethany's holistic approach to life is reflected in the programs and services offered to meet residents' nutritional, physical, social, and emotional needs.

The Village is located on a 100-acre, park-like campus in Centerville, Ohio, just minutes away from the State Route 48/Interstate 675 interchange. The community's rolling terrain includes a beautiful lake surrounded by wooded nature trails. A replica of the original farmhouse, home to Bethany's first eight residents, provides overnight accomodations for guests of residents.

Bethany's five levels of care are provided in five corresponding facilities: The Cottages, The Homestead, The Tower, The Pavilion, and The Health Care Center.

Ideally suited to active, independent residents, The Cottages offer a close-knit neighborhood of homes arranged along a wooded area of the Bethany campus.

The Homestead is recognized as an active center of campus life. The apartments in this handsome building are comfortable, secure, and spacious. The Homestead offers a number of basic services, including one daily meal exquisitely prepared in the dining room.

The comfortable studios and suites of The Tower offer a high level of convenience and security to moderately independent Bethany residents. Many basic services are provided, including housekeeping, laundry, and meals.

The cheerful studios of The Pavilion are specially designed for those residents who require ongoing assistance with activities of daily living. At The Pavilion companions are ready 24 hours a day to provide extra assistance tailored to each individual's needs.

Quality nursing care is provided around the clock by a caring team of professional and devoted volunteers in The Health Care Center. This intense level of care is supported by a wide range of activities and services consistent with Bethany's holistic approach.

Bethany is one of the few retirement communities in the area with a Special Needs Program for people with Alzheimer's and related dementia disorders. Residents of other Bethany facilities receive temporary nursing care, as needed, in a special area of the Health Care Center.

Activities and attractions for Bethany residents include

Manors of the Valley facilities provide affordable housing for elderly and disabled persons. St. Mark Manor in Dayton is designed specifically to meet the needs of persons with hearing impairment.

marked nature trails, arts and crafts, gardening, both voice and bell choirs, college classes, dances, movies, and bingo. Bethany's innovative Main Street Promenade provides residents an opportunity to browse in the gift shop, snack in the cafe, join in the fun in the game room, or watch the chirping, colorful birds in the aviary. Transportation is available to take Bethany residents to many nearby shopping areas, doctors' offices, and social activities.

Bethany's pastoral services staff regularly visit Bethany residents and also conduct Bible studies and special classes. Though Bethany's ties to the church are strong, residents come from a variety of religious backgrounds. The Village provides worship opportunities for people of all faiths, as well as a quiet chapel for daily meditation.

The Community Services division of LSS provides people in the community with a number of important ministries, including Chaplaincy and Pastoral Care, Consumer Credit Counseling Service, Family Services, HandiVan, and Once Around Shops.

The Chaplaincy and Pastoral Care program is one of the oldest ministries sponsored by LSS. It began in 1922 when a resolution was passed by the Joint Synod of Ohio requesting that a pastor be named whose time would be devoted to visiting people in area jails, county homes, and hospitals. This program continues to be a vital ministry throughout the area.

Consumer Credit Counseling Service provides debt management assistance for clients with overextended credit and offers mortgage counseling and community education programs. This service assists more than 1,300 families each year.

Family Services offers individual and family counseling and adoptive placement services. LSS provides counseling for problem pregnancies and conducts support groups for pregnant and parenting teenagers.

HandiVan, in cooperation with area churches, provides transportation for elderly and disabled adults in northern Montgomery County and Miami County.

Once Around Shops typically serve more than 10,000 people each year with clothing assistance, a food bank, and emergency financial help. Another ministry carried out through the Once Around Shops is the Holiday Toy Box. This program provides new toys, hats, and gloves for more than 5,000 Dayton-area children in need during the Christmas season. Holiday Toy Box is supported by community-minded partners such as the Dayton-area General Motors plants and unions.

The Cottages at Bethany Lutheran Village are ideally suited for active residents who are able to live independently.

Manors of the Valley is a vital ministry providing affordable housing for elderly and disabled persons who have limited financial means. More than 600 residents live in Manors of the Valley facilities in more than a dozen communities in Ohio, Indiana, and Kentucky.

The We Care Homes ministry strives to meet the needs of people with mental retardation or other developmental disabilities. We Care Homes provides residential services and life-skills training in a group home setting for 65 clients in Hamilton and Butler counties. Supported-living services are provided for individuals in Hamilton County who live independently or with their families. Varying levels of support are tailored to the individual's needs.

The Once Around Shops provide clothing and emergency assistance for persons with limited resources.

PARTNERS IN EXCELLENCE INDEX

Commitment to Progress Index